V...
to ... ...
Larry, Mary, and
Daniel — a wonderful
family
_ Bill

P9-CJW-954

Reclaiming Childhood

|||||||||||||||||||||||||||||||||||||||||||||||||||||||||||||||

William Crain

Reclaiming
Childhood

Letting Children Be Children in Our

Achievement-Oriented Society

TIMES BOOKS

HENRY HOLT AND COMPANY

New York

Times Books
Henry Holt and Company LLC
Publishers since 1866
115 West 18th Street
New York, New York 10011

Henry Holt® is a registered trademark of Henry Holt and Company, LLC.
Copyright © 2003 by William Crain
All rights reserved.
Distributed in Canada by H. B. Fenn and Company Ltd.

Library of Congress Cataloging-in-Publication Data
Crain, William, date.
    Reclaiming childhood : letting children be children in our achievement-oriented
society / William Crain.—1st ed.
        p. cm.
    Includes bibliographical references and index.
    ISBN 0-8050-7154-7 (hb)
        1. Child rearing.   2. Child development.   I. Title.
HQ769 .C9175 2003
649'.1—dc21   2002020398

Henry Holt books are available for special promotions and premiums.
For details contact: Director, Special Markets.

First Edition 2003

Designed by Jo Anne Metsch
The illustration on the title page is from Arnheim 1954/1971, 173,
and the illustration on page 187 is from Crain 2000, 96.

Printed in the United States of America
1   3   5   7   9   10   8   6   4   2

For Ellen

Contents

||||||||||||||||||||||

Preface xi

Introduction: Our Obsession with the Child's Future 1

1: Following Nature's Plan: Child-Centered Parenting
   in the Early Years 10
2: The Child as a Dramatist 31
3: The Child as a Naturalist 43
4: The Child as an Artist 69
5: The Child as a Poet 91
6: The Child as a Linguist 107
7: How Did the Future Gain Its Grip
   on the Modern Mind? 123
8: Questioning Technology 143
9: Responding to the Standards Movement:
   The Child-Centered Alternative 153
10: Parents' Questions 173

APPENDIXES: PORTRAITS OF NATURAL CHILDREN
A. A Child of Nature: Huckleberry Finn 189
B. Children Facing School: Sally Brown and
   Peppermint Patty 199

Notes 209
References 233
Acknowledgments 257
Index 259

Preface

||||||||||||||||||

OUR CHILDREN began attending public elementary schools in the late 1970s in Teaneck, New Jersey, a large, racially integrated suburban community. The schools had a fine reputation, but neither our children, nor the other children I knew, liked school very much. They found most of their schoolwork dull and overly abstract.

From talks with parents, I found that the problem was widespread—in Teaneck and in other communities. Parents often observed that their children had begun life curious and eager to learn, but after a few years of school their enthusiasm had faded.

Soon the standards movement started picking up momentum, and I worried that the new academic demands and standardized tests would cause children much greater unhappiness. Even kindergarten, once a playful introduction to school, was becoming largely academic. At all grades, children were spending more and more time on tedious, test-driven education. In 1987, I decided to run for the Teaneck Board of Education to try to address the trends at my local level.

I anticipated how the school community would justify the new academic demands. Our school officials, like our nation's leaders, said the new steps were necessary to prepare students for a competitive future. But I also learned that the community's commitment to the future was more emotional than I had thought. I attended numerous meetings of parents, teachers, and school officials, and hardly a meeting concluded before someone found it necessary to remind the others that "the purpose of education is to prepare children for the future." Hearing this, the entire room typically fell silent, with everyone nodding as if they had been reminded of some profound truth and moral obligation.

How might one respond to this view? I didn't find it particularly easy, and I felt alone in my questioning. Indeed, the situation is not too different today. Even though pockets of parents and educators have become critical of the standards movement and its emphasis on standardized testing, few critics question the standards movement's overall goal of preparing children for the future. Instead, they argue that we have been thinking about the future too narrowly, too exclusively in terms of tests and academics. They urge us to think more broadly about preparing children for life and lifelong learning, or about producing well-rounded and compassionate adults who can think critically and participate in civic affairs. Only rarely does one hear anyone say, "Maybe it's time to question our emphasis on the future. Maybe we need to start paying attention to children's present feelings and interests."

I found inspiration from a handful of great educators and psychologists in the child-centered tradition initiated by the eighteenth-century philosopher Jean-Jacques Rousseau—a tradition that includes John Dewey and Maria Montessori and contemporary scholars such as David Elkind. But I increasingly found myself reading and reflecting upon the thoughts of Rousseau himself.

Rousseau warned that a preoccupation with the child's future blinds us to nature's plan for healthy development. Nature, he argued, inwardly guides children through a series of stages, and during each stage children develop different capacities. We need to observe children's spontaneous interests and tendencies and give them a chance to develop their potentials at their current stage.

Rousseau only began to sketch out what childhood is like. He wrote generally about children's urge to develop their senses and bodies through play and physical activity. He didn't see the remarkable creativity of young children's play and artwork or other special qualities of the childhood years. But he advanced the proposition that childhood is important in its own right, and that children should be able to experience the joy and fulfillment that comes from developing the capacities that are meaningful to them.

I served on the school board for nine years. During that time, our nation's top political and educational leaders urged the educational "reforms" we hear so much about today—greater academic demands, longer school days, more technology in the classrooms, and greater parental efforts to boost children's achievement. As I discussed these goals with parents and teachers, I found myself thinking in terms of the kinds of questions Rousseau asked. How will the changes affect children in their present lives? Will they have time to develop the special qualities of childhood? Will they be able to make their own discoveries? And finally, what can I recommend to parents and teachers who want to help their children have fuller, happier childhoods? These questions are at the heart of this book.

Reclaiming Childhood

Introduction:
Our Obsession with
the Child's Future

TWO MOTHERS were sitting on a park bench in a fashionable part of New York City while keeping an eye on their toddlers at play in a sandbox. One mother looked pensively at her little boy and then turned to the other woman and asked, "Do you really think he is Princeton material?"

This mother's concern may strike us as a bit extreme, but it reflects our culture's fundamental view of children. We are so preoccupied with their future that we cannot see and value them for who they are, children.

A focus on the future dominates every aspect of children's lives. In education, an intense anxiety about the future has driven the standards movement. Beginning with the 1983 federal report *A Nation at Risk,* political and corporate leaders have repeatedly warned that the nation's schools must do a better job of preparing children for the twenty-first-century economy. Our nation's economic preeminence is at stake. In response, almost every state in the nation has toughened academic standards and installed rigorous tests to measure students' progress. States are increasingly making grade promotion contingent upon specific test scores. In 2002 the federal government mandated testing grades three through eight. And to ensure that students will have the skills and knowledge they will need for the future, schools everywhere are increasing academic demands on children at very young ages—even in preschool.

The standards movement has not made life pleasant for children. Teachers are so busy preparing children for tests that there is little time for projects and activities that children find exciting and meaningful, such as building things, gardening, and participating in the arts. The tests also make many children very anxious. But in today's world children's present interests and feelings count for little in comparison to the all-important goal of preparing them for the adult workplace.

Our nation's policy makers recognize that some children will have difficulty keeping up with the others. This is most true of children living in poverty. But here again we see how contemporary thinking focuses on the future. Young children who receive poor nutrition, health care, and housing are invariably described as children *at risk* for future problems. (For example, poor children are at greater risk for high-school dropout, teen pregnancy, and unemployment.) The implication is that if poverty only affected children as children, the problems wouldn't matter.

Even child advocacy groups put a strong emphasis on the child's future. For example, the Children's Defense Fund, while reminding us of our moral obligation to help poor children in their present lives, has highlighted poverty's long-range effects. The organization has issued a report, *Wasting America's Future,* which estimates that child poverty will cost the nation billions of dollars in future workforce productivity. The Children's Defense Fund warns that such economic losses will prove to be especially damaging at this point in our nation's history: "As the U.S. population ages, our young children are becoming an increasingly precious resource we cannot afford to waste."

When the Children's Defense Fund refers to children as a "precious resource," it invokes a term we hear all the time—as in the expression "Our children are our most precious resource." The popularity of this cliché is rivaled only by the slogan "Our children are the future." Both slogans urge us to value children, but not as children, in their present lives. They urge us to value them for what they can contribute in the years ahead.

As a group, those who are most worried about children's futures are undoubtedly parents. Middle-class parents in New York City feverishly compete to get their children into the nursery schools that will put their kids on the track to Ivy League colleges. They might sense that there is something wrong with preparing four-year-olds for the schools' IQ admissions tests, but the parents want the best future for their children. And around the nation, as David Elkind reports, parents are trying to give their children "a leg up on the competition" by starting them on formal academic instruction at very young ages. One parent, Elkind observed, asked a prospective nursery-school director, "What is your science curriculum?" Another screamed at her child's first-grade teacher, "You can't give him a 'satisfactory.' How will he ever get into MIT?"

Recently, parents have been presented with a new worry. A number of public officials have highlighted the importance of environmental stimulation for early brain development. Reporting on recent research, the officials say that stimulation in the first three years can determine the child's entire future. Although the research does not justify this claim, the official pronouncements have elevated parental anxieties, and educational companies are selling more tapes and instruction kits for children in the first three years of life. After all, as one newspaper article put it, "SAT scores may be at stake."

All this adult anxiety about children's futures is affecting children's emotional well-being. Pediatricians are reporting worrisome levels of achievement-related stress among elementary-school children. Many children are so anxious about their school performances that they are having difficulty sleeping and are suffering from headaches and bouts of anxiety. The *New York Times* recently reported that a rising number of teachers are quitting their jobs partly because they believe the test-related stress is unfair to children.

But stress is only half the story. Children also are being deprived of the experiences they need to grow well. As Jean-Jacques Rousseau said over two centuries ago, children naturally develop different capacities at different stages of life. When we focus too intently on what children will need for the future, we rob them of the chance to develop their capacities at their current stage.

Consider the child between the ages of about three and eight years. A considerable body of research suggests that during this time children are naturally motivated to develop their bodies and senses and, as Howard Gardner emphasizes, the artistic side of their personalities. Young children love to sing, dance, draw, make up poems, and engage in dramatic play. They may even create imaginary companions. During this time, moreover, their artistic abilities blossom in breathtaking ways. For example, children between the ages of about five and eight years routinely produce drawings that are fresh, lively, and beautifully balanced. In fact, many great painters, such as Picasso, Klee, and Kandinsky, have said that they try to recapture the creative attitude they had as young children.

Then, toward the end of this period, the child's mind typically undergoes a transition. The child's dominant orientation becomes less sensory, freely playful, and artistic and becomes more rational and logical. The fantasy and magical qualities of the earlier years fade. As the song "Puff the Magic Dragon" says,

Puff must retreat because his human playmate is growing up and becoming more sensible. The child becomes significantly more comfortable with academic instruction. In developmental psychology, this change is known as the "five-to-seven-year shift," and a wide range of research documents the reality of it.

But today's schools pay no attention to this developmental sequence. Obsessed with preparing children for a competitive, high-tech workplace, schools are emphasizing academic instruction and rational problem-solving skills in kindergarten and earlier. Schools also are assigning a considerable amount of homework. Some have even eliminated recess. As a result, children have little time for play and the arts, and they cannot perfect their talents in these realms. On some level the child must conclude, "What matters most to grownups is not me, and the creative impulses that feel so strong and natural to me, but grownups' own ideas of how I must think." The child must feel like he or she is being forced into an external, rational mold—like the prisoners of the mythological Procrusteus, who cut or stretched his victims' arms and legs to make them fit his iron bed.

A similar situation has developed with respect to the child's affinity to nature. Many of the great Romantic poets called attention to the child's special sensitivity to the natural world. Wordsworth, Shelley, Whittier, and other poets said that children develop feelings of oneness with animals, trees, wind, earth, and waters, and they experience nature as a source of endless wonder and delight. A small but growing body of research suggests that childhood is indeed a time of special sensitivity to nature. Researchers have found, for example, that young children, up to the age of seven years or so, actually dream about animals more than humans or other topics. It seems that up to the age of twelve, children have a great urge to explore and find comfort in natural settings.

But children cannot develop their tie to nature in a vacuum.

They need experiences with the natural world, and today we are so busy preparing children for the technologically advanced workplace that we fail to give them the experiences they need. We see no point to letting the child ramble through weeded lots or dabble leisurely at the edge of a stream. Instead, educational-policy makers encourage more time at computer terminals and longer school days and school years, all of which mean more time indoors. And children's after-school hours are filled with video games, electronic toys, and television, keeping them in artificial, indoor environments. All the while, we keep paving over the earth, cutting down trees, and installing artificial surfaces. In today's synthetic, high-tech world, the child's bond with nature may never fully develop. A childhood potential may atrophy, impoverishing the child's personality.

I believe, then, that we are so obsessed with preparing children for the future that we are depriving them of the chance to develop their artistic orientation, ties to nature, and other distinctive traits of the childhood years. I am suggesting that we are, in effect, stunting their growth, and future research may show that the effects show up in increased depression, suicidal ideation, restlessness, and other symptoms of unfulfilled lives.

To remedy the situation, we must begin to appreciate the special virtues of childhood. When it comes to the child's feeling for nature, for example, we need to consider an attitude like that expressed in the motion picture *The Yearling*, based on Marjorie Kinnan Rawlings's 1938 novel about a Florida farm family.

In the story, the mother, having watched her previous children die at early ages, has hardened herself against children and her sole offspring, an eleven-year-old boy. She criticizes him for constantly running off and bringing animals home. He should start becoming a serious adult, she says, "doing a man's share of work." But the father asks the mother to ease up on the boy.

Boy ain't a boy too long. Leave him kick up his heels a little now.

I've seen our boy stand agaze and breathless at the wonderment of the bird and the critter, the wind, the rain, the sun and the moon. Just like I stood when I was a boy. Don't be afraid to love the boy.

The father's attitude might seem old-fashioned and sentimental, but there is wisdom in it. He recognizes that childhood has its distinctive interests and passions, and he wants to protect them. He doesn't see childhood as merely a preparation for the future, but as a time that is valuable—indeed, precious—in its own right.

A CHILD-CENTERED PERSPECTIVE

THIS BOOK BUILDS on a specific intellectual and educational tradition. It is a tradition that began with Jean-Jacques Rousseau and includes people such as Maria Montessori, John Dewey, Jean Piaget, Constance Kamii, and David Elkind. Whether their topic is parenting or education, these writers' fundamental orientation is *child-centered*. They believe, that is, our top priority should not be our own goals and ambitions for children. Instead, we should give the greatest weight to the capacities that children are naturally motivated to develop at their present phase of development.

To help children develop, child-centered writers say, we should take our cues from children themselves, paying special attention to their spontaneous interests and feelings. Children take a keen interest in tasks that enable them to develop their

emerging powers, and they work on them with great enthusiasm and concentration. And when they are finished, they are
often happy and at peace, for they have been able to develop
their powers. We should take these emotions as clues to the
activities children need.

Child-centered writers, finally, ask us to respect the child's
efforts to learn on her own. They point out that a young child
drawing a picture or building blocks solves many technical
problems on her own, and they urge us to resist the temptation
to intervene with our advice, instructions, and corrections. Our
job is to give the child opportunities to learn what is most
important to her, and to then step back and allow the child to
figure things out for herself.

Over the years, several child-centered writers have spoken
out against what they have seen as excessive adult pushing and
prodding. For example, in 1971 Louise Bates Ames wrote a passionate article entitled "Don't Push Your Preschooler." As the
standards movement picked up steam in the 1980s, David Elkind,
in particular, wrote eloquently on the need to protect childhood
against early academic pressures. As a guide for parents and teachers, Elkind presented the classic stage theories of Jean Piaget and
Erik H. Erikson as models of slower, more natural development.

At this time, as we begin the twenty-first century, research
evidence permits us to say more about the special qualities of
childhood. I will try to capture these qualities in descriptions of
the child as an explorer, a dramatist, a naturalist, an artist, a poet,
and a linguist. My hope is that these descriptions will serve a
purpose similar to that of a nature field guide. Just as accounts of
trees, birds, and mountains help people appreciate nature, I hope
my descriptions will help readers recognize the remarkable
strengths of childhood.

This book is intended, above all, for parents. If parents can
more fully appreciate their children in their present lives, this

appreciation will strengthen and embolden their children. Children will gain a basic confidence that will enable them to pursue their current interests vigorously and move forward in life.

But parents must do more than just appreciate children, as helpful as this appreciation is. Parents must also help children grow and learn. In this book, I recommend ways of helping children pursue their spontaneous interests and make their own discoveries.

This book, finally, talks about schools. Schools are such a large part of children's lives that we, as parents, must become involved with them. We must understand the pressures schools put on children and understand the alternatives we can lobby for.

||||||||||||||||||||||||||||||||||||||||||||||||||||||||||||||||||||||||||||

CHAPTER 1

Following Nature's Plan: Child-Centered Parenting in the Early Years

N EW PARENTS face many uncertainties. This is especially true in the United States and other nations that emphasize progress and change. Unlike parents in more stable, traditional societies, U.S. parents do not always feel they can turn to their own parents and grandparents for child-care advice. Instead, today's parents search for newer and better ways, looking for the latest scientific findings and approaches. But the experts aren't always in agreement, and parents can easily become confused and anxious. How long should one breast-feed? Should one feed on a schedule or on demand? Is it good to let a baby cry? Should one teach the baby to walk? Are flash cards and *Baby Mozart* videos a good idea? To these, as to a myriad of other questions, advice varies.

To make matters worse, parents are constantly reminded of their tremendous responsibility. Magazines and books tell parents that they are their children's first teachers, and what they do will have a tremendous impact. Popular book titles suggest that it's up to the parents to start teaching the child everything important: *Teach Your Child How to Think, Teach Your Child Decision-Making, Teach Your Child the Language of Social Success,* and so on. It's easy for parents to believe that if they don't do everything correctly, their children will become failures for life—and it will be the parents' fault.

Parental uncertainties and anxieties are not new. The famous baby doctor Benjamin Spock and the psychoanalyst Erik H. Erikson wrote about the problem in the 1940s and 1950s. When my wife and I began raising a family in the late 1960s, we had anxieties similar to those of young parents today.

Our insecurities make life unpleasant for us, but they also affect our children. According to Erikson, babies can sense our level of relaxation, and they need to experience a sense of calm within us in order to trust the world as a comforting place. Erikson implied that parents gain an inner assurance through a faith in something larger than themselves, such as religion. But not all parents have a deep religious faith. How can parents acquire the inner calm and confidence that is so important?

I believe that the person who offered the best recommendations was the pediatrician Arnold Gesell. Gesell said the first thing that we, as parents, need to recognize is that the baby's development is not really in our hands. Children enter the world with an inborn growth schedule that is the product of several million years of biological evolution. They are preeminently "wise" about what they need and what they are ready and not ready to do. Thus, we should adopt a *child-centered* approach: Instead of trying to force the child into our own predetermined patterns, we should take our cues from the child herself. If the baby is hungry, we should feed her; if she wants to play, we should go ahead and play with her; if she is sleepy, we should let her sleep and not rouse her to be fed. The baby follows nature's laws, so we can safely follow the baby's cues. Thus, there *is* something in which we can place our trust—nature herself.

Initially, when parents are still expecting the birth of a child, this approach might seem to be just another theory. But once they begin watching their infants grow, parents can become deeply impressed by the implicit wisdom of nature's inner guidance. This was certainly the case with me. As I watched our own children, as well as those of our friends, I saw how babies spontaneously engage in behaviors that I never would have imagined teaching, such as rocking back and forth a couple of weeks prior to crawling. I saw how babies investigate objects with rapt and spellbound attention. I saw that when parents follow the baby's signals and needs, babies work out their own stable schedules of feeding, sleep, and wakefulness. I felt a humble pleasure in watching nature work.

Although Gesell published his major works in the 1940s and 1950s and wrote romantically about nature's inner guidance, he also conducted some of the most rigorous scientific studies to date on infant development. In his more technical writing, he spoke of nature's guidance as *biological maturation.* Maturation is an inner, genetic force that determines the sequential nature of development. In utero, the genes direct embryonic growth in fixed sequences, and we can see fixed sequences after birth as well. Children begin to roll over, sit up, crawl, stand, and walk according to a set schedule. When, under the direction of the genes, the child's nervous system has grown to a certain point, the child will feel an inner urge to engage in each new activity.

The environment, to be sure, plays a role. But maturational theorists believe its role is primarily supportive; it ensures that children have opportunities they need to perfect their inwardly emerging capacities.

Maturational theorists recognize that while development always follows specific *sequences,* children do grow at different *rates.* Not all children sit up, crawl, or walk at the same age. But maturationists believe that individual growth rates, too, are largely determined by the genes.

Gesell, finally, initiated the current research interest in inborn temperament. He observed that while some children grow rapidly and are blithe and alert, other children have different temperaments. Some children, who grow more slowly, like to take their time and ponder matters. Others, who grow unevenly, are often moody and alternate between disinterest and flashes of brilliance. Gesell emphasized that every child has a unique, inborn growth rate and temperament, and he urged us to respect each child's individuality.

Not all child-centered theorists emphasize the concept of maturation. Jean Piaget, in particular, believed we can describe a great deal of intellectual development simply in terms of the child's curiosity. Children become intrigued by problems they can't quite solve in their usual ways, and as they work on these problems, they construct new cognitive structures. This construction process isn't directly governed by the genes. But Piaget agreed with the maturationists that the child's development comes from within. It doesn't come from adult teachings or environmental influences, but from the child's own spontaneous interests and efforts to create new ways of understanding the world. Thus, Piagetians also urge us to take our cues from the child. We help children the most by giving them opportunities to work on problems they find most interesting.

Today, the child-centered philosophy is most strongly promoted by the prominent writings of Mary Ainsworth and other attachment theorists. Like Gesell, attachment theorists argue that infants are biologically prepared to guide us with respect to the experiences they need. When we respond to their signals and cues, they develop healthy and secure attachments to us. They enjoy being with us, and they also use us as a secure home base from which to venture off and explore the surroundings.

DOES THE CHILD-CENTERED APPROACH LEAD TO "SPOILING"?

THE CHILD-CENTERED philosophy strikes many people as too permissive. It would seem that if we always take our cues from the child, the child will become spoiled, thinking that she can always be in control. However, the research evidence, at least with respect to infancy, has supported child-centered theory. In a classic study, Sylvia Bell and Mary Ainsworth asked what happens when mothers respond promptly and consistently to babies' cries (rather than acting on their own ideas of when it is all right for them to cry). The clear finding was that responsiveness does not lead to spoiling. On the contrary, by the age of one year these babies, in comparison to those of less responsive parents, cried less and were more independent. They enjoyed being held, but if the mother put them down, they didn't cry or protest but ventured off into exploratory play. They would check back on the mother's presence from time to time, as is natural at this age, but they were basically quite independent. Apparently, when babies' signals are heeded, they become confident that they can always get help when needed and therefore can relax and venture forth and explore on their own.

Other studies have supported this finding with respect to babies' cries and other signals (such as reaching to be picked up and gestures of greeting). When parents respond consistently and sensitively to babies' signals, babies develop feelings of trust in their parents' care, and this trust frees them to venture out into the world with considerable independence.

Of course, as babies grow and become increasingly mobile

and active, their behavior can get out of hand. They can do things that are unsafe to themselves, or harmful or disrespectful toward others. A child-centered approach doesn't advocate complete indulgence. We don't have to allow a two-year-old to scribble on the walls because he's developing his inner artistic urges.

Often it is easy enough to set limits and still allow children to develop their naturally emerging capacities. It's easy enough to say, "Walls aren't for drawing, paper is. Here's some paper." At other times, such solutions aren't so obvious. In general, it seems useful to distinguish between moral and intellectual behavior. It is appropriate to set limits with respect to the moral infractions—behavior that hurts or disrespects others. But we do not want to limit the child's intellectual explorations. (A helpful book on limit setting is Haim Ginott's *Between Parent and Child*.)

When it comes to the child's intellectual explorations, the child-centered approach trusts the child's own sense of what is important. On some level, children know what they need to learn in order to grow. As Ralph Waldo Emerson put it, "It is not for you to choose what he shall know, what he shall do. It is chosen and foreordained, and he only holds the key to his own secret." Thus, parents watch for children's spontaneous interests and give the child opportunities to pursue them.

Often the child's interests may be very different from those of adults. For example, adults increasingly want their young children, beginning as early as one or two years old, to learn numbers, letters, and other skills relevant to their academic futures. But young children demonstrate a passion for other activities— such as running, climbing, jumping, drawing, water play, exploring nature, and make-believe play. Young children's enthusiasm for such activities comes from the children themselves; the activities seem to enable them to actualize their growth.

Even when it comes to recreation, children have their own

interests. I remember when I first took our daughter, then three years old, to the Bronx Zoo. I was sure she would want to see all the large-animal exhibits. But we had hardly begun walking up the long path to the zoo itself when she spotted a worm. She stopped and looked at it, completely absorbed, for about fifteen minutes. She finally decided to walk along, but had taken only a few steps when she became interested in a long chain that fenced off the sides of the path, and she swung on it for several more minutes. All in all, it was over an hour before we arrived at the animal exhibits, and I was surprised that her interest in them was only modest. They seemed too far off for her; she was much more interested in such things as a squirrel and a feather that were right next to her. Gary Nabhan has reported something similar in natural settings. Whereas adults scan nature's vistas and panoramas, young children focus on the objects and wildlife immediately before them—a pine cone, a flower, an ant. They want to learn about small objects and details.

A child-centered philosophy asks us not only to respect the children's own interests, but to allow them to make their own discoveries. Frequently, we are in a hurry to explain things to children or instruct them. For example, when on a walk with a child and the child stops to observe something of interest, such as a flower or a dog, the adult often labels it and explains how it is similar to something else in the child's experience. But the child wants to examine it on her own. Similarly, when children begin to draw, adults often try to improve their drawing. The adults' behavior, in this case, is extremely misguided, for young children routinely develop their drawing talents in remarkable ways on their own, without adult intervention. We shall discuss children's drawing in some detail in chapter 4, but for now I want to state that at least until the child is seven or eight years old, it is best to make sure children have materials and time to draw, and then step back and let them work on their own.

The psychologist Louise Ames once noted that often it isn't parents, but grandparents, who best exemplify the child-centered attitude. Grandparents derive endless pleasure from just watching their grandchildren go about the business of being children. Whether a child is trying out her first steps, trying to balance one block on another, making up a song while playing with a truck, or watching an insect, a grandparent may sit and watch, smiling, as if something quite wonderful is occurring. Grandparents do not rush in to teach and correct the child—they just enjoy observing. And children often feel good about being in the presence of grandparents. Many parents think children like grandparents because the grandparents spoil their grandchildren. Some parents say, "Of course my son likes his grandparents; they let him get away with murder." But I suspect the real reason is that grandparents have a broader sense of the life cycle. They recognize the special qualities of the childhood years and the child's own efforts to discover what is important to her.

Nevertheless, the child-centered approach strikes many people as too laid-back, especially for today's high-charged society. The child-centered approach seems more appropriate for an earlier era, when the pace of life was slower. Today everyone is anxious to prepare children for a competitive future, and to begin as soon as possible. Adult-directed philosophies dominate the books on parenthood and child development. I will briefly review some major models and then expand on the child-centered alternative.

ADULT-DIRECTED APPROACHES

Diana Baumrind's "Authoritative Parent"

Pediatricians, educators, and even popular magazines draw on psychological research, and there is no research on parenthood more prominent than that by Diana Baumrind. Nearly every child psychology textbook highlights her findings on effective parenting.

On the basis of parent interviews and home observations, Baumrind reported that the most self-reliant, self-controlled, and task-oriented four-year-old nursery-school children had parents of a certain type. The parents weren't "authoritarian" parents who were bossy, intrusive, and unaffectionate. Nor were they "permissive" parents who helplessly allowed their children to do whatever they wanted. Instead, the effective parents were "authoritative." They combined firm control with warmth and a desire for the child to become independent.

On the surface, Baumrind's research seems to weigh against the child-centered approach. Her highly effective "authoritative parent" generally sounds more controlling and directive than a child-centered philosophy would advocate.

But Baumrind's findings are much more complex than textbook summaries say. Her major study described not three types, but eight. Moreover, some lenient parents had extremely competent children. These were not the parents whom Baumrind labeled "permissive." The permissive parents seemed confused. But other parents were very clear about their views. They valued a democratic family that respects the voice of every family member, including that of the youngest child. As one would expect, their children were often independent in nursery school. More surprising, perhaps, the children generally did what the parents wanted. The children weren't following parental orders (the parents rarely gave any). Instead, the children seemed to feel that because their choices were respected and the parents were reasonable, they would pay careful attention to what the parents wanted. Thus, a close look at Baumrind's actual data may reveal significant support for child-centered parenting—parenting that credits the child with her own wisdom about her needs.

Early Academics

In the United States today, there is a major emphasis on early academic learning. Parents, with their eyes on the future, would like to begin teaching their children intellectual skills early on, giving them a head start on academic success. President George W. Bush wants to make Head Start much more academic.

The question of accelerating intellectual development is long-standing in psychology, and research has yet to say for sure how much speeding up is possible. Generally speaking, it seems that efforts to accelerate cognitive growth in day care and preschool do produce some gains, but the gains are temporary. There also is evidence that parents who talk a lot to their children raise their children's vocabularies, especially if parents focus their words on the children's interests. However, adult teaching can backfire. When adults assume too much control, they diminish children's curiosity, which seems essential for cognitive growth.

Moreover, some research warns against introducing academic material too soon. Kathy Hirsh-Pasek found that academic preschools, compared to more play-oriented preschools, produced kindergartners who were less creative and more anxious about their performances. They also liked school less. These children showed some academic gains in preschool—they knew their numbers and letters better than the others—but these gains dissipated during kindergarten. The negative effects of early academic instruction weren't overpowering, but other research points in a similar direction.

Scaffolding

An increasingly popular approach to advancing the child's development is that of the Russian psychologist Lev Vygotsky. Vygotsky actually wrote his major works during the 1930s, but there is keen interest today in his proposal to teach children in the "zone of proximal development." This is the forward progress children can make when, instead of working alone, they work with the assistance of more competent people. Assistance is often described as "scaffolding"; we help the child along for a while and increasingly remove our assistance as the child gets the hang of a new skill.

Scaffolding advocates want to avoid total or excessive adult direction. But from a child-centered perspective their approach still presents problems. For one thing, when we try to move development forward, we shorten the time the child has to pursue her current interests. For example, as I will argue in detail later, childhood is a time when children need leisurely time to explore the natural world. If we are always moving the child forward, trying to advance her intellectual skills, we can deprive the child of this time.

In addition, scaffolding advocates don't always recognize the extent to which their method might foster intellectual dependency. Consider the following example, which is a central illustration in Laura E. Berk and Adam Winsler's popular book, *Scaffolding Children's Learning*. An adult is "scaffolding" the efforts of a young child, Jason, as Jason tries "to put a difficult puzzle together."

JASON: I can't get this one in.
ADULT: Which piece might go down here?
JASON: His shoes. *(Looks for a piece resembling the clowns' shoes but tries the wrong one)*
ADULT: Well, what piece looks like this shape?
JASON: The brown one.
ADULT: There you have it! Now try turning that piece just a little.
JASON: There!

Jason then happily succeeds with several pieces. But note the extent to which the adult has directed Jason's efforts. When Jason confronts a new problem, he is likely to look for help once again.

The puzzle, to be sure, was difficult, and it therefore required adult assistance. But from a child-centered perspective, we would question why it was so important that the young child work on this task in the first place. Child-centered educators value the problems that children are determined to solve themselves. Quite often, these are not store-bought toys and games. Instead, they are the countless problems children encounter in their spontaneous activities—drawing, modeling with sand and dirt, using props for dramatic play, pouring liquids, sorting pebbles or coins, creating stories and poems while they play. Quite often, young children become so deeply engrossed in their activities that they hardly pay attention to the adults around them—let alone ask the adults for help.

The Birth-to-Three Movement

There has been a new call for adult intervention in children's early development. The goal is not to accelerate specific skills, but to stimulate neural connections. At a major White House Conference in 1997, Hillary Clinton, the actor Rob Reiner, and some neuroscientists called attention to research suggesting that environmental experiences in the first three years alter the brain for life. They urged all caregivers to take advantage of this special window of opportunity nature provides for stimulating the child's brain development.

In a nutshell, the scientific argument is this. During the first three years after birth, the brain is furiously at work creating neural connections. In fact, the two-year-old's brain already has twice as many synaptic connections as the brain of the adult. But by the age of three years or so, this period of exuberant brain development is over. During the next several years, a pruning process dominates; large numbers of synaptic connections are lost. The connections that are retained are those that have been exercised through experience. Whatever the child sees, hears, touches, tastes, or thinks activates synaptic connections and cements them in; the rest wither away. Thus, if we want children to form richly wired brains, we must give them rich experiences in the first three years of life, before the pruning process gets too far along.

The "birth to three" message rapidly spread through the media. Numerous science writers, private firms, foundations, and governmental agencies have urged parents to take advantage of this extraordinary window of opportunity nature has provided. Parents, they say, should give their children as much sensory and intellectual stimulation as possible in the first three years, during this period of exuberant brain growth. Otherwise, the window will shut and the educational advantages that parents might have provided their children, including their children's hopes of getting into Ivy League colleges, will be lost forever.

Many scientists, however, are more skeptical. One attempt to put the birth-to-three movement in perspective is that of John T. Bruer. In his book *The Myth of the First Three Years,* Bruer makes these points.

First, most of the brain research is not that new. It's over two decades old.

Second, our knowledge about brain development, in the first three years and after, is still sketchy. There's much we do not know.

Third, it is true that some scientists hypothesize critical periods, time periods when the organism is most receptive to environmental stimulation. But it is wrong to think of birth-to-three as the one-and-only, all-encompassing critical period. Instead, there seem to be several specific critical periods, and only some of these occur during the first three years. For example, there might be a critical period with respect to color vision during the first three years; babies need to see colors during this time if they are to develop this capacity. But other critical periods, such as those with respect to language learning, occur later.

Fourth, critical periods do not govern most learning in life.

Fifth, significant aspects of brain development occur long after the age of three years. For example, the prefrontal lobes, which influence intellectual processes such as planning and reasoning, do not seem to even begin pruning until puberty.

Sixth, it's wrong to think of sheer numbers of synapses as good and pruning as bad. Pruning may bring order into synaptic connections, enabling us to stay goal-directed and avoid distractions.

Bruer's points are sensible, but the birth-to-three message is still going strong. It also is creating considerable parental anxiety. Parents have the impression that the first three years of life are somehow critical, and they should be doing something, but the advice they are given is confusing and contradictory.

Some birth-to-three experts advise parents to just use common sense. But other experts recommend that parents provide as much stimulation as possible—a "full court developmental press every minute during the birth-to-3 developmental season." To help them stimulate youngsters, parents will find bookstores and toy stores selling flash cards, "Brilliant Beginnings" instruction kits, classic-music videos, and new books with practical advice.

Sometimes the same expert gives contradictory messages. An example is the book *Start Smart: Building Brain Power in the Early Years*. In its early pages, the book cautions against overreacting to the birth-to-three message. What babies need most is simply our loving care. But the book leaves the overall impression that parents should bombard young children with stimulation: talk, stories, TV, songs, dances, puzzles—everything possible. Some of the stimulation involves problem-solving instruction that far exceeds the three-year-old's capacities.

In a more academic book, *What's Going On in There?*, Lise Eliot offers parenting advice in light of a vast amount of research, both on brain development and parenting practices. But Eliot's advice often requires parent to walk a difficult tightrope. She suggests that parents stimulate children, but not overstimulate them. Parents should be "demanding," but not "pressuring."

Eliot recommends ways of "sustaining babies' interests" and "encouraging children's attention." In particular, parents can rotate toys and trade toys with friends and neighbors so the children won't tire of them. But once again, parents must worry about overdoing things. They shouldn't present so many toys that the child becomes confused and loses focus. Parenting becomes a very difficult balancing act.

THE NATURAL EXPLORER

THE BIRTH-TO-THREE child-rearing advice, then, is often confusing and difficult to follow. I believe this has happened because the experts have sometimes lost sight of what young children are like.

Most notably, the experts generally assume that adults must encourage babies' and toddlers' attention and sustain their interest. But simple observation suggests otherwise. Without any urging on our part, babies investigate common objects—a wad of paper, a pair of eyeglasses, keys, pots and pans—with rapt attention. They examine such objects for several minutes, oblivious to all other stimulation. In fact, the intensity of the infant's concentration often seems much greater than that of most adults. I have often been struck how the expression of the baby when examining objects is similar to that of great athletes and artists during their peak efforts.

What's more, as babies begin to walk and become toddlers, they go through a period in which they are the boldest of explorers. They rush down hallways, opening closets and cupboards. They energetically climb chairs, couches, and stairs, seeing what they can find. And they march along sidewalks and across lawns, elated by their ability to move about on their own and taking pure delight in their discoveries. A flower, a bird, a puddle of water—the world is full of new wonders. If they slip or fall, they simply get up and keep on moving. The psychoanalysts Phyllis Greenacre and Margaret Mahler referred to this time as one in which the child has a "love affair with the world."

Toddlers become so exuberant in their explorations that Mahler and her colleagues have been moved to call the early toddler period "precious" and a "pinnacle of perfection." The younger baby, to be sure, also explored the world with great intensity. But for the first several months, the baby was confined to the mother's lap, so his explorations were restricted. And when the baby was able to crawl away from the mother, he also was concerned about the mother's presence. Thus, although the baby certainly explored energetically, he also frequently checked back to make sure the mother was still there. Now, when the baby can walk, and with a basic trust in the mother reasonably well established, the baby feels a boundless freedom to venture forth. As Mahler's colleague Louise Kaplan says, it's as if the baby's deep and persistent urge to explore is finally released. The youngster often becomes so consumed by his explorations that he forgets about his mother altogether. Occasionally, to be sure, the child does still remember her and gives a quick glance back at her. But he ventures forth with such courage and joy that the world seems to smile on this new conqueror.

This period of full-tilt exploration lasts from about twelve to eighteen months. During the months and years that follow, childhood continues to be marked by intense curiosity and exploration, but childhood is mixed with new doubts and new concerns about one's place in the social world. There isn't quite the same never-ending exuberance of the toddler on the move.

The elation and courage of the young toddler also character-izes some of our adventures as adults, as when we sail new waters, hike over new terrains, climb steep cliffs, and dive into unexplored waters. The difference is that the toddler's elated explorations occur day in and day out. The child's whole waking life is one wonderful adventure.

It would seem, then, that adults might find it easy to just enjoy the youngster's courage and exuberance. But this is not the case. Instead, adults generally assume that they must instruct or help the child. They think they must show the child how to jump, climb stairs, open boxes, and so on, even though the child learns such activities with great pleasure on her own. And, as we have seen, even advanced scholars assume that adults need to improve the infant's and toddler's curiosity.

Of course, some infants and toddlers become bored and list-less. But when this happens, it's generally wrong to assume that the problem somehow lies with the child. Rather, it's likely that adults are imposing their own interests on the child and curtail-ing the child's natural way of learning.

For example, in Manhattan it is now rare to see a toddler or young child walking outdoors with her caretakers. Adults push the children everywhere in strollers. While pushing, the adults often try to engage their children in educational conversations ("Now today is Friday. What comes after Friday?"). But the children are hardly interested. I am sure that if the children could express themselves in words, they would say, "Here I am, eager to move about on my own and explore what I encounter, but the adults pick me up and force me to ride. And all the while, they talk about things that *they* think are important, but which I can't even see. There's a fascinating world to explore. Why do they rob me of the opportunity?"

The child-centered philosophy, then, holds that we help children learn by respecting their own ways of learning. Like a tree whose branches grow toward the sunlight and whose roots reach out toward water, the young child eagerly reaches out for the experiences she needs to develop. Thus, we should bring the baby and toddler into contact with a world in all its richness and then give the child a chance to explore what is most interesting to her. And instead of trying to assist or direct the child's investigations, we should give the child a chance to learn on her own.

OUR UNOBTRUSIVE PRESENCE

QUITE OFTEN, THE child-centered approach is criticized for going overboard in its emphasis on independent learning. This approach seems to be so opposed to adult guidance or assistance that it wants us to leave the child completely alone—a recommendation that sounds like neglect.

Actually, there are many ways that we, as parents or caretakers, can help children learn on their own. We can, for example, give them educational materials that arouse their curiosity and then let them work on the materials themselves. This is an approach that is integral to Montessori and some Piagetian nursery schools. But for children under the age of three or so, such materials are fairly scarce; the available materials do not compare to the countless resources—physical and social—that children find fascinating in their everyday worlds.

What I would like recommend here is not specific materials, or even a specific technique. Rather it is an attitude, a way of being with the child.

The philosopher Søren Kierkegaard, in a brief comment on the baby's first attempts to walk, said that for the parent, "The art is to be constantly present and yet not be present." That is, we must be present for the child's safety, yet not in the sense of imposing our anxieties, instructions, or assistance on the child. We need to stay sufficiently in the background to give children the freedom to learn by themselves.

This attitude—this *unobtrusive presence*—is helpful in a wide range of situations. A young child can only explore many new settings or try out new activities, such as climbing stairs, running downhill, or wading in water, because we provide the opportunities and stay nearby for protection. But the child can only learn freely and independently if our presence is unobtrusive.

Maria Montessori also tried to describe this attitude and offered some examples of it. She described, for instance, ways in which sensitive parents accompany their toddlers on walks. Such parents do not force the child to keep with them, or pick them up and put them in strollers if they can't keep up. Instead, the parents follow the child's pace, stopping whenever the child stops to examine things, giving the child opportunities to explore. As the parents stand patiently by, they quietly enjoy the fascination that the child shows for the most common things—a leaf, an insect, a puddle of water. These parents are clearly not neglecting the child, nor are they controlling the child's learning. Rather, their patient, unobtrusive presence gives the child the chance to investigate the world on her own.

Although the caretaker's unobtrusive presence is helpful in a variety of circumstances, it seems to emerge most naturally in one particular context. This is when children, soon after they can crawl, begin what Mary Ainsworth calls "using the parent as a base from which to explore." If, for example, a mother takes her nine-month-old son to the park, he will typically stay close to her for a while, but then become increasingly interested in the environment and take little excursions away from her to investigate it. From time to time he will look back at her, or actually return to her before venturing forth once again—as though to reassure himself that she is still there for him. The mother senses that it is just her stable presence that the child desires. He wouldn't want her moving about or shadowing him or trying to control him through verbal commands. It is simply her calm and stationary presence—what Margaret Mahler called her "quiet availability"—that gives him the courage to explore the world on his own.

Here, the adult's actions are limited. The parent's behavior is like that of parents in many species of animals, whose method has been characterized as "watching all the time, but acting only when the baby demands it." Sometimes, however, we may wish to be more active, as when we bring infants into contact with objects that are beyond their reach. If, for example, an infant girl shows an interest in a high door handle, we can lift her up so she can reach it. At this point, however, it is often best to become still, to do nothing more than hold her. Having set the stage for learning, we turn the action over to the child.

The child also wishes to investigate other people, and here again our unobtrusive presence is most helpful. I remember one day when I was watching a kids' soccer match while holding our five-month-old daughter. We were standing next to another spectator, a boy about ten years old. Our daughter looked intently at him, and then she reached for his face and began touching it. She was completely absorbed in her deliberate study of his face. I expected the boy to pull away or change the interaction to some "baby talk" game. But I was surprised that the boy just stood perfectly still and gave our baby a chance to explore in her own way. He just stood quietly, with a slightly amused smile. He somehow knew that this is how babies learn about people, and he gave her an opportunity to do so.

Our unobtrusive presence usually requires a good deal of patience. It takes patience for us to just stand by while a baby perfects the skills of walking or stair climbing or investigates a flower. It requires patience for us to hold still while a baby explores us. But we soon find ourselves taking silent pleasure in the intensity of the child's actions. I believe we get the sense that the child is engaged in activities that are vital to her growth— and we are quietly giving growth a chance to occur.

I have described one way of helping children learn on their own. It is only one way. As mentioned earlier, we can also provide toys and materials that engage children's independent efforts. We can also interact more fully with children in ways that facilitate learning without infringing on their independence. For example, Daniel Stern and others have described how infants and mothers often begin playing together, with the mother loosely imitating the baby's sounds and gestures and also varying them in ways the baby finds interesting and enjoyable. The baby is exposed to new stimuli, but the baby also plays a large role in regulating the pace, intensity, and rhythm of the interaction. Nevertheless, it is frequently just our patient and unobtrusive presence that gives the child the security and the freedom to explore the world on her own.

||||||||||||||||||||||||||||||||||||||||||||||||||||||||||||||||||||||||||||||||||

CHAPTER 2

The Child as a Dramatist

Then dawns the Invisible.

—EMILY JANE BRONTË

ONE AFTERNOON our daughter Sally, who was two years old, pointed to a spot on the top of our vacuum cleaner and said, "Deed." I couldn't see what she was pointing to and tried to get her to clarify what it was. But she just kept pointing and saying, "Deed!," becoming increasingly emphatic and irritated with me for failing to respond to what she saw. I was shaken. Was she hallucinating? It didn't make any sense. I decided to just push the episode sufficiently out of my mind to get on with my tasks for the day.

The next afternoon, Sally and I were in the park, and I gave her a ride on the small merry-go-round. When she got off, she said, "Want ride, Deed?" Then she pushed the merry-go-round for her imaginary companion.

It was not long before Sally talked to both Deed and a new companion, "Bissa." No one in our family had any idea where Sally might have got the names. Her companions were less than an inch tall, sometimes resting in her pockets or holders in the car. They went away sometime before she was eight years old.

The afternoon Sally pointed to Deed made a deep impression on me. There is no doubt that she saw Deed. But what struck me most was the sheer creative power. She seemed to create something out of nothing.

Imaginary companions are but one aspect of the child's make-believe play. Such play begins when the child is about 1½ or 2 years old and involves the child's early use of symbols. That is, children use objects or actions to symbolize something they imagine. For example, Piaget reported that when his daughter Jacqueline was this age, she one day pretended that a piece of cloth was a pillow and acted out the process of going to sleep. On other occasions she moved her finger across a table and called it a horse and crawled on all fours, saying, "Meow." As children move into their third year, they begin using dolls, sticks, rocks, and other objects to create elaborate dramas, even speaking in different tones when acting out the roles of the different characters.

But within children's world of make-believe, there is nothing so striking as the imaginary companion. Not only are they visible to children; they become central figures in children's lives. In an early study by Louise Bates Ames and Janet Leonard, a parent described her three-year-old son's imaginary playmate, Dig-a-dig chicken. The boy played with Dig and talked about him all the time. Dig was sometimes as big as Daddy and sometimes so small he could fit in tiny places. Dig himself had a little boy. The child built a house for Dig, which he wouldn't let anyone knock down, and whenever the family went anywhere, the child asked if Dig could go too. Children also frequently set places for their companions at the dinner table, place extra pillows for them on their beds, and host numerous events for them—especially elaborate birthday parties.

Imaginary companions become very real presences in family's lives. In John and Elizabeth Newson's study in Nottingham,

England, the parents of four-year-olds often made statements such as the following.

[Our daughter] has Janet. It's a little girl. She came out with her—oh, more than a year ago. Everything's Janet—and yet she doesn't know anybody called Janet. But I mean—we can be watching television, and if my lad sits too close, it's, "Your squashing her—get off!" And he *has* to get off, and all! I think we've all got used to Janet now.

As in my case, many of the English parents said that they became worried. They thought their child's imagination might have crossed over the edge. But the parents were reassured when they learned that other children went through the same phase.

One of my students, a mother of a 2½-year-old, told our class that she was unnerved by her daughter's experience of her imaginary friends, such as Bo Bar.

No one in our family knows where the name came from, and this pretend friend is so *real* to her. Like the other day, my daughter and I were dancing, and she said, "Bo Bar, come over and dance with us too." I saw the movie *The Sixth Sense,* about the boy who sees dead people, and I started to get freaked out about my daughter. Then I saw in the nursery school that other children have imaginary companions, too, so I became less upset. But I still don't like to think about it too much.

Marjorie Taylor, a psychologist at the University of Oregon, has reviewed much of the research to date. Most studies have focused on children between the ages of two and seven years, when children (and/or their parents) most commonly report the presence of imaginary companions. Taylor estimates that nearly half of all children create an imaginary companion at some point before they are seven years old. If one includes stuffed animals and dolls that children treat as animate, the percentage is somewhat higher—about 60 percent. Girls tend to create them slightly more often than boys. Tracy Gleason, Anne Sebanc, and Willard Hartup at the University of Minnesota have found that children who create imaginary companions typically create more than one. Sometimes children have several companions at the same time; sometimes they create new companions after reporting that one has died or gone away.

Most imaginary companions are people, usually children. But a sizeable minority—perhaps a third—are animals.

Some children also impersonate animals. For example, they move about on all fours, barking or meowing, eating out of a dish or bowl on the floor, and even urinating in animal fashion. When spoken to, the child will either bark or meow back, or just look at the human in a quizzical manner. The child gets deep into the role. While the child is a dog or cat, the child doesn't appear to understand human language.

One New York City mother and father spent a year getting their four-year-old daughter ready for the Stanford-Binet intelligence test required for admission to prestigious nursery schools. But when the test examiner asked the child her name, she said, "Amanda," the name of their cat. Then, to every question the examiner asked, the child simply responded, "Meow."

It is often believed that children who create invisible companions are lonely and isolated—or even emotionally disturbed. Several research studies have found that the children who create invisible companions, compared to other children, are more frequently firstborn or only children, a finding that supports the loneliness hypothesis. But this finding isn't perfectly consistent, and children who have imaginary companions have as many playmates as other children do.

Generally speaking, researchers have not found dramatic

personality differences between children who invent companions and children who do not. Some researchers have found no differences. When investigators do find differences, the children with the invisible companions are generally judged to be more sociable, intelligent, and creative. They are more likely to engage in more imaginative make-believe play in general and to watch less TV. Children with imaginary companions also perform better on role-taking tasks—tasks that ask them to understand other people's perspectives.

Summarizing the findings, Marjorie Taylor says, "The invention of an imaginary companion should not be interpreted as a symptom of emotional or interpersonal problems. In fact, children who create imaginary companions tend to be particularly sociable individuals who enjoy the company of others and are somewhat advanced in social understanding."

DO CHILDREN BELIEVE INVISIBLE COMPANIONS ARE REAL?

AS I MENTIONED above, when our daughter created Deed, it was clear to me that she actually saw the tiny person, and other parents have had the same impression. As one parent in Nottingham, England, said of her four-year-old, "He has Candy, a dog. When I go on a walk with *my* dog, we take Candy; we have to take Candy to the edge of the pavement. I think he can really see his dog. In fact, I said to my husband, I think *I* can see this dog!"

What is more, children's pretend companions can take on lives of their own. When Marjorie Taylor and her colleagues asked preschool children if there was anything they didn't like about their imaginary companions, the children "had plenty of complaints. 'She puts yogurt in my hair.' 'He hits me on the head.' 'She won't share.'" Some imaginary companions talk too loud. Some "don't show up when the child wants them to, whereas others are annoying because they never go away." We might think that the children who create them have control over them, but this isn't what the children say.

Taylor describes the experience of one mother who took her three-year-old daughter to a horse show. The child loved horses and had a pretend pony of her own. The child was sure that her pony would be with all the other horses at the horse show, but "a thorough search of the grounds indicated that the pony must have had other plans for the day." The child was so upset that the mother had to cut the outing short. "The situation was exasperating for the mother who saw a seemingly obvious solution to the problem. Why couldn't her daughter just pretend the pony was there? For some reason, this didn't seem to be an option."

Thus, children frequently experience their invisible companions as having minds of their own. This fact is often taken as evidence that children believe their companions are real.

Indeed, some cultures believe that the companions are in fact real. The experience of psychologist Antonia Mills in India brings the point home. Initially, when Mills asked the adults she surveyed if they knew of any children who had imaginary companions, the adults all said, "No." But Mills thought about her question and changed her term from "imaginary companions" to "invisible companions." Then several adults said, "Yes," they knew children who had them. In the parts of India that Mills surveyed the companions are seen as real spiritual beings or real people from past lives. When children are about seven years old, the adults pressure the children to stop talking to the invisible presences. The adults fear the children might take on past identities rather than pursue their current lives.

Readers who entertain the possibility of reincarnation will be interested to know that children themselves sometimes refer to past lives. In the Newsons' study in Nottingham, England, the parents reported that their four-year-olds often talked about a mysterious time "before I was born," "when I was a man," and "when Daddy was a little boy." One mother said, "He's always on about a horse that he had before he was born. It's ever so strange—he's always talked about it ever since he *could* talk. It makes you wonder."

My undergraduate students from the Dominican Republic, Colombia, and other Latin American countries tell me that their traditional cultures also hold that invisible companions are real. They are guardian angels. Parents teach children to pray to them every night before bed and the angels protect them throughout their lives. But only young children see them. My students tell me that the invisible companions generally disappear when the children are about seven years old. Parents believe that this happens because children become immersed in school and social activities.

Of course, in the United States and other societies dominated by Western science, invisible companions are generally considered imaginary. The unsettled question is whether *children* believe they are real. Since children often describe their companions as taking on lives of their own, it would seem that children do believe in their reality. But Marjorie Taylor disagrees. She notes that when researchers interview children about their invisible companions, the children often spontaneously tell the interviewer, "They're not real, you know." Taylor adds that adult writers sometimes experience their characters as having minds of their own. Taylor asks, "Do we want to claim that adult novelists believe their characters are real?"

Overall, Taylor says, young children's "mastery of fantasy" is impressive; they handle the reality/fantasy distinction about as well as adults. She characterizes the view that children confuse fantasy and reality as "negative."

However, I wish Taylor wasn't so concerned with finding the

similarity between young children and rational adults. What needs emphasis is the creative imagination of young children. Young children routinely create vivid characters and dramas, and the characters become so animated that they take on lives of their own. In these respects the ordinary child thinks in ways that characterize only the most creative adults.

THE FATE OF IMAGINARY COMPANIONS

IMAGINARY COMPANIONS, like make-believe play in general, appear to be most common in the years from about 2½ to 6, reaching a crescendo toward the end of this time. Dorothy and Jerome Singer call it "the high season of imaginative play." Then the child's imaginary life fades. In the Newsons' study in England, only 3 percent of the seven hundred seven-year-olds were identified by their parents as having imaginary companions, compared to 22 percent of these children at the age of four years.

The seven-year-old becomes more rational. In Piaget's theory, the child is entering the stage of concrete operations and now thinks logically about the real world before her. The child becomes suspicious of appearances and knows, for example, that even though water poured from one container to another appears to have increased, the amount must be the same since one hasn't added anything or taken anything away. The child also distinguishes dreams from reality, living from nonliving things, and fact from fancy. Exercising her more logical mind, she now questions magic and myths such as Santa Claus. She asks, "How come Santa used our wrapping paper?" "How come Santa has the same handwriting as Daddy?" One of our sons asked, at the age of seven, how Santa could get to all the homes he saw in one night, and how Santa got into those that didn't have chimneys.

The age of magic, from about two to seven, gives way to the age of reason.

The child's play, too, undergoes a change. She no longer spins tales aloud to herself, regardless of whether others are listening or not. Solitary play gives way to social games with rules, in which the child adjusts her behavior in response to that of her opponents and teammates. She is becoming adjusted to social reality.

As mentioned earlier, these changes are part of a broad "five-to-seven-year" shift, in which the child generally becomes more rational and realistic. Considerable evidence documents such changes in Western societies, and some evidence indicates that the change is culturally universal. Although the evidence is still tentative, the five-to-seven shift also seems to correspond to neurological growth, particularly refinements of the frontal lobes.

Thus, imaginary companions give way as the child's mind becomes more logical and rational and the child adapts to the social world. But some major researchers, including Marjorie Taylor and Dorothy and Jerome Singer, aren't so sure that children always give up their imaginary companions at the age of seven or so. Some children may simply keep them more private. Such a change would coincide with Vygotsky's theory on the internalization of language. Four- and five-year-olds talk out loud as they engage in solitary play. Then, at age six or so, their speech begins to become quieter and more abbreviated, and by the age of seven or eight, others cannot hear it at all. Self-directed speech has gone underground and is differentiated from public speech. In a similar way, some children may still have imaginary companions, but keep this fact to themselves.

Taylor and the Singers also emphasize that some children, during middle and late childhood (from about age seven to twelve), create *paracosms,* entire imaginary societies or worlds. The Brontë children, including Emily, Charlotte, and Anne, created two imaginary worlds for the toy soldiers given them by their father. The characters engaged in magnificent dramas, some of which were incorporated into their adult novels and poetry.

Taylor and the Singers also point out that adults occasionally have imaginary companions. Many adults, like adolescents, enjoy games such as Dungeons and Dragons, believe in ghosts and the paranormal, and participate in activities such as Civil War recreations.

All in all, Taylor and the Singers try hard to build a case for continuity between the make-believe play of the young child and fantasy after this period. But compared to young children, the percentages of people who engage in the highly imaginative activities seem small. It's important to recognize that there is a time, early childhood, when imagination reigns.

THE ADULT'S ROLE

RECENT RESEARCH HAS called attention to the adult's contribution to imaginative play. Indeed, some psychologists believe that adults initiate the child's make-believe play. For example, a parent might tell a one-year-old who is moving toward a cardboard box, "Oh, you want to go into your house." In this way, the parent suggests the possibility of pretending. Some parents also explicitly direct children's play. If a child is holding a doll, an adult might say, "Pat your baby," or, "Tell your baby to chew her food." Several psychologists have described such parental coaching as "scaffolding"; the parents get the child started in make-believe play before the child can take over and engage in it by herself.

However, it's not at all clear that adults actually have this effect. Two major studies—one by Wendy Haight and Peggy Miller, the other by Miller and Catherine Garvey—indicate that it's often the child, rather than the adult, who initiates the early episodes of make-believe play. What's more, the most stunning instance of make-believe play, the imaginary companion, is clearly the child's creation—not the parent's. Parents are surprised by what the child comes up with.

What researchers have documented is that, once children begin make-believe play, parents can enrich it. They do so by playing along with children, responding to the child's initiatives in a lighthearted way. When adults are too intrusive or controlling, they dampen the child's fantasy play.

Recommendations

Based on research studies and personal observations, I believe parents can promote make-believe play by taking these steps.

1. Most fundamentally, we foster imaginative play by our positive attitude toward it. Accept it and enjoy it. Don't criticize it or discourage it.

2. Provide props, such as blocks and dolls. The best toys are often rather simple, allowing for the child's imagination to reign. At the same time, children also find their own props, using sticks, rocks, paper clips, and anything imaginable to represent fantasy characters in a drama. Commercial toys are usually overly structured—they do too much for the child. They seem exciting on the TV commercial, but the child soon tires of them.

3. Give children opportunities to play in nature's outdoors. In one study, Mary Ann Kirby found that four-year-olds engage in particularly rich imaginative play in spots they can use as hideouts (such as empty spaces beneath large

bushes). Andrea Taylor and her colleagues found that poor inner-city children engage in richer fantasy play when they can play in green settings in their neighborhoods.

4. Play along with the child if she asks, but allow the child to direct. (In the Newsons' study in England, a mother said she plays shop with her four-year-old. When asked what role she plays, she said, "Oh, I'm a mere customer—I can't be the shopkeeper!")

Marjorie Taylor reports several instances in which an adult's effort to exercise some control over a child's imaginary companion's behavior led the child to abandon the companion altogether. Taylor says, "Perhaps the key to the child's enjoyment of the parent's participation is that the child retains the role of the director." The parent fosters dramatic play by acting something like a good-natured stage manager. The parent provides some props and fills in a role when needed, but lets the child direct.

|||||||||||||||||||||||||||||||||||||||||||||||||||||||||||||||||||||||||||

CHAPTER 3

The Child as a Naturalist

Live free, child of the mist.

—H. D. THOREAU

ONE MORNING, my four-year-old neighbor, Jonathan, stepped out of his front door and shouted, "Hi," to me. The next moment he heard a bird's call and returned the call, as if to say hello to the bird, too. He acted as if nothing could be more natural.

Children seem to have a strong affinity for nature. Like Jonathan, they often assume that they have a companionship with other living things. Indeed, many of the great Romantic poets—Wordsworth, Blake, Shelley, and others—looked back on childhood as a time when wind, brooks, grass, and other elements seemed to sing, speak, and move with them. Between the child and nature, Wordsworth wrote, there is a "primal sympathy," and nature provides the child with both comfort and ceaseless wonders.

The child's attraction to nature seems to begin very early. The infant or toddler, for example, will often express pure joy at the sight of an animal such as a dog or a bird. The child may break into an enormous smile and try to hold the animal, and energet-ically follow it wherever it goes.

Similarly, infants and toddlers are enthralled by sand, mud, and water. At the beach, for example, they spend hours com-pletely engrossed in handling the sand. They find something incredibly meaningful in the simple experience of handling it.

The power of the child's attraction to nature often mystifies adults. We presumably went through a period when we felt the same way about nature—about the sight of a dog or a bird, the feel of sand—but the experience is now buried deep within us. Our outlook is dominated by other matters—our jobs and ambitions, our plans and daily schedules. As Wordsworth put it:

> Waters on a starry night
> Are beautiful and fair;
> The sunshine is a glorious birth;
> But yet I know, wher'er I go,
> That there hath past away a glory from the earth.

Even so, we might expect that most adults would cherish the child's special joy and wonder in the natural world. But this is not my impression.

For the past decade, in Manhattan and in suburban New Jer-sey, I have tried to pay close attention to what happens when children, walking along with their caretakers, become interested in some aspect of nature. I have been most struck by adults' impatience. For example, I recently saw a girl, about two years old, walking with her caretaker across a Manhattan square. The girl registered little emotion until she spotted a pigeon, and then she lit up. She pointed at the bird as if she had discovered some-thing of enormous importance and tried to follow it about. But the adult merely said, "Yes, a pigeon. Now come along." The child complied for a few steps, then changed direction and began following the bird once again, this time provoking a sterner response.

More broadly, the relentless forces of modernization are taking nature away from children. Everywhere we turn, we see construction crews removing the weedy waysides, woods, fields, and ponds that children once loved to explore. In their place, real estate developers are creating indoor malls, office buildings, and housing developments with parking lots, cement walkways, perfectly manicured lawns, and neatly landscaped flowerbeds. Anything wild is being removed.

In New York City, the parks department even plans to replace all grass playing fields with artificial turf. Grass fields, the parks department says, become too muddy and difficult to maintain. Grass fields are not, of course, models of nature's diversity. But the soil and grass are alive and interact with the surrounding waters and ecosystems, hosting subtle varieties of vegetation, birds, and other life-forms. Upon hearing of the plan, a nursery-school teacher exclaimed, "But where are our kids going to find their worms?"

As we remove nature out-of-doors, we keep enriching children's indoor environments. We provide children with all the latest videos, television programs, video games, and computer technology. In a recent study, Gary Nabhan and Sara St. Antoine found that even in the remote Sonoran Desert along the United States/Mexico borderland, most of the eight- to fourteen-year-olds in their sample said they had learned more about wild animals from TV and movies than from direct experience in the out-of-doors. Most of the children, who were from Native American as well as Latino and Anglo backgrounds, had never spent a half hour alone in a wild place or had collected natural treasures such as feathers, rocks, and bones from their desert surroundings.

Is declining contact with nature a cause for concern? Are

children really in danger of losing something important in their lives? If so, what, precisely, is at risk?

For answers, we turn to developmental psychologists and other social scientists. But the information they provide is sparse. Researchers have largely ignored the fact that the child lives in a natural world at all. Every year, thousands of studies investigate children's thinking about math, scientific concepts, language, and people, but relatively few have examined children's experiences of the natural world.

I believe that this neglect occurs because the concerns of psychologists and other social scientists basically reflect society's dominant goals and values. Our society wants children to achieve success in the human-made world. We want children to learn the cognitive skills that enable them to succeed in a high-tech workplace. We also want them to learn to interact well with other people. But the development of the child's relationship with the natural world is hardly a national priority.

On the topic of nature and childhood, there are only a handful of theoretical writings. Maria Montessori, Edith Cobb, and Joseph Chilton Pearce have speculated that childhood is a special time for developing a feeling for nature. More recently, the biologist E. O. Wilson and his colleagues have advanced the *biophilia hypothesis.*

Biophilia means love of living nature, and Wilson suggests that humans have a moderate, genetically based attraction to other living things. Our interest in nature, Wilson suggests, makes sense when we consider the environment in which our species evolved. For more than 99 percent of human history, our ancestors lived in a natural environment—not a mechanical world. Thus, a curiosity about and sensitivity to nature must have conferred survival value on human populations.

Contact with nature, the biophilia theorists further assert, is vital for human self-actualization and self-fulfillment. Nature has inspired much of our art and our poetry, and we often feel most content and restored in natural settings.

But, the biophilia theorists emphasize, our attraction to nature isn't terribly strong. It isn't nearly as strong as the hunger drive or the sex drive, for example. Our attraction to nature, moreover, is only partly genetic and requires experience with nature sometime prior to adolescence to develop and flourish. That is, there is probably a "sensitive period" during which children are highly motivated to make contact with nature, and if their experiences during this time are impoverished, their feelings for nature will never be as strong as they might have been. As David Orr says, "If by some fairly young age . . . nature has not been experienced as a friendly place of adventure and excitement, biophilia will not take hold as it might have. An opportunity will have passed and thereafter the mind will lack some critical dimension of perception and imagination."

The writings of Wilson, Montessori, Cobb, and others on children and nature are sketchy and speculative, but they suggest two important questions for research to address.

1. Is childhood a time of special sensitivity to nature? Are there specific ages when children are most highly motivated to seek nature out and make contact with it?
2. How might this contact help the child develop?

ARE CHILDREN ESPECIALLY SENSITIVE TO NATURE?

Environmental Concerns

If childhood is a time of special sensitivity to nature, we might expect children to show especially strong environmental concerns. Some polls suggest that they do. In one U. S. telephone poll, Peter D. Hart Research Associates found that most young people (grades four through twelve), as well as their parents, believed that the individual in their family who was most concerned about the environment was the young person. The young people frequently lobbied their parents to recycle and to purchase environmentally responsible products. The youngsters also were typically more worried than their parents about the general deterioration of the planet's ecosystems.

A nationwide Louis Harris poll gives more specific information on the ages when environmental concerns might be the strongest. This poll's results are summarized in table 3.1, below.

TABLE 3 . 1

Harris Poll (1993). Children
Concerned "A Lot" about the
Environment*

Grade	Concerned "A Lot"
4–6	67%
7–8	54%
9–10	53%
11–12	50%

*Children were asked whether they were concerned "a lot, a little, or not at all."

As we can see from the table, the children in grades four to six were more concerned about the natural environment than the adolescents (grades seven to twelve).

When my coworkers and I asked New York City children to make up an ideal government for an imaginary island, we found that six- to ten-year-olds expressed more environmental concerns than the eleven- to sixteen-year-olds. When Sung Ha Suh gave the same interview to children in Chile, she obtained similar results. More informally, I have repeatedly been struck by the passionate environmentalism of children. I often testify at public hearings in efforts to protect trees and wildlife, and I have learned to expect children to walk up to the speaker's podium to make statements such as, "Stop cutting down the trees. How would you like it if someone cut you down?"

Animal Dreams

Children are especially interested in animals. In the previous chapter, we saw that animals are prominent in their make-believe play. In addition, research has found that children, compared to adolescents, talk more about animals when they create stories. But the strongest evidence comes from children's dreams. Psychologist David Foulkes asked children to sleep a few nights a year in his sleep lab at the University of Wyoming. When the sleeping children showed rapid eye movements (REMs), which signal dream activity, Foulkes woke them up and asked them what they were dreaming about. (Foulkes began his study with three- to five-year-olds, and I would worry that the entire experience might frighten young children, but Foulkes said it did not.) Foulkes found that the three- to five-year-olds frequently dreamt about animals—38 percent of the time. The children dreamt about animals more often than they dreamt about people or any other topic.

Foulkes initially doubted his finding. He knew that children are interested in animals, but he didn't expect this interest to be so great that animals would populate their dreams. But he continued to bring the children to his lab over the years and found that animal dreams were nearly as common at ages five to seven years. After the age of seven or so, animal content began to decline, and among Foulkes's older children, between the ages of eleven and fifteen, it was rare. Their dreams were primarily about other people and the self in various activities.

Some of the children's animal dreams were exciting. For example, one child dreamt that a horse broke a fence and freed the pigs and other horses. But most of the dreams had a simple quality—a bird singing, frogs in the water, chickens eating corn, a dog barking, a horse running, a calf in its barn.

When I have told people about Foulkes's finding, they often say, "Yes, but he studied children in Wyoming, a rural area where children have much more experience with animals than children in cities and suburbs do." However, Robert Van de Castle and other researchers have found similar results when urban and suburban children reported their dreams to teachers and parents. Animals are much more common in the dreams of children—especially young children—than in adolescents or adults. The children dream primarily about dogs, cats, and horses, although they sometimes dream about snakes, bears, wolves, lions, spiders, and other wilder animals.

Foulkes, like many psychologists, is puzzled by children's fascination with animals. Do animals represent their impulsive nature? Foulkes believes that young children most commonly dream about animals before the age of seven years or so because they are unable to clearly symbolize themselves. They use animals as a stand-in for the self. Foulkes calls animal dreams "compensations for a symbolic defect" and says that they reflect the child's "cognitive immaturity."

How readily a major psychologist puts a negative slant on children's dreams! One could just as easily view the child's dreams about animals in a positive light, as revealing a fundamental truth. As the poet Gary Snyder says, children recognize that they are young animals. As we grow older, and become socialized to Western values, we lose sight of the fact that we belong to the natural world. Instead, we prize the self and achievements within our insulated social worlds, regarding the lives of other species as quite secondary.

Foulkes observes that a small number of his subjects, going against the dominant trend, continued to dream a lot about animals in their early teenage years. These young people, who were usually girls, were good-natured, relatively indifferent to social approval, and prone to introspection and fantasy. Were these the budding poets and artists who draw on nature as a source of inspiration?

Shelters

In any case, several strands of evidence suggest that children's interest in nature is generally stronger prior to the entry into adolescence—prior to the age of eleven or twelve. In their actual behavior, too, such a difference has been found. Whereas children love to build hideouts and shelters in natural settings, these activities decline sharply after eleven. This decline has been observed in rural New England; in Devon, England; and on the island of Carriacou in the West Indies. David Sobel, who studied this behavior in England and the West Indies, suggests that young people become less interested in finding "homes" in the natural world and more interested in finding their place in the social world.

Not all studies have found that children have especially strong concerns about nature. Some studies have produced more mixed results, although these studies have often used questionnaires that the children might not fully understand. In addition, there is a need for more research with respect to very young children, under the age of seven years or so, to see if their interest in nature is especially intense. But generally speaking, the research evidence so far suggests that childhood is indeed the time of strongest attraction to the natural world.

HOW DOES RICH CONTACT WITH
NATURE BENEFIT CHILDREN?

EVEN IF RESEARCH showed beyond a doubt that children have
a particularly strong interest in nature, psychologists, parents,
and educators would want to know how rich contact with
nature specifically helps the child develop. Valuable leads are to
be found in a small but important number of studies that have
examined children's spontaneous behavior in nature's outdoors.
These studies are often informal, but they are rich in detail.
After culling through them, I believe it is possible to suggest at
least three ways in which nature helps children develop their
potentials.

1. Nature stimulates powers of observation.

In a pioneering study conducted between 1971 and 1973, Roger
Hart investigated the outdoor behavior of the four- to twelve-
year-olds in a rural New England town. Hart interviewed the
children, observed their free behavior, and followed them about
as they led him to their favorite places. As he had expected, the
children engaged in lots of active play—running, jumping, and
climbing—and they loved to hike in and explore their natural
surroundings. But Hart was surprised by the patience and care
with which the children simply observed nature. For example,
some children spent long stretches of time quietly watching the
fish, frogs, salamanders, and insects in the ponds, brooks, and
river. Sometimes a child would kneel by the water for many
minutes with his or her hands cupped, waiting for a catch. As a
result of their observations, the children came to know the loca-
tions and habits of the water species in remarkable detail.

    Adopting a similar methodology, Robin Moore found that
nine- to twelve-year-olds in urban sections of England liked to

go to the parks and undeveloped, weedy areas to collect objects such as rocks and acorns and simply to observe. They took considerable pleasure in quietly looking at birds, ponds, flowers, bees, ladybugs, lizards, mice, and other small animals. Moore said that as the children showed him their favorite places, he often felt as if he were on a nature tour with an expert guide. The children showed him plants and small animals in places that initially appeared to be nothing but neglected wasteland.

Nature's effects on children's perceptions became very clear during a project Moore initiated in Berkeley, California, in 1972. Moore and community members (including children) began transforming an all-blacktop, 1½-acre elementary schoolyard into a new playground that included a half-acre nature area with ponds, streams, wooded areas, and meadows. Five years later, Moore interviewed the fourth graders who had experienced the change, and their comments speak of a sensory awakening.

The children said that whereas the all-blacktop yard was "boring," the nature area was a wonderful place just to sit or to "go on little trips and look at things." One child said she especially liked to see the sunlight through the trees, and another liked to taste, smell, and look at the plants. Many children were especially interested in the animal life at the ponds.

"I love to look at the frogs," Lela said, "They're t-h-a-t big and all green. Last time I saw one it jumped right out of the water."

The children also attended to the sensual effects of the water itself. "It's like a cool breath of air blowing in your face," one child said. "I feel like I'm swimming and I'm not even in the water."

In the classrooms, the teachers encouraged the children to discuss and document their observations, and the children were aware of how much they were now learning. As one said, "You would never say, 'Let's go outside and learn about a cement yard.'

There's only one thing to know about a cement yard. It's a cement yard, period. [Now] there's always something new to find out."

2. Nature fosters creativity.

In Hart's study in rural New England, the children loved to build things. They built tree houses in the sturdy maple and apple trees, and they constructed model towns and highways in the loose dirt beneath the trees. They also energetically built clubhouses, hideouts, forts, and other shelters on the ground—frequently beneath the canopies formed by large bushes or tall grass.

Actually, the younger children, between the ages of four and seven years, didn't so much build shelters as find them. But the older children, the eight- to twelve-year-olds, engaged in a good deal of actual construction, using sheets, discarded lumber, fallen branches, and other "loose parts" to help build their structures. In the winter they built shelters out of snow.

As I have noted, children's shelters have drawn the attention of other researchers. Children seem to eagerly build shelters indoors, as when they drape a sheet over a bunk bed to make a cozy tent. And children also build shelters in urban areas, too. Researchers have yet to systematically compare the amount of shelter building in different environments, but I have the strong impression that it is greatest in relatively wild, outdoor settings. For example, city children seem to build shelters most often when they have access to undeveloped, open space such as fields with tall grass. Children become excited by the possibility of exploring wild areas, and they feel an urge to build an outpost or base from which to venture forth. As David Sobel says, they create a place to be at home in the outdoors.

Nature also inspires children's art and poetry. Parents and teachers know how commonly the sun, trees, clouds, birds, and other aspects of nature appear in children's drawings. Most adults are less familiar with children's poetry, but nature's inspiration seems very powerful. After examining four anthologies and collections of poems by children (some of which were written down by attentive parents), I estimate that over two-thirds of the poems deal with the natural world. I will discuss children's poetry in more detail in chapter 5, but for the moment I would like to point out that much of it reveals the kind of keen observation we discussed earlier. The children's senses are wide-awake. For example, eight-year-old Wendy Hancock calls attention to a sound that could easily be missed.

> The storm is over and gone away,
> Not a bird sings, not a twig moves.
> There's driftwood on the beach and
> the sea is low,
> After the storm
> After the storm.

> But there *was* a sound,
> Was it a rabbit scurrying
> Or a dog barking?

> No, no, no,
> It was the whisper of the trees
> Far away,
> Far away.

With disarming simplicity, such poems remind us what it was like to be alert and responsive to the natural world around us.

3. Nature instills a sense of peace and being at-one with the world.

I have described how natural settings prompt quiet observation and how children's alert observations contribute to their poetry. But nature also creates states of quiet and calm that differ from alert observation. In rural New England, Hart found that the children spent considerable time simply resting in a seemingly introspective manner. This was particularly true at "froggy ponds," sluggish brooks or ponds that sometimes contain frogs, insects, or other small wildlife. At water's edge, the child often stared into the water in a daydreamlike state, aimlessly dabbling dirt or water as he or she did so. In these moments of quiet, the children seemed to feel a fluid connection between themselves and the water—a oneness with the world.

Nature's quieting effect is striking in Robin Moore's study of the Berkeley schoolyard. When the yard was entirely asphalt, there was constant fighting and bickering. But in the new nature area the children played together more harmoniously, and they were much quieter. This was true of both the boys and the girls, who had previously played apart. In the nature area, they commonly joined together in relaxed conversation. As one child said, "It feels good there. Really quiet. Lots of kids just like to sit around and talk."

I think the children often felt calm in the nature area because they sensed that they were in the midst of a nurturing presence. It was as if they had become members of a very loving family. Describing the nature area, the children said things such as, "It makes me feel at home." "Being alone doesn't bother me now." "It's just a good-natured place." "It seems like one big family there." As Moore said, the nature area gave the children a new sense of belonging.

Sometimes the children experienced particular moments of

heightened connection to the natural environment. When a pond is still, Kelli said, "It makes me feel speechless, it's so quiet there. It makes me feel warm inside . . . I just feel nice about myself." Moore called special attention to this girl's empathy with her surroundings. Nature's quiet produced a similar state in her; she felt "speechless." She also felt very good inside, albeit in a way that was difficult to put into words.

Childhood feelings of calm and connection also are prominent in Louise Chawla's study of twentieth-century adult autobi-ographies. Those writers who remembered intense experiences with nature as children highlighted feelings of calm and rooted-ness in the world—feelings that lasted a lifetime. As Chawla noted, an especially eloquent description of such feelings is found in the autobiography of Howard Thurman, an influential African-American minister.

Thurman, who grew up in Daytona, Florida, in the early 1900s, frequently felt lonely as a boy. When he was seven years old, his father died, and his mother was distant. But Thurman felt comforted by the night, which provided him with a kind of maternal reassurance.

> There was something about the night that seemed to cover my spirit like a gentle blanket . . . [At times] I could hear the night think, and feel the night feel. This comforted me and I found myself wishing the night would hurry and come, for under its cover, my mind would roam. I felt embraced, enveloped, secure.

Thurman felt a similar relationship with an old oak tree in his yard; leaning against it gave him a feeling of peace and strength. The woods, too, befriended him. But his most intense experi-ences came at the seashore. When he walked along the shore one night, and the sea was very still,

I had the sense that all things, the sand, the sea, the stars, the
night, and I were one lung through which all life breathed.
Not only was I aware of a vast rhythm enveloping all, but I
was part of it and it was part of me.

Even the storms seemed to embrace the young Thurman,
and his experiences of unity with nature as a boy gave him

> a certain overriding immunity against much of the pain with
> which I would have to deal in the years ahead when the ocean
> was only a memory. The sense held: I felt rooted in life, in
> nature, in existence.

I have described three ways that rich contact with nature helps
children develop. Nature stimulates children's powers of observation, promotes their creativity, and instills feelings of peace and
oneness with the world. These benefits are important. Yet, as
mentioned earlier, nature's presence in children's lives has been
diminishing. Even while Hart and Moore were studying children's
outdoor activities in New England and England, they observed
that adults were rapidly replacing natural areas with pavement,
concrete, and neatly manicured lawns. The Berkeley nature area
was a bold, but rather isolated effort to reverse a sweeping trend. In
the remainder of this chapter, I will suggest three ways the absence
of nature in children's lives is affecting mental health.

IMPLICATIONS FOR MENTAL HEALTH

Attention Disorders

Many children today have difficulty paying attention. They have
trouble focusing on tasks and are restless in general. In about 3 to 5
percent of U. S. children, the problem is so severe that it receives a

psychiatric classification: Attention deficit/hyperactivity disorder. But in varying degrees the problem is much more widespread and has caused alarm among many health professionals.

Researchers generally assume that the cause of the problem is genetic or physiological. But we have seen that in natural settings children are capable of remarkably patient and careful observation. So we should also consider environments. Today's outdoor environments may be too sterile and boring to appeal to the child's senses and engage the child's powers of careful observation. What's more, today's indoor environments probably exacerbate attention problems. Channel changers and video games invite the child to constantly change or accelerate stimulation.

Recent research indicates that more time in natural settings can alleviate attention problems. Nancy Wells found that economically disadvantaged children had better attention spans after their families moved to housing with greener surroundings. In addition, Andrea Taylor, Frances Kuo, and William Sullivan found that middle-class children had fewer attention problems after spending time in green settings such as parks rather than non-green settings such as malls or parking lots.

Fighting

Problems with attention are frequently associated with fighting. And fighting, too, might partly be the product of sterile outdoor environments. In fact, this was what the children in Moore's study said when discussing the all-asphalt schoolyard. On the barren asphalt, "Kids get bored, so they mess around a lot. . . . Kids even smash glass, not because they're bad but because they need something to do." "Kids get really irritable and cranky. And then a fight can start." In contrast to the monotonous asphalt, the beautiful nature area, with its shaded dirt paths, brush, and ponds, invited sensory explorations and creative activities such as constructing model buildings with sticks and sand and making leaf boats.

The children in Moore's study also spoke about nature's power to ease tensions. They described the nature area as a place where kids could rest and feel good about everything, including one another. "Nature makes kids good with each other," and, "Now if kids have a fight, they can go in the trees and be friends again." The children's comments bring to mind the maternal quality noted earlier. In the nature area the children felt "like one big family." "It makes me feel at home." It is as if nature were a gentle mother who brings children into her loving arms.

LONELINESS

WE OFTEN HEAR the term "Mother Nature," but it's largely a cliché. Among Western adults, it has primarily been poets who have talked about the earth's maternal presence with any depth of feeling. For example, Mary Oliver's poem, *Sleeping in the Forest,* begins, "I thought the earth/remembered me, she/took me back so tenderly."

In addition, we hear impassioned statements about Mother Earth from traditional Native Americans. The Lakota writer Luther Standing Bear said, "Wherever the Lakota went, he was with Mother Earth. No matter where he roamed by day and night, he was with her. This thought comforted and sustained the Lakota and he was eternally filled with gratitude."

Today few of us have any sense of such a connection. And I wonder if we aren't lonelier because of this.

Loneliness is widespread. Individuals feel disconnected, adrift, and isolated, and the problems are becoming visible at younger and younger ages. Several great social theorists, such as Emile

Durkheim and Erich Fromm, have felt that isolation and loneliness is the characteristic pathology of modern times.

Scholars have searched for explanations. Some have speculated about the loss of communal ties that characterized traditional societies. Other scholars have looked to problems with the modern family. When, for example, parents become too preoccupied with their work lives, children grow up feeling neglected and alone.

Contemporary psychoanalysts such as Margaret Mahler, D. W. Winnicott, and Heinz Kohut have suggested that the roots of isolation can be found in early mothering. In healthy development, these writers say, the mother's empathic responses to the baby's needs contribute to the baby's sense of being harmoniously at one with the world. As children grow they become more independent, but the early sense of unity with the mother stays with them and helps them weather separations, rejections, and losses. When, in contrast, children lack early feelings of pleasurable unity, they may grow up feeling very alone and adrift in the world, and any threat of rejection makes them feel like they are falling apart.

All these explanations have merit. Rarely, however, has anyone raised the hypothesis that modern loneliness has to do with our estrangement from nature. The studies of Hart, Moore, and others suggest that in natural settings children develop strong feelings of peace and connection. Nature seems to act like a new mother, calming and comforting the child, and making the child feel she belongs in the world. As Howard Thurman wrote in his autobiography, experiences with nature made him feel rooted in life itself. Shouldn't we consider the possibility that people feel alone and adrift today because they grow up in such artificial environments that they lack connections to nature as a comforting, maternal presence?

RECOMMENDATIONS

HOW CAN WE enrich children's contact with the natural world?

1. Give the child opportunities to explore.

From a child-centered perspective, we best enrich children's experience of nature not by direct teaching, but by providing them with opportunities to make their own discoveries. We need to allow children to be explorers and adventurers.

But this requires patience. If, for example, we are walking a two-year-old child to the store, the child's sudden wish to stop to examine a leaf or a bug might initially strike us as whimsical or as an unnecessary distraction from our goal. It is important to remind ourselves that the child's interest is likely to be much deeper than ours. When possible, we should stop and give the child opportunities to explore what is so meaningful to her.

2. Don't overrely on labels.

The existential psychologist Ernest Schachtel pointed out that we frequently close off the young child's experience through the use of labels. When a two- or three-year-old points at an insect, or asks, "What is that?," we often assume that we have satisfied the child's curiosity by labeling it. We say, "That's an ant," as if that were all there is to know about it. After answering the child's question, we should give the child time to observe the ant fully.

Parents are sometimes eager to talk to the child about what he sees, and to turn the moment into a lesson. A parent might say, "Do you remember the ants in the book at home? That's a worker ant; its job is to find food for the colony." We consider our verbal explanations to be educational, but they may distract the child from what he is attending to. If a little boy is silently absorbed in watching the ant, let him continue. Let him learn in his own way and make his own discoveries. As Ralph Waldo Emerson said, "Be not too much his parent. Trespass not on his solitude."

3. Unobtrusively protect the child's safety.

Some parents restrict children's explorations of nature because they are concerned about the child's safety. This is a very legitimate concern, especially for children under the age of seven or so. Young children do not seem ready to venture off by themselves to wade in ponds, climb rocks, or to wander off paths to examine insects or other living things. But with a little effort, we can usually strike a balance between safety and the child's need for adventure. It is usually enough to sit or stand a short distance from the child, keeping a watchful eye on her while she explores her surroundings in her own way. We do not need to do more than this—simply maintain an unobtrusive, watchful presence.

Older children, after the age of seven or so, can venture farther from adults. But older children still need some adult protection. They often need a parent, teacher, or park staff member to be unobtrusively present while they explore natural settings.

4. Defend nature in the local community.

The most essential action we can take is to protect nature around us. Children won't be able to connect with their natural surroundings if no natural surroundings are left.

Defending nature is difficult. Powerful forces want to develop the open space in our communities. Real-estate developers can make a great deal of money by building more stores, apartment buildings, and parking lots. So they cut down trees, remove brush and tall grass, and pave over paths and ponds. But if children are to explore nature, we must argue on behalf of preserving natural surroundings. We must write letters, attend community meetings, and speak to local officials.

Real-estate developments, to be sure, typically include some vegetation in their landscaping. But the landscaping uses only a limited number of plantings—usually turf grass and a few varieties of plants—and there is a great emphasis on neatness. Conventional adult taste prefers clean cement, manicured lawns, bordered flowerbeds, and paved paths. The landscapes seem almost fabricated. There is nothing even remotely wild.

To really explore nature, children need what Robin Moore calls "rough ground"—weedy lots, dirt roads, ponds, wooded fields, unpruned trees, tall grass. Such settings tend to be relatively diverse and unpredictable. We can't be sure, for example, what species of insects, flowers, or birds might find a home in a weedy vacant lot. Thus, a child exploring such an area can make truly original discoveries.

Proposals to maintain rough ground will meet with objections: "The area will become overgrown"; "It will look unkempt"; "Children will get dirty." But rough ground is important if children are to experience nature in its richness, so we need to appeal to community groups to permit some areas to remain relatively wild. We can point out that relatively wild areas give a community a rustic look and possess a special beauty as they host a variety of wildflowers and species. Natural habitat gardeners have shown how it's possible to let some areas grow wild within the confines of an overall design. And we can appeal to people's concern for other species, which will continue to have the habitats they need to survive.

5. Replicate Moore's Berkeley project.

In the United States, so much land has been paved over already that I believe we need to replicate Moore's Berkeley project widely. That is, we need to take up asphalt and create nature areas. Moore says that such projects do not always require formal designs. "Rip up some asphalt, surround it with a sturdy enclosure, add some fertile soil and leave it alone. . . . Make it a spot for kids and wildlife to colonize together." For those more comfortable with planning, the organization Learning Through Landscapes provides publications that have guided the design of numerous nature parks in the United Kingdom.

6. Value "loose parts."

In suburban communities, parents often purchase prefabricated tree houses and mount them in their backyard trees. Other parents purchase playhouses that sit on the ground. The parents are well-intentioned; they want to provide their children with outdoor structures that children have traditionally enjoyed. But the adults don't give the children the chance to create their own structures.

It is important, therefore, to consider the extent to which outdoor environments permit creativity. Scholars such as Roger Hart and Robin Moore point to the value of "loose parts"— objects such as fallen branches, discarded wood, cardboard boxes, and old furniture that children find and use for their own building. Loose parts contrast with most store-bought toys, modular construction kits, and computer software—all of which have a largely predetermined structure. Hart says that too many parents want children to have the toys and equipment that "our technological society throws before them in more and more sophisticated mechanical forms; forms which demand nothing from the child beyond the ability to learn to use them for the purpose they were built."

7. Encourage nature studies.

All my recommendations thus far suggest ways we can give children opportunities for discovery and creativity. I have assumed that the adult's role is limited so the child can be an independent adventurer.

However, the situation today may call for some adult intervention, especially with older children. Today, as in earlier times, infants and young children are typically avid explorers of nature around them. But by the time a child is eight or nine years old, the child may have spent so much time in front of the TV set or playing electronic games that she is more comfortable indoors than outdoors. In earlier eras, she might have picked up exciting outdoor nature activities from other children, but today her peers also spend lots of time indoors. And when she goes outdoors, the highly manicured environment doesn't invite much investigation. Thus, some adult interventions may be necessary to wean her away from the TV set and introduce her to nature's wonders and possibilities.

If you live near a nature center, there is a good chance that it provides the kind of setting and programs that will rekindle the child's enthusiasm for exploration. After visits to nature centers, the child is likely to start investigating her home surroundings. What is more, nature educators generally try to respect independent learning. For example, they might ask stimulating questions such as "How many things can you hear in this field with your eyes closed?"; "If you cup your ears so they are like a deer's, do things sound different?"; "Can you find your way to the rabbit's home?" After asking the question, the adult turns the investigation over to the child, allowing the child to make her own discoveries.

This approach, incidentally, is one favored by the original societies of naturalists in America, the Native Americans. For example, the Lakota writer Luther Standing Bear told how the older people would ask children to sit still when there was apparently nothing to see, hear, feel, or smell. Then, after waiting, the child typically detected something—a rustle of the wind, a gentle scent, the faint call of a bird. The child was rewarded with the pleasure of his or her own discovery.

If there is no nature center nearby that seems appropriate, we can act as nature educators ourselves. Several nature books for children describe projects that give children wide opportunities to learn for themselves. In addition, we can introduce activities such as building shelters. We can start a shelter and then turn the rest of the building over to the children. Roger Hart, who has studied nature studies programs worldwide, has told me that municipalities in Europe sometimes hire "play leaders," who serve this function. Hart encourages communities to hire play leaders in the United States, but they are still rare. In the meantime we as parents can adopt the role.

8. Encourage poetry.

As a final recommendation, I would like to put in a special word for poetry. Earlier, I indicated how children's poems are creative activities that draw upon their keen observation of nature. The process of composing poems, in turn, undoubtedly refines and strengthens children's keen observations and feelings with respect to the natural world. Chapter 5 will take up this topic in more detail.

CONCLUSION

I HAVE SUGGESTED that children are especially drawn to nature and benefit from rich contact with it. I also have speculated that the modern child's isolation from nature contributes to some common emotional problems, and I have recommended ways of bringing the child into contact with nature. Among these recommendations, I have urged efforts to preserve and restore nature in our communities. I trust it goes without saying that we ought to preserve nature not just for the sake of our children's development, but also for the sake of all other living things.

CHAPTER 4

The Child as an Artist

*Once I drew like Raphael, but it has taken me a whole
lifetime to learn to draw like children.*

— PABLO PICASSO

YOUNG CHILDREN, between the ages of about two
and eight years, throw themselves into artistic activities. They love to sing, dance, draw, make up poems
and stories, and engage in dramatic play. And, as Howard Gardner
emphasizes, their talents routinely blossom in breathtaking ways.
Much of their dramatic (make-believe) play is rich and imaginative, and their songs, drawings, and poems are often beautiful
and enchanting. In this chapter, I will describe the development
of children's drawing.

Toward the end of their second year, children begin to scribble.
No one teaches them to scribble; they just begin doing so. Over
their next several years, they pour out drawing after drawing,
creating new and interesting pictures.

Several psychologists who have studied this process have
looked at it from the perspective of gestalt theory. Gestalt theorists, such as Rudolf Arnheim and Rhoda Kellogg, believe that
innate forces influence the sequence and kinds of forms children
produce. These theorists recognize that innate determinants are

not the whole story. They recognize that children also freely experiment with new forms, and cultural factors also influence what children draw. But gestalt psychologists believe that innate forces prompt all children to proceed through a basic sequence, and their drawings are guided by an inner, innate sense of aesthetic principles such as symmetry and balance. Children try to produce good forms—good "gestalts."

THE PRIMORDIAL CIRCLE
(TWO TO THREE YEARS OF AGE)

THE FIRST CLEAR form to emerge from the two-year-old's scribbles is the circle. Initially, children scribble in a back-and-forth motion (see figure 4.1a). Then children begin drawing clearer circles. These are often spiral-like, concentric circles; the child begins drawing a circle and keeps widening it (see figure 4.1b).

The gestalt psychologist Rudolf Arnheim said that the emergence of the circle is a great event in life.

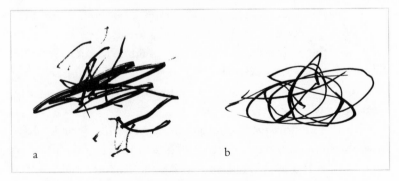

Figure 4.1. Early scribbles with back-and-forth motions (a)
give way to more circular forms (b).

To see organized form emerge in the scribbles of children is to watch one of the miracles of nature. The observer cannot help being reminded of another process of creation, the shaping of cosmic whirls and spheres from amorphous matter in the universe.

When children draw concentric circles, they initially have trouble controlling their motions. As Gardner says, they seem driven to keep expanding the spiral and cannot stop. It takes a month or two before they can slow down and direct their hand movements well enough to draw a single discrete circle (see figure 4.2).

Arnheim believed that the creation of single, discrete circles is also a very special achievement.

To be able to make—all by himself—something so clear, so orderly, and perfect must be an extraordinary experience for the child. In fact, he tries it again and again, working with evident pleasure and concentration and producing a great number of what adults may dismiss as repetitions.

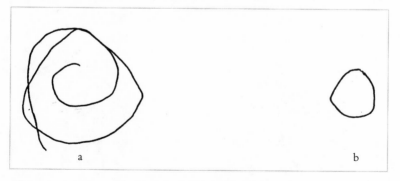

Figure 4.2. Two-year-olds initially have difficulty stopping their circular movements (a). It's an achievement when they can make a single, discrete circle (b).

Arnheim believed that the circle is the most basic shape in the human mind. For this reason, we, as adults, use the circle to represent objects when their form is unknown to us. "Spheres, disks, and rings figure prominently in the early theories about the shape of the earth and the universe, not on the basis of observation as because unknown shape and spatial relationships are presented in the simplest way possible."

Once children can draw discrete circles, they can put them together to represent figures. They draw circles within circles to create facelike figures (see figure 4.3). These figures look a bit like ghosts, but the child isn't trying to draw ghosts. The child is simply working with the form she has mastered so far.

SUNBURSTS AND MANDALAS (THREE YEARS)

RHODA KELLOGG'S RESEARCH suggests that children do not immediately begin developing human figures further, however. Instead, they experiment a little while with other forms. A very common form is the radial or sunburst pattern—the circle with rays. Note how the sunbursts in figure 4.4 are well-balanced.

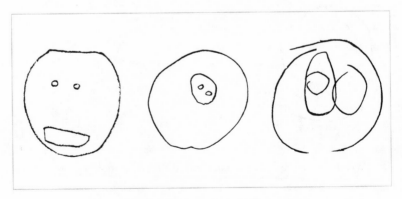

Figure 4.3. Early faces. *From Kellogg 1969, 94.*

Figure 4.4. Sunbursts. *From Arnheim 1954/1971, 173.*

Another common form at this time is the *mandala*. In adult artwork, mandalas are perfectly balanced patterns of circles, crosses, and squares that the psychoanalyst Carl Jung believed represent the human search for the unity of life. Three-year-olds' mandalas are, of course, very simple; they often are simply circles with crosses inside (see figure 4.5). But Kellogg proposed that the same urge toward unity and balance is at work.

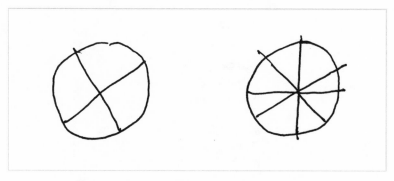

Figure 4.5. Early mandalas. *From Kellogg 1970, 36.*

TADPOLES (THREE TO FIVE YEARS)

THEN, AFTER EXPERIMENTING with such forms, children draw more complete humans. They start attaching legs to the heads and face to produce what researchers call *tadpole* figures (see figure 4.6). The striking feature of the tadpole is that the legs extend directly from the head. There is no trunk. Sometimes children also draw arms, but when they do, the arms also extend directly from the head. They still omit the trunk.

Three- to five-year-olds draw human tadpoles with great frequency. But they also draw many suns, animals, and trees and plants, using the basic structures that they have developed so far to create their pictures (figures 4.6 and 4.7).

Figure 4.6. Tadpole figures. *Bottom figures from Crain 2000, 96.*

Figure 4.7. Young children's drawings of a dog (a) and flowers (b and c). The children use the tadpole and sunburst forms they have mastered earlier. *The dog is from Arnheim 1954/1971, 176.*

It is possible that the sequence I have reviewed is not perfectly invariant. Kellogg herself noted that there might be exceptions. Some children might begin drawing tadpole humans prior to sunbursts or mandalas. But this hasn't been a matter of great importance to researchers. Instead, what has intrigued them is the striking feature of the tadpole human—the missing trunk. And on this matter, gestalt psychologists such as Kellogg and Arnheim disagree strongly with most researchers.

The Tadpole Controversy

Most researchers assume that the tadpole reflects a deficiency on the child's part. For example, Norman Freeman suggests that young children have an "ordering problem" similar to that they show on many memory tasks. When asked to recall a series of numbers, young children find it easier to recall the first and last number than a middle number. Similarly, when drawing, they know what comes first (the head) and last (the legs and perhaps the arms), but they forget what comes in the middle (the trunk).

The gestalt psychologists, in contrast, do not see tadpoles as deficient at all. As the gestalt researcher Henry Schaefer-Simmern said, the child isn't primarily interested in copying reality or "putting together memorized parts." The child is more concerned with the creation of balanced and harmonious form. Indeed, the tadpoles often possess a pleasing elegance and simplicity. With just a few well-placed lines, the tadpoles capture the essence of an animated human being. Such simplicity is one of the goals of art.

At present there isn't solid research evidence that decisively supports either the deficiency position or the gestalt position. What is clear is that three- and four-year-old tadpole drawers know more about human anatomy than they draw. They know that people have stomachs, chins, necks, and so on. They can readily put the body parts in the correct positions when making puzzles. Even while drawing, they may talk about numerous anatomical features of their figures ("Has cheeks, chin, big body, weensie hand . . .") but draw nothing but a simple tadpole person.

Informal observation suggests that what happens is something that would fit with gestalt theory. When drawing, children often enter into a state of deep concentration. Whether they talk or fall silent, they pay little attention to the people around them, and they certainly don't look at others as models for their work. Instead, they draw in a half-conscious state in which, as Howard Gardner says, impersonal forces seem to be at work. Psychologist Claire Golomb gives an example of a boy who, after drawing a tadpole figure, examined it attentively and said, "Never seen hands coming from the head." He spoke as if he wasn't entirely responsible for what he drew. It might be that children's drawing is guided by a deep, inner sense of patterns—the sense of patterns that gestalt theory postulates.

Such anecdotes hardly prove that the gestalt position is correct and the deficiency position is wrong. More research is needed to sort out the merits of these positions. But I do believe that there is a sense in which the deficiency position is very misleading. It turns our attention away from the remarkable qualities of young children's drawings.

It is not just that three- and four-year-olds' tadpoles have a simple elegance and charm. During the next few years, as children progress beyond tadpoles, they routinely create drawings that are fresh, lively, and beautifully composed. Howard Gardner, whose research has done so much to draw attention to the young child's artistic talents, has called the next few years the "golden period of artistic development."

THE GOLDEN PERIOD (FIVE TO EIGHT YEARS)

FIGURE 4.8 reproduces a drawing by our daughter, Sally, when she was 4½ years old. The drawing has a lively yet gentle rhythm, achieved by counterbalancing the movement of each figure's

Figure 4.8. Sally's drawing at age 4½ has a lively yet gentle rhythm.

hand with that of the opposite foot. The effect is so pleasing that one hardly notices the "unrealistic" aspect of the figures, such as the shape of the hands or the postures themselves.

In figure 4.9, Gardner shows the likeness between a drawing by a six-year-old boy and a painting by Paul Klee. The boy uses wonderfully balanced form to express the gaiety of a girl jumping rope. If anything, the child's drawing is livelier than Klee's.

These children's drawings (in figures 4.8 and 4.9), while striking, are not unusual. All children seem to go through a period, from the ages of about five to seven or eight years, when they create numerous pictures that are energetic and harmonious.

Many great painters (as well as poets and other artists) have

Figure 4.9. A six-year-old boy's drawing (left) is lively, free, and
beautifully balanced. Howard Gardner compares it to a
painting by the modern master Paul Klee
(right). *From Gardner 1980, 5.*

themselves said that they try to recapture the outlook of the
young child. This was true of Klee, as well as Picasso, whose
words I quoted at the opening of this chapter: "Once I drew
like Raphael, but it has taken me a whole lifetime to draw like
children." Below are some others' comments.

> The artist . . . has to look at everything as though he saw it for
> the first time; he has to look at life as he did when he was a
> child.—Henri Matisse

> [The artist] is a passionately child-like and play possessed
> being.—Thomas Mann

> The artist, who throughout his life is similar to children in
> many things, can attain the inner harmony of things more
> easily than others.—Wassily Kandinsky

Not everyone agrees that we should liken children's art to that
of adult masters. Several people have pointed out that although
children's works express the freshness, vitality, and harmony that

adult artists value, children achieve these qualities unconsciously. Adult artists, in contrast, engage in considerable conscious planning and design. Even Klee, who made a great effort to recapture the qualities of children's art, pointed out that the adult work was more consciously planned.

Others, such as the psychologists Glyn Thomas and Angele Silk, have argued that the value placed on children's art is historically and culturally relative. Young children's art, they say, wasn't valued until the twentieth century, when western artists derived inspiration from it.

This qualification isn't entirely correct. Delacroix and Baudelaire, two giants of the nineteenth-century art world, said artistic geniuses recapture the fresh and zestful outlook of children. But we do need to recognize broad cultural and historical differences in aesthetic preferences. Some research indicates, for example, that Chinese art experts value technical control over the liveliness of young children's drawing. Still, to the extent we prize art that is fresh, lively, and harmonious, the spontaneous drawing of young children is a stunning achievement.

THE AGE OF PRECISION (EIGHT TO TWELVE YEARS)

THEN, AT THE age of about eight years, a change occurs. Children's drawings become more geometrically precise and realistic. Their drawings, as Gardner says, become "increasingly faithful to their target, increasingly neatly colored in. But . . . the sense of life, power, and vitality" wane.

The change is illustrated by two drawings by my neighbor Andy, in figure 4.10. The first, which Andy drew when he was six years old, is lively and freely expressive. The second, which Andy proudly created when he was nine years old, is more rigidly geometric. It pays more attention to detail, but it is stiff.

Figure 4.10. Andy's drawings illustrate the shift from a livelier to a more geometric style. *From Crain 2000, 105.*

Our daughter Sally's drawings also illustrate the same basic shift. Earlier I commented upon the liveliness of the drawings she began producing when she was 4½ years old (see figure 4.8). By the time she had reached the age of eight years, Sally's drawings had become more geometric and precise. For example, the drawing in figure 4.11 reveals Sally's use geometric perspective to portray a room in realistic detail, but the drawing is rather rigid. Although it has a touch of humor, it lacks the expressive movement and rhythm of her earlier works. Sally had entered a period, lasting into early adolescence, when her drawings were more stilted and stylized. And, as Gardner points out, this basic development is pervasive. A number of studies suggest that when children are at the age of seven or eight years, their drawings become more technically competent but less "flavorful."

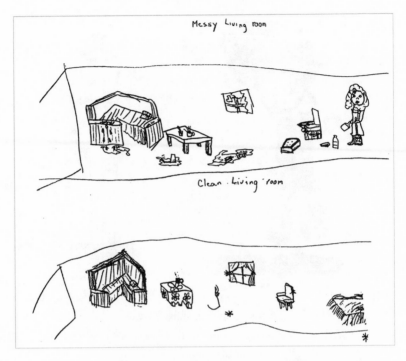

Figure 4.11. At age eight, Sally works on geometric perspective
and the details of a messy versus a clean room.

Explaining the Transition

What accounts for this change—this shift to precision? One fac-
tor may be schooling. Schools emphasize technical skills and
accuracy, and the school culture may affect children's drawings.

But it's likely that drawings reflect a more general, natural
change in the child's mental life. Sheldon White and others have
gathered a good deal of evidence that between the ages of about
five and seven years, children become more rational, level-
headed, and objective. This "five-to-seven-shift" seems to take
place in a wide variety of cultures, including those that don't

rely on formal schooling. And the evidence for this shift supports the insights of major developmental theorists, such as Piaget and Erikson. After the age of seven or so, these theorists hold, the child's thinking becomes less zestful and fanciful. Instead, the child examines the world systematically and objectively. The child looks for regularities and lawfulness—an orientation that would seem to manifest itself in the concern for geometric precision in her artwork.

Since Piaget's theory has been central to so much writing and research in child development, I will comment on how he sees this general cognitive change.

In Piaget's theory, the change occurs when the child advances from the stage of preoperational thought (lasting from about two to seven years) to the stage of concrete operations (from about seven to twelve years). The child's thinking frees itself from a reliance on appearances, as illustrated by the conservation-of-liquids task. A child is shown two identical glasses, A1 and A2, which are filled with liquid to the same height. After the child agrees that the amount of liquid is the same, the experimenter (or the child) pours liquid from A2 into container P, which is shorter and wider (see figure 4.12). The preoperational child

Figure 4.12. Conservation of liquids task. A child sees that beakers A1 and A2 contain the same amount of liquid. He then pours A2 into P and claims that A1 now has more because it is taller. *From Crain 2000, 122.*

says A1 has more than P because it is taller. Occasionally the child says P has more because it is wider, but in either case the child focuses on the "look" of things, the striking visual dimension. The child doesn't realize that the amount must be conserved, that it must be the same.

At the stage of concrete operations (after the age of seven or so), the child's responses are no longer dominated by her perceptions. She now responds logically, explaining, for example, that the water is the same because none has been added or taken away.

This task is but one of many that Piaget devised to tap the sweeping development that occurs as children move from pre-operational to concrete operational thought. For example, he tried to show how children overcome egocentrism. Just as they no longer view conservation tasks from a single, striking perspective, they no longer view social situations from their own immediate perspective. Children also overcome animism. They no longer assume that trees, flowers, rocks, and other objects possess feelings and intentions just like they do. What's more, they no longer see dreams as real, but as internal events that are separate from the real world.

In these and other ways, the world of the child after the age of seven or eight becomes very different. It is no longer dominated by appearances and fantasies. It is now rational and objective. The child's thinking, to be sure, isn't fully developed. It is only rational and logical insofar as it deals with real things or people. It is not until adolescence that young people enter Piaget's final stage (formal operations) and start thinking logically about purely hypothetical topics. But the thinking of the eight-to-twelve-year-old, compared to that of the younger child, is more rational and objective—much more the kind that we value in our scientific, technological society. Piaget considered it to be a major advance, as do psychologists in general. Not all agree with the specifics of his stages, but they consider the rationality of the eight-to-twelve-year-old to be an unambiguous step forward.

The study of artistic development throws this widespread view into doubt. It seems pretty clear that the seven- or eight-year-old's new rational intelligence alters her drawings. The drawings become more precise, geometric, and technically competent. But they lose the freshness and vitality that great artists have admired. We need to ask whether there are valuable qualities in the younger child's outlook that she loses in the process of growing up.

Piaget pointed out that the young child is more swayed by appearances and perceptions than logic. Because Piaget focused on logic and rational thought, he viewed this perceptual orientation as negative. But don't artists put a great value on perception? Young children seem to have such intense vision that they can remember small details if they wish. They also have a strong sense of synesthesia, how qualities can cut across the senses (for example, a four-year-old girl said, "Father talks boom, boom, boom . . . as dark as night! But we talk light, like the daytime . . . bim, bim, bim"). Many artists say synesthesia enriches paintings, music, and other art forms. Finally, young children are fanciful and perceive everything as dynamic and expressive, as when they find faces on the sun and on flowers, balloons, and other objects. The young child's cognitive bent, in short, is precisely that which artists value.

PROMOTING ARTISTIC DEVELOPMENT

HOWARD GARDNER, Ellen Winner, and their colleagues have sketched out a view of how, ideally, drawing might develop, and how education might help. In a nutshell:

Initially, when children are between the ages of about two

and seven years, their art unfolds so wonderfully on its own that it should be given free reign. Instruction is unnecessary.

During middle childhood (between the ages of about eight and twelve years), children focus on technical skills such as geometric precision, detail, and perspective. They seem eager to master these skills and to learn the culture's technical and stylistic conventions, so at this time, art education can be effective.

Finally, during adolescence, young people are in a position to integrate technical skills with a renewed expressiveness and originality.

But Gardner and his colleagues observe that this sequence is hardly ever realized in our society. Instead, a good deal of discouragement sets in. In middle childhood, children draw much less than they did when they were younger, and in adolescence they usually stop drawing altogether. I believe there are two reasons for this.

First, our society as a whole doesn't value the arts. Our nation's leaders worry tremendously about children's progress in reading, math, and science; our nation's competitive future, the leaders say, hinges on achievement in these academic areas. Federal commissions urge our students to lead the world in math and science, but no national leader has called for the United States to lead the world in the arts.

In the 1990s, to be sure, the federal government and several state governments developed curriculum standards that included the arts. But in actual practice, most elementary schools only offer art classes one period every five or six school days. And even then, the classes are increasingly devoted to art history and appreciation rather than artistic activity. In middle school and high school, art usually becomes an elective, and one that most students do not take. Parents don't encourage their teenagers to take art classes because, unless a student is particularly talented in art, art courses won't help the students get into the most competitive colleges. Students are advised to concentrate instead on honors and advanced placement courses in math, science, literature, and the social sciences.

A second reason children lose interest in art has to do with their personal interactions with adults. Early on, children find that when adults take an interest in what they draw, the adults are frequently critical. Picasso and Klee tried to learn from young children's spontaneous drawing, but most adults want to improve it. In preparation for this chapter, I collected scribbles from five two-year-olds, and in every case the parent or the preschool teacher had been trying to direct or improve the child's scribbles. The adults urged the children to draw rounder circles or straighter lines or to scribble within the outlines of predrawn figures. Similarly, when children draw tadpoles, almost all the parents I know have tried to correct their drawings. They have told their children to include a trunk and to draw the arms and legs from the trunk instead of from the head. The parents want their children to draw the way they (the parents) think is best—realistic copies of people and things. They fail to consider the stunning beauty of the child's spontaneous work.

The same adult-directed approach is common in the schools. As Seymour Sarason says, "[In] kindergarten, the child is 'taught' what is acceptable in his or her creations. Far more than not, children are told what to draw or make and to judge those works according to criteria set by the teacher." Even sophisticated books on art education suggest ways of getting children to make more realistic drawings.

Of course, the young child's inner urge to draw is strong, and to a considerable extent early artwork will unfold in its own way in spite of adult criticism and direction. But the adult reactions take their toll, confusing the child and causing the child to doubt herself and her abilities.

How, then, can we as parents help?

1. *Give young children opportunities to draw; then step back and enjoy their work.*

We must first make sure that young children have free time and materials for drawing and painting. Then, if we can just look at children's spontaneous drawings in a fresh way, allowing the drawings to speak directly to us, we will witness small miracles. Our children's artwork will fill us with pride and happiness. Our children, in turn, will sense our enjoyment. They will feel that their creativity—and they themselves—are appreciated. They will gain an inner confidence that will help them move boldly forward.

This is not to say that providing children with opportunities for the arts is easy. Today there is so much academic pressure on young children—even four- to seven-year-olds—that time for the arts is crowded out. This is true at school and at home. Children have a good deal of homework, which tires them, and to relax they just watch TV. In our school communities we need to work against excessive academic demands and to hold the line on TV so children have the time and energy to fulfill their deepest creative impulses.

2. *Keep verbal comments brief.*

Parents sometimes wonder, "How much should I talk to my child about her drawing?" "What should I say?" Art doesn't lend itself to verbal analysis, and this goes for children's art as well. In the young ages, children don't usually ask us for many comments, let alone help. Their drawing is inwardly driven, and they become so deeply engrossed in it that they pay little attention to the outside world. But they do sometimes show us their finished works or indicate that they'd like a response, and we should respond.

I believe it's best to avoid general evaluative comments such as "You're a good drawer" or "That's a great painting." Even positive evaluations raise the possibility of negative evaluations in the future, and after a while the child can become so worried about external evaluations that she doesn't focus intently on her work. Instead, we should comment on particulars in the drawing with observations such as "That sun sure seems happy," "That's a tall tree," "I bet those birds like that tree," "She loves to jump rope." The child usually smiles and says, "Yup," and is fully satisfied. The child's mind is apparently filled with a variety of images and thoughts about her drawing—sometimes an entire story—and our simple statements connect us to the story in a way that the child likes.

Occasionally a child will seem unhappy with something about the drawing. We can ask general questions, such as "Would you like to tell me more about the drawing?" As a general rule, it's best to try to let the child lead us as to how much feedback she wants. In chapter 10, I discuss the method of active listening that can help the child take the lead in expressing her concerns.

3. *Lobby for the arts in the schools.*
   Since school is such a large part of children's lives, it would be helpful if schools fostered children's creativity by providing more time for the arts. Then children would have much more positive feelings about school. We can advocate for the arts at PTA meetings, school board meetings, and school forums. We can elect school board members who want more time for the arts.

   We can also lobby for a particular kind of art instruction. Parents do not directly hire teachers. But we can circulate writings and express ideas on the educational approach we think is best. If we can get our approach included in the school system's policies, the policies will influence the selection of particular teachers and methods.

My hope is that all schools will hire and develop art teachers who recognize the wonders of the young child's spontaneous art and are reluctant to interfere with it. The teacher might introduce the child to a variety of materials, giving a bit of explanation of how they work, but then allow the child to work with the materials on her own.

Although the golden period for drawing typically ends at about eight years of age, drawing and active participation in artwork contributes greatly to the richness of the growing child's life. After the age of eight or so, direct instruction, as Gardner says, becomes more appropriate. Children want adults to help them with techniques that make their art more precise and realistic. But the best instruction continues to be gentle and flexible; it presents the child with ideas and gives the child the freedom to utilize them as she sees fit. It always strives to avoid making the child feel criticized and inadequate.

I hope, finally, that we can encourage adolescents to take courses in the arts. Young people find the arts fulfilling and replenishing. They often talk more freely when working on an art project and experience relaxation that is generally missing in today's high-pressured world. Art courses might not help most students compete for Ivy League college admissions, but students' present lives are important, too.

|||||||||||||||||||||||||||||||||||||||||||||||||||||||||||||||||||||||||||||||||

CHAPTER 5

The Child as a Poet

If I find a moon,
I will sing a moon-song.

—HILDA CONKLING

(a g e   f o u r   y e a r s)

IN COMPARISON to children's drawing, less is known about their poetry. But it promises to reveal just as much about the remarkable nature of the early childhood years.

One of the first scholars to call attention to children's poetry was the Russian poet and writer Kornei Chukovsky. In his 1925 classic *From Two to Five*, Chukovsky said that young children are natural "versifiers" and that every child goes through a stage in the preschool years when he or she is "an avid creator of word rhythms and rhymes."

Chukovsky said he first became aware of the young child's natural poetic bent when he saw his four-year-old son running around in the garden on a broomstick, shouting to his sister:

> I am a big, big rider,
> You're smaller than a spider.

The boy liked his poem so much that he repeated it over and over as he galloped about—even after his sister, who was less enthusiastic about the poem, had left the area. After a while he was called to dinner and led to the table, but "his poet's blood had not yet calmed down." Scanning the sight with his spoon in hand, he exclaimed:

> Give me, give me, before I die,
> Lots and lots of potato pie.

Chukovsky said children usually like to make up poems when they are active—running, jumping, hopping, or skipping. "When they make soap bubbles and see them soar, it is natural for them to jump after them, crying out not once but many times:

> How high ai, ai, ai,
> Up in the sky, ai, ai, ai.

Such exuberant poetry, Chukovsky added, is most common in the spring. Running about on fresh grass, they pour forth "verse to express their exhilaration."

Children seem to begin forming the rudiments of poetry early in life. Chukovsky observed that infants who are not even a year old, who still spend much of the day in their cribs, already amuse themselves "with rhythmic jabbering, repeating again and again some favorite sound." He noted that after the age of one year or so, infants often repeat to themselves rhymed syllables such as "alia, valia, dalia, malia."

Others have made similar observations. In 1928 Harriet M. Johnson, a pioneer in the development of nursery schools, noted that a significant aspect of language between about fourteen and forty-two months is its "markedly rhythmic forms"; young children love to create sound patterns that have a beat, regular emphasis, or cadence. As Johnson's nursery-school children played or ran about, they chanted things such as

Up a lup a dup,
Up a dup I go.

Munna, munna, mo,
Munna, munna, mo.

Very young children, Johnson concluded, frequently speak just for themselves, using sounds to accompany their activities. At these times, they are less concerned with meaning than rhythm, sound, repetition, and form. After Johnson's work, other researchers have supported her findings.

Although babies and young children talk a lot to themselves, they also communicate with others, and today there is a keen interest in mother/infant dialogues. Daniel Stern and others, using technologically advanced film techniques, have shown that when these conversations are happy and lively, mothers often tune in to the rhythmic and musical nature of the baby's vocalizations and actions. For example, a mother says, "Ka, bam, ka bam, ka bam" to accompany the baby's rhythmic rattling.

After children reach the age of two years or so, their poems increasingly take on clear content, describing events and scenes in the surrounding world. These poems frequently have a simple beauty. For example:

Bells are ringing,
Frances is singing.
—*Frances Kent (age two years, two months)*

Poetry may include not only musical elements such as rhythm, beat, and repetition, but also heightened visual imagery and feelings. Young children create striking images, too, as when a three-year-old girl exclaims:

Open, open the gates—
The sun is coming up in the sky!

There is much to learn about how children's poetry develops from this point. Are there particular ages when children are most enthusiastic about poetry? The poet Georgia Heard, teaching poetry in public schools, noted, "When I read poetry to kindergartners and first-graders, they sway and nod their heads and snap their fingers." Heard thinks, "We all need to revive those old responses to poetry and trust them again." Is the imagery of younger children—before the age of eight years or so—fresher and more original than that of older children? Some research suggests that younger children's metaphors are more inventive and less conventional, but we do not know about their actual poetry. The answers await new investigations.

NATURE'S INSPIRATION

STILL, THE ANTHOLOGIES available do strongly point to one conclusion: Young children's poetry is greatly inspired by nature. Timothy Rogers's 1979 anthology, *Those First Affections,* contains 220 poems, primarily by British children between the ages of two and eight years, and I estimate that 85 percent deal with the natural world. Chukovsky's book includes thirty-two poems by children between two and six years, and I would classify 66 percent as dealing with nature. In two books that include poems by New York City children between the ages of five and eight years, published in 1989 and 1970, I estimate that 56 percent and 74 percent refer significantly to nature.

I find Rogers's collection of poems (most of which were written down by attentive parents) especially impressive. Many poems describe the sounds of the wind. For instance:

'Whump!' goes the wind on the
window,
And the window goes 'Whamp!'
—*a four-year-old*

Eight-year-old Richard Correll tells us:

Fruit trees whisper
To the rustling wind. . . .

And eight-year-old John D'Addona tells about a storm:

The thunder is tremendous
Shooting across the sky
With desperate thoughts in its mind

Other poems express a fascination with the sounds of water—
brooks, rivers, fountains, and the ocean—as well as other sen-
sations in nature. Four-year-old Hilda Conkling (who grew
up to become an adult poet) asks us to listen to the voice of a
brook:

There is going to be the sound of
Voices,
And the smallest will be the brook:
It is the song of water
You will hear.
A little winding song
To dance to. . . .

In several poems, children create images of nature's happiness.
For instance:

It was such a lovely day,
They slept in the garden
And the children smiled asleep
And the birds were laughing up in the
Sky
—*Roberta Nesham (age 3½)*

The above poem is reminiscent of some of Blake's, in which aspects of nature (in this case birds) share children's feelings. Throughout Rogers's anthology, one is repeatedly struck by how the children feel a connection or kinship between themselves and the natural world.

In several poems the children even speak directly to animals and plants. Two-year-old Thomas Broadbent seems to ask a spider a basic question of existence:

Bu'fly, bu'fly
Fell in a pond
Why spider, why spider, why?

Here's a poem by four-year-old Hilda Conkling that speaks directly to a flower:

Sparkle up, little tired flower
Leaning in the grass!

Did you find the rain of night
Too heavy to hold?

ANIMISM

MANY OF THE children's poems are animistic; they attribute voices and emotions to nonhuman objects. Trees whisper, a brook sings, thunder is desperate, a flower is tired.

In Piaget's view, animism is a characteristic not just of children's poetry. It is a general feature of young children's thinking (prior to the age of seven or eight). Some researchers have questioned this, but I believe Piaget is correct. When researchers ask young children questions in the manner of testers, children may not reveal animism; they give the answers adults believe are correct. But when investigators let children talk among themselves, they talk about how trees become unhappy and feel pain, how animals experience all the emotions that people do, and so forth.

Animism is devalued in our modern, technological society. Our society makes sharp distinctions between the human and the nonhuman, between the animate and the inanimate worlds. Indeed, Piaget said that animism reflects the young child's cognitive immaturity—specifically, the child's egocentrism. Young children egocentrically assume that the wind, flowers, brooks, and animals think and feel just as they do. Piaget said that children overcome their animism as their thinking matures. As they become more rational, they distinguish human experience from the impersonal workings of the rest of the world.

But animism has a positive side; it contributes to artistic expression. Poets, painters, and musicians don't try to separate themselves from the world and analyze it in objective, impersonal terms. They try to feel the underlying unity between themselves and the world and capture the feeling tone of things. They want to feel the somber mood of a landscape, the joy of a sunny day, the caress of a tonal pattern, the upward striving of a Gothic column, and the fatigue of a leaning flower.

A psychologist who had important things to say about animism was Heinz Werner. Actually, Werner didn't usually refer to the term *animism;* he preferred to use the closely related term *physiognomic perception. Physiognomy* means face, and Werner called perception of the expressive, dynamic, emotional aspects of stimuli physiognomic because it is so often the face that reveals emotion to us. Werner contrasted physiognomic perception with "geometric-technical perception," which responds to the objective, measurable dimensions of stimuli such as height, area, hue, and decibel level.

Werner agreed with Piaget that children tend to see the entire world physiognomically or animistically. To a young child, a cup lying on its side is tired; a stick being broken hurts. Thus, physiognomic perception emerges quite naturally in children's poetry (and sometimes in their drawings, too, as when they draw faces in the sun).

Werner also agreed with Piaget that as children grow up, they tend to replace physiognomic perception with more scientific thinking and geometric-technical perception. This, Werner added, is especially true in modern, technological societies. We, as modern, rational adults, tend to regard most physiognomic perception as silly. We might recognize that artists use it, but we generally consider artists to be an eccentric lot.

But Werner, in sharp contrast to Piaget, didn't believe that animistic or physiognomic perception dies out after childhood. In continues to grow, if slowly and imperceptibly, and we can still see the world physiognomically as adults, especially when we let ourselves enter a relaxed or playful frame of mind.

To demonstrate this, Werner and others have presented adults with lines such as those in figure 5.1 and have asked, "Which line is happy and which is sad?" From a rational, scientific perspective, the question is meaningless; lines are nothing but abstract forms. They cannot feel anything. But most adults, to their surprise, perceive the line on the left as rising in a happy manner and the line on the right as falling and conveying sadness.

Sounds, too, express moods to us. One sound rises cheerfully; another falls in a heavy, somber mood. One sound glides along gently; another explodes violently. Colors convey moods too, as when we are affected by the serenity of a shade of blue. Most of us don't spend much time reflecting on such matters, but poets, musicians, painters, and other artists try to help us appreciate them. They want us to feel the expressive qualities of lines, sounds, color, and other sensory impressions—the same expressive qualities that are in brooks, sky, wind, and the entire world.

Most modern adults believe that when we perceive expressive qualities in the physical world, we are projecting our own emotions onto it. But Werner and gestalt psychologists deny this. Their view was forcefully stated by Rudolf Arnheim, who said that although physical objects might not exactly possess human emotions, the entire world shares the same dynamic, expressive

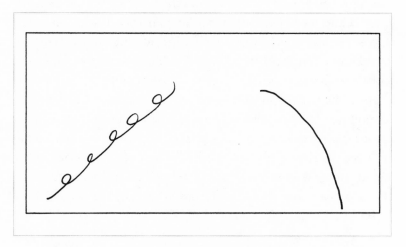

Figure 5.1. Lines express feelings. Which line is happy and which is sad? *From Crain 2000, 97.*

forces. Motifs such as rising versus falling and gentle versus explosive underlie all existence. Thus, when four-year-old Hilda Conkling urges a leaning flower to "sparkle up" because it looks tired, she is not just projecting her own emotions onto the flower. Just as human energy rises and falls, so too does that of a plant, and there is a similarity between the expressive gestures.

Similarly, when eight-year-old John D'Adonna says that the thunder shoots across the sky "with desperate thoughts in its mind," his characterization is not simply a projection of human attributes onto the thunder. Thunder, of course, cannot experience desperation exactly like humans do, but there is a basic similarity in the way tension mounts and gains no outlet except through explosion.

Arnheim said that perception fulfills "its spiritual mission only if we . . . realize that the forces stirring in ourselves are only individual examples of the same forces acting throughout the universe. We are thus enabled to sense our place in the whole and the inner unity of that whole."

Our unity with nature—and the threats to it—has concerned many adult poets. The early Romantic poets such as Wordsworth and Goethe warned that the modern, scientific attitude was distancing us from the natural world by asking us to view nature as nothing but impersonal matter. This detached view of nature, these poets sensed, would make it easy for humans to abuse and exploit it.

In recent years, when the damage that human societies have inflicted on the earth has become so glaring, many poets write about our relationship to the earth with even greater urgency. They say we must regain our bonds to the earth if we are going to save it. Barbara Deming says,

> Teach us to listen . . .
> We are earth of this earth, and

we are bone of its bone
This is a prayer I sing, for we have
forgotten this
and so
The earth is perishing.

The children's poetry I have presented expresses this feeling of closeness and connection to nature. Children listen to what the wind and waters express and even talk to plants and animals.

But in the children's poetry I have reviewed, the children seem to have had ample contact with nature's outdoors. This is not always the case. Most urban children lack rich experience with the natural world, and it's my impression that this absence is reflected in the anthologies of their poems. While urban children do express feelings for nature, their nature poetry isn't as full and flowing. Moreover, as noted in chapter 3, suburban and rural children also seem to be rapidly losing contact with nature. They increasingly live in indoor environments dominated by TVs, computers, and video games. So we must wonder how long children's nature poetry will flourish.

For now, it's important to note that some children's poetry, like that of adults, explicitly calls for the preservation of natural things. Howard Gardner's six-year-old daughter, after a trip to a farm, wrote (with her parents' assistance with the spelling):

> A horse is a wild animal
> A horse should be free
> A horse should be left like it was built to be.

The following poem is by a fourth-grade boy who was fortunate enough to attend the Berkeley, California, elementary school when the community took up asphalt and created a nature area. In his poem, the boy expresses his developing bond with nature, as well as his sense of the threat that modern society poses.

> I am setting in between three
> green trees and a rock,
> with grass surrounding me and
> my friends the trees. When I
> listen to the cars zoom by I feel
> in my body a faint cry.
> —*Brendan*

FACILITATING CHILDREN'S POETRY

POETRY CANNOT BE forced. Eight-year-old Gillian Hughes (in Rogers's anthology) puts it this way:

> A poem has got to be born.
> It cannot come out when you want it
>   to;
> It must be born.
> When you want to make a poem you
>   cannot make it,
> But when you do not want to make it,
>   it comes.

Thus, we do not help children through teaching in the ordinary sense, by asking children to write a poem and giving guidance and criticisms. Our help must be more indirect. We create an environment—prepare the soil—in which children's poems can emerge and flourish. Here are four recommendations for parents.

1. *Give children contact with nature.*

   Since nature inspires so much of children's poetry, our first task is to make sure children have rich exposure to nature. Encourage visits to parks and summer camps. Take them for picnics in the countryside. Drive them to the beach, lake, or foothills in the winter, to see what nature is like when left to itself, without people about. Sign children up for nature studies programs. Above all, protect nature in one's community. Once children have experiences with the natural world, they seem naturally to compose poems about it.

2. *In children's first year, enjoy baby talk with them.*

   Daniel Stern's research suggests that our early "baby talk" appeals to infants' own sense of rhythm, beat, and other musical elements. For example, a mother's spontaneous repetitions of Hello ("Hello, Heelloo, Heelloooo") give babies pleasure because of rhythmic qualities. Baby talk is controversial; some authorities recommend it, while others believe it is infantilizing. But it comes naturally to parents, and it probably strengthens many of the musical rudiments of poetry. At least for the first year or year and a half, I encourage it.

3. *Sing songs and lullabies.*

   Lullabies appeal to children's inner rhythms of peace and contentment. Their soothing melodies give children the sense that the world is an empathic and comforting place. For this reason, our lullabies seem to inspire some of children's own early poems. For example:

   > Hushabye, hushabye, it's dark in the
   > morning,

Flowers are up in the sky.
—*Lucinda Broadbent (two years old)*

4. *Recite poems.*

Some poems are expressly intended for children, and we read them directly to them. As a young boy, "Twinkle, Twinkle Little Star" made a strong impression on me. I think this was because the poem confirmed a sense of wonder. The poet Georgia Heard fondly remembers "Peas porridge hot." But, as Heard points out, children also like more difficult poems, especially when we read them with feeling because they mean something to us.

We do not have to read all poems directly to children. It is often helpful to just read poems to ourselves, or to other adults, when children are present. In this way, children have more freedom to choose what they like. Sometimes they will ask us to read or recite a poem again, even though it wasn't expressly intended for them. Whether we read "children's poems" or "adult poems," it is important to keep an eye on what children respond to and let their responses guide our selections.

Of course, if we ourselves compose poems, it is all the better. Without saying a word to our children, we model behavior they, too, may find worthwhile.

POETS SUCH as Georgia Heard and Kenneth Koch, who have taught poetry in the New York City elementary schools, also favor an unobtrusive approach. As Koch says:

Children have a natural talent for writing poetry and anyone who teaches them should know that. Teaching is really not the right word for what takes place: it is more like permitting the children to discover something they already have. I helped them to do this by removing obstacles, such as the need to rhyme, and by encouraging them in various ways to get tuned in to their own strong feelings, to their spontaneity, their sensitivity, and their carefree inventiveness.

In actual practice, Koch often gives the children initial prompts, such as beginning poems with "I wish" or "I dream." Heard consults with the children as they write. She might ask the child if he is satisfied with the poem and what else he might say. If the poem is too conventional, Heard tries to get the child to think of images that reflect what he himself strongly feels.

I recommend that parents avoid even these minimal interventions. A parent, in comparison to a guest poet in the classroom, is of profound emotional importance to a child. When a parent directs the child's poems, the effect is much more powerful. It can much more easily stifle the child's spontaneity. The child starts thinking less about her own images and more about pleasing the parent.

As parents, it's preferable that we only create the facilitating preconditions for children's poetry—to expose children to natural settings, to join them in their early vocalizations, and to read poems aloud to them. In such ways we establish a favorite environment for poetry, but we then allow the poems to emerge from the children themselves.

Of course, when children tell us their poems, we should react. We should listen carefully. Careful listening is itself a meaningful response that we sometimes neglect. We also should allow ourselves to be moved—by the humor, the happiness, the sorrow, or whatever the poem expresses.

As in the case with children's drawings, it's best to avoid evaluative comments such as "You're a great poet" or "That's an excellent poem." General evaluations of this kind generate too much self-consciousness. The child becomes too concerned

with her personal evaluation to focus intently on the images in
her poems. If we sense that a child wants some verbal feedback,
we can respond to a particular feature of the poem. We might
say, "That bird sure flew fast," "I get a sense of how cold it was,"
"The wind sure seemed angry," or "I really hear the wind whis-
pering." In this way we share in the child's experience—a reac-
tion that gratifies any poet.

||||||||||||||||||||||||||||||||||||||||||||||||||||||||||||||||||||||||||||||

CHAPTER 6

The Child as a Linguist

The young child has succeeded in a
remarkable type of theory construction.

— NOAM CHOMSKY

EVERY SO often, a scholar comes along who revolu-
tionizes the way we think—an Einstein, Darwin,
Marx, and Freud. Are there any such people among
us today? It is undoubtedly too early to tell, but there is one person who is thought by many to be a strong candidate—Noam
Chomsky.

Prior to Chomsky, the study of children's language was a
pretty dull affair. It was assumed that children learned to speak
through imitation and parental teaching, and few people had
any sense that children's speech is anything special. Research
basically consisted of counting nouns and verbs.

Then, beginning in the 1960s, Chomksy's work began cir-
culating through academic circles. Chomsky's focus was on
grammar—specifically, the syntax or rules we use to create sentences—and he showed how we all use these rules in a highly
creative way. We constantly use them to generate and compre-
hend sentences we have never heard before. These rules are
exceedingly complex and abstract, but Chomsky began to make

their general nature clear. What's more, Chomsky suggested that the ordinary child can employ most of these rules by the age of five or six years. If Chomsky was right, the ordinary child—at a time when adults are teaching her the ABCs—demonstrates a mastery of language that is so abstract and complicated that we must credit the child with being a linguistic genius.

Chomsky opened people's eyes. Soon, researchers remembered that vocabulary growth itself was remarkable. Between the ages of eighteen months and six years, children learn an average of nine new words a day. It's clear that this occurs without careful instruction—there's no time for it. Children must be very sensitive to words. But if Chomksy is right, vocabulary growth is actually a rather minor achievement. What is truly remarkable is the rapid development of syntax or grammar—the elaborate, abstract, often-hidden rules for producing and comprehending correct sentences.

Chomsky himself hadn't studied children's speech in a formal way. He made observations, but he primarily worked on technical articles and books on adult grammar. But a growing number of psychologists saw the importance of his work and began to study how grammar might develop in children. One of the pioneers in this research was Roger Brown, who unobtrusively tape-recorded the spontaneous speech of three young children for several years. Among other things, Brown recorded how the children began using *tag questions,* and a brief look at the tag questions of one of Brown's young subjects, Adam, will illustrate the remarkable nature of children's speech.

One day, when Adam was 4½ years old, he uttered the following tag questions:

Ursula's my sister, isn't she?
I made a mistake, didn't I?
Diandros and me are working, aren't we?

He can't beat me, can he?

He doesn't know what to do, does he?

The "tags" are the little questions on the end. Adam's tags illustrate an unerring grasp of several rules. Let's consider just a few. First, to create the tags, Adam must reverse the negative or affirmative statement in the first part of the sentence. When Adam says, "I made a mistake," an affirmative statement, the tag must be negative, "Didn't I?" When he begins with a negative statement, such as "He can't beat me," the tag must be positive, "Can he?" Adam does this correctly every time.

Also, Adam must locate the subject of the sentence and then convert it into the correct pronoun in the tag question. In the sentence, "Diandros and me are working, aren't we?," Adam correctly sees that the subject is the phrase "Diandros and me," and he converts it into "we."

More impressively, Adam recognizes that unless the verb in the main sentence is a form of *to be* or *to have,* one must move the auxiliary verb to the front of the tag question. Notice, however, that in the sentence, "I made a mistake," there is no auxiliary verb present—at least on the surface. So to create the tag "Didn't I?" Adam must create the auxiliary "did." This rule is so deeply hidden in English grammar that no one was even aware of it until Chomsky pointed it out. But Adam correctly employs it every time.

Thus, Adam is simultaneously employing several operations at once, and I have only illustrated some of them. It is truly remarkable that he can perform tag questions at 4½ years of age, but he isn't at all unusual in this respect.

An interesting aspect of Adam's tag questions is how they emerged over time. Adam produced no tag questions at all until he was 4½, and then he suddenly burst out with them. In one hour he created thirty-two such questions, whereas the average adult frequency is three to six. He seemed to be exercising his newly acquired ability.

The development of tag questions illustrates Chomsky's main point: Children master complex linguistic rules and procedures in a very short time. They seem to master most of the intricacies of grammar by the age of six or so, and the rest by puberty. This is not to say that they are consciously aware of grammatical rules, but they develop an intuitive, working knowledge of the complex and buried rules of their native language. And this is not all. If a child finds herself in a new land, where another language is spoken, the child masters the second language, too. It's a common observation, Chomsky says, that a young child of immigrant parents picks up a second language in the streets from other children, with amazing rapidity, and soon speaks this new language as fluently as the other children. In the meantime, the child's parents struggle away, finding the process far more tedious and difficult.

How is it possible for the human child to accomplish so much in so short a time? Chomsky believes it is futile to try to explain the language acquisition in terms of environmental variables, such as parental teaching or modeling. Children, Chomsky says, hear only a fragmentary body of speech, yet form rules that extend well beyond what they hear exemplified. Chomksy believes that the explanation must come from a consideration of how the child is biologically programmed for the task—how the child's brain is designed to pick up grammar and language.

The problem, in Chomsky's view, is like that of understanding the remarkable behavior patterns of various species. Birds fly, spiders spin webs, beavers build dams, monarch butterflies and sea turtles navigate enormous distances—and humans speak. One wouldn't try to understand why birds can fly—while humans cannot—by considering ways in which parent birds do a better job of teaching or modeling flight behavior. One would want to know how the bird is designed or engineered for the task. Similarly, in Chomksy's view, one needs to know how a child's brain is engineered to pick up language.

Chomsky proposes that the human child comes to the task with a built-in sense of what a correct grammar must look like. So, to the extent that the child extrapolates rules from what she hears, she is guided by an inner sense—an inner ear—that tells her that certain rules are fine and others are wrong. This innate knowledge, to be sure, cannot be the whole story, for children learn different languages depending on where they grow up. The child growing up in China typically learns Chinese, not English or Spanish, so the knowledge of a particular language cannot be built into the brain. It must be learned. But Chomsky believes that every child possesses an innate sense of the underlying form of all languages—the universal grammar—and automatically knows that certain speech is grammatically permitted and other speech is simply wrong. So the major task of linguists, Chomsky says, is discovering just what the rules of universal grammar are.

Over the years Chomsky has changed his ideas somewhat. He has never abandoned the concept of universal grammar, but he has altered his conception of how much creative discovery the child engages in. In his early writing, Chomsky suggested that the child raises hypotheses, searches for regularities, and forms rules—all the time guided by an inborn sense of what kinds of rules are permissible. But as Chomsky's work progressed, he increasingly speculated that the number of discoveries the child must make is limited. In Chomsky's later view, the child only needs to find out a small number of key points about the kind of grammar his or her native language employs. Once this information is received, huge segments of the adult grammar automatically fall into place, like the instant formation of a crystal structure after receiving a single drop of liquid.

I believe Chomsky's earlier thoughts were closer to the mark—that the child does engage in a great deal of formulation and reformulation of rules on the road to adult grammar. Let us briefly look at what the research on infants and children tells us.

THE GROWTH OF GRAMMAR

Early Language

Right at birth, babies seem tuned into language. Careful film analyses suggest that infants make very slight body movements to speech, and their movements vary with the boundaries of sounds and words. They seem to dance to language. Such movements are not made in response to other sounds, such as tapping.

At about one month of age, babies begin gurgling and cooing, and by six months or so they are usually making babbling sounds, such as "ba ba" and "da da." Babies' early vocalizations appear to be highly similar throughout the world. As we noted in chapter 5, their early babbling soon takes on rhythmic, musical qualities.

One-Word Utterances

At about one year, babies begin producing single words. Some researchers believe that they are trying to use single words to express entire sentences. For example, "cookie" might mean "I want a cookie" or "There is a cookie," depending on the context. At about fifteen months babies begin using different intonations when they are asking questions as opposed to making statements.

Two-Word Utterances

At about a year and a half, children begin two-word utterances. Some typical utterances are listed in table 6.1.

TABLE 6.1

Some Typical Two-Word Utterances

Type	*Example*
1. NAMING	THAT DOGGIE
2. REPETITION	MORE JUMP
3. NEGATION	ALLGONE BALL
4. POSSESSION	MY TRUCK
5. ATTRIBUTION	BIG BOY
6. AGENT-ACTION	JOHNNY HIT
7. ACTION-OBJECT	HIT BALL
8. AGENT-OBJECT	MOMMY BREAD (MEANING, "MOMMY IS CUTTING THE BREAD")

Researchers have been fascinated by the possibility that there are underlying structures to the two-word utterances. For example, Martin Braine proposed that the child forms a "pivot grammar," using one word, such as "allgone," as a pivot and using many other words in an open class—"allgone boy, allgone sock, allgone boat, allgone milk. . . ." Later research showed that not all English-speaking children use a pivot grammar, but it does seem that some children form a "grammar" of this sort, and pivot grammar illustrates the creative way children form rules.

Developing Grammar

Between two and three years of age, children put three or more words together, and their speech more clearly manifests the kinds of rules they are forming. In some cases, English-speaking children show that they are sensitive to the universals of human language. Most notably, their pauses indicate that they know that languages don't deal with strings of words, but with phrases. For example, children say things such as "Put . . . the red hat . . . on." The pauses indicate a sensitivity to the fact that the noun phrase "the red hat" stays together. The child won't pause in other places; he won't say, for example, "Put the . . . red hat . . . on."

Children also form rules for word endings—rules that are more consistent than those of adult grammar. They say things such as "I runned," "He doed it," and "She goed." Children see that the rule for forming the past tense is to add the "ed" sound, and then they overregularize the rule, applying it consistently and ignoring the exceptions in the adult grammar. They also overregularize plurals, saying things such as "foots," "mans," and "mouses." They discern that the rule for plurals is to add the *s* sound and apply it across the board, assuming that the adult language is more consistent than it is.

Children's overregularizations are found in many languages, and they often last well into the elementary-school years. Here is an example of how a child stubbornly sticks to an overregularization, despite the parent's attempt to model the "correct" word ending.

CHILD: My teacher holded the baby rabbits and we patted them.
PARENT: Did you say your teacher held the baby rabbits?
CHILD: Yes.
PARENT: What did you say she did?

CHILD: She holded the baby rabbits and we patted them.
PARENT: Did you say she held them tightly?
CHILD: No, she holded them loosely.

Why does the child ignore the adult's wordings? Does the child actually think the adult is wrong—that the adult is violating the rule? This might be the case. In any event, children clearly stick to the general rules. They value rules, not exceptions.

Overregularizations give children's speech a unique flavor. But children are actually overregularizing adult rules. In other instances, children form rules that are very different from the adult speech they hear.

Edward Klima and Ursula Bellugi found that children consistently develop nonadult rules with respect to negatives. Initially, children speak as if the rule is, Place the negative in front of the rest of the sentence (or after it). For example:

No play that.
No fall!
No want stand head.
Car go no.

A bit later, they form a new rule: Put the negative after the subject and before everything else.

He no bite you.
I no want envelope.

The study of children's negatives and other speech forms led Klima and Bellugi to conclude, "It has seemed to us that the language of children has its own systematicity, and the sentences of children are not just an imperfect copy of those of an adult."

Transformations

Between about three and six years of age, children's begin making transformations. A transformation occurs when a speaker shifts the form of a sentence, as when one turns a statement into a question or the passive tense. For instance, one might transform "Susan rode the bike" into "Did Susan ride the bike?" or "The bike was ridden by Susan." Tag questions, which we discussed above, are examples of transformations. The entire topic is of central importance to Chomsky's theory. Indeed, Chomsky's theory is sometimes called "a theory of transformational grammar."

Children don't develop adult transformations instantly, and they seem to go through stages somewhat like those with respect to negatives. For example, they go through a stage when they say things like "Where I can put it?" and "What he wants?" They put a "Where" or a "What" at the front of the sentence, but instead of reversing the auxiliary verb and the subject ("Where can I put it?") they then maintain the subject-verb-object word order ("Where I can put it?")

Sometimes adults ask children to imitate their correct (adult) grammar, but the children seem to stick to their own way of speaking. For example:

ADULT: Adam, say what I say: Where can I put them?
ADAM: Where I can put them?

English-speaking children, then, go through stages when they form their own, spontaneous rules. These rules seem to be the same from child to child. It is possible that the children's speech is guided by innate organizing tendencies. This possibility will gain strength if, as linguist Dan Slobin hypothesizes, cross-cultural research finds universal similarities in children's speech.

PIDGINS AND CREOLES

SOME OF THE most exciting linquistic research has been conducted by Derek Bickerton on *pidgins* and *creoles.*

A pidgin comes about when adults from diverse linquistic backgrounds are suddenly thrown together, as happened on some slave plantations. To communicate, the workers developed pidgins—choppy strings of words lacking most of the qualities of true grammar. For example, pidgins lack operations for making transformations. Unless the speakers are talking about something very familiar to them all, they soon become confused. A creole is a pidgin that has been developed into a true grammar.

But, according to Bickerton, adults are incapable of creating a creole. Only children have this power!

Bickerton's most intensive study was of people who immigrated to a plantation in Hawaii at the turn of the twentieth century. They came from Korea, the Philippines, and many other countries to harvest an abundant sugar crop. Bickerton studied historical records and interviewed people who were still alive. He found that the adult immigrants created a choppy pidgin to communicate, and their children created an elegant creole—and they did so in a single generation.

Bickerton reports that creole grammars are highly similar around the world. He also notes that creole sentences sometimes have the look of children's spontaneous speech. These resemblances, in his view, are no accident. Creoles reflect the innate grammatical structures children use to reshape the choppy pidgins they hear.

We must still consider Bickerton's ideas as tentative hypotheses, but he certainly is pointing to a creative power that has impressed others. Chomsky called attention to children's ability to pick up a second language with amazing rapidity during their play with other children, whereas adolescents and adults labor at the task. Children's ability to create a creole out of a degenerate pidgin confirms their remarkable linguistic power. Further evidence of this power comes from the observations of hearing-impaired children.

EVIDENCE FROM CHILDREN'S SIGN LANGUAGE

IN HIS BOOK *The Language Instinct,* the psycholinguist Steven Pinker describes what happened in Nicaragua, beginning in 1979, when the country tried to create schools for deaf students. The schools attempted to teach lip reading to youngsters, who were ages ten years and older. These efforts generally failed, but the youngsters informally put together a kind of pidgin sign language by pooling the makeshift pantomimes and gestures they used at home. Then the new children who joined the school, at the age of four years or so, reworked the pidgin sign language and turned it into a much more elaborate and elegant grammar. In effect, the young children created a creole. With their new grammar, the children could tell jokes, compose poems, and describe distant events—all of which was far beyond the capacity of the earlier pidgin. Here again, a single generation of children created a grammar.

Some of Chomsky's followers believe that the child's special power with respect to language takes place during a genetically determined critical period, perhaps from birth to about six or seven years of age. During this time the mind is especially geared to pick up and create syntactic rules—the rules of grammar for forming sentences. It is possible that some kind of capacity extends beyond this—until adolescence—and then the ability drops off sharply.

SHOULD WE TEACH CHILDREN LANGUAGE?

NOT EVERYONE IS deeply impressed by the child's unique linguistic power. Several psychologists still assume that the adult role in teaching language is pivotal. Some also recommend ways for parents to accelerate children's linguistic development.

For example, William Fowler has created a program in which parents expose children to phases of language development a little before they would ordinary reach them. Fowler reports that his program accelerates language development and also boosts early school achievement. But, as Lise Eliot observes, Fowler's research needs careful replication.

Many psychologists have concentrated on the role of *motherese*. Motherese is a special kind of speech that caretakers use when talking to children. Although adult-to-adult speech is plagued by fragmentary sentences and convoluted phrases, motherese is clear, simple, and gramatically correct. In Roger Brown's research, Adam's mother often responded to Adam's speech in this clear way.

ADAM: See truck, Mommy. See truck.
MOTHER: Did you see the truck?
ADAM: No I see truck.
MOTHER: No, you didn't see it? There goes one.
ADAM: There go one.
MOTHER: Yes, there goes one.

The mother's speech is short and perfectly grammatical. It is simple enough for Adam to imitate, which he does at one point (although a bit imperfectly). When the mother says, "There goes one," Adam says, "There go one."

Motherese seems to come to us quite naturally. It is prevalent in cultures around the world, although not in all. The Kaluli in New Guinea, for example, don't believe in using it. Current evidence indicates that parents who use a particularly large amount of motherese can speed up language development a bit. But motherese is hardly essential for normal language development. On average, the Kaluli children, who don't hear motherese, learn language at about the same rate as U. S. children.

In general, I find the concern over speeding up language development to be misguided. Chomsky and his followers have made a strong case that the ordinary child's mastery of complex grammar is phenomenally rapid as it is. The child's syntactic development far outpaces her development in logical reasoning, for example. Those who want to accelerate it must assume that speed is such a supreme value that nothing can be fast enough. If they came across a group of children who were walking at five months of age, their first question would probably be, "How can we get them to walk even earlier?"

INCREASING CHILDREN'S VOCABULARY

OTHER PSYCHOLOGISTS HAVE focused on how parental speech can increase the child's vocabulary. Betty Hart and Todd Risley have shown that children's vocabularies are larger when mothers talk a lot to their children. The mother's talkativeness is also associated with higher IQ test scores (which is hardly surprising because vocabulary and IQ scores are strongly related). A high degree of maternal talkativeness also is more common in upper-middle-class communities than in poor and working-class communities.

On the basis of such findings, some scientists have developed programs to help parents talk more to their children. Some psychologists believe that this is a good way to alleviate "some of the potentially damaging consequences of poverty."

Such proposals may have promise. But we need to keep efforts to increase vocabulary in perspective. Vocabulary is valued in academic settings, but it is not the most significant feature of children's linguistic development. Indeed, it is quite minor in comparison to the child's grasp of the complex and abstract rules of syntax.

Moreover, I see two ways in which parents' efforts to build children's vocabulary can be counterproductive.

First, parents' efforts to teach children words can distract children from quiet contemplation. A child often likes to spend long stretches of time inspecting things—other children at play, animals, ponds, sticks, flowers—and adult talk can get in the way. Recently, I saw a mother and her two-year-old daughter walking down the sidewalk when the child stopped to look at two dogs. The child was enthralled. After a while, the child said, "Two dogs." The mother saw a teachable moment and coaxed the girl into singing a "two's song"—"two dogs, two horses, two ducks. . . ." The child halfheartedly joined in as the mother happily moved them along. The mother might have helped her child's vocabulary, but we'll never know how much the child was prevented from learning what had fascinated her.

Even when young children talk, their talk is often meant for themselves, and adult conversation can be distracting. For example, young children talk a lot while they draw, spinning their own stories. If adults try to engage them in extensive conversation, it disrupts the web of images in the child's mind.

Second, efforts to improve children can produce feelings of inferiority, which in the case of language are totally inappropriate. Strong evidence suggests that the ordinary child's achievements are phenomenal. Whatever the child lacks, it is trivial in comparison to the complex syntax the child is in the process of mastering. This is true of all children, whatever the socioeconomic background. In fact, if the child is living in a poor neighborhood but has immigrant parents, the child is probably acquiring the complex syntax of at least two languages (and at least twice the vocabulary the English-speaking researcher is aware of).

In rare cases, of course, the child may have a linguistic problem. But when it comes to ordinary children, any assumption that we must correct some important deficiency should be abandoned. We should talk in ways that children find enjoyable. This may enhance the pleasure they take in words and foster their vocabulary. But we need to overcome any presumption that we, as adults, are in a position to teach the child the core structure of language. When it comes to deep and abstract syntax, the child has been given a linguistic power that is greater than our own and deserves our utmost respect. If, when we look upon the individual children in our lives, we would every so often remind ourselves that "this young child is accomplishing an astonishing linguistic feat," our appreciation would work wonders.

||||||||||||||||||||||||||||||||||||||||||||||||||||||||||||||||||||||||||||

CHAPTER 7

How Did the Future Gain Its Grip on the Modern Mind?

I hear from afar the shouts of that false wisdom,
counting the present as nothing,
and pursuing a future that flies as we pursue it.

— JEAN-JACQUES ROUSSEAU

I WAS STANDING on the sidewalk with our three-month-old puppy when a man walked by with his mature dog. Our puppy energetically greeted the dog, and even though the latter stood rather elegantly aloof, our puppy scampered back and forth, doing whatever she could to start some play. After watching our puppy a moment, the man said, "I sometimes wish they could stay that age forever."

There is something special about human children, too. I have described several of the special strengths of childhood and have suggested that in some cases, the child's qualities actually seem superior to those of most adults. Children's drawings, for example, go through a period of lively harmonies that great artists try to recapture. Children's feeling for the natural world seems particularly empathic and intense. Their make-believe play and language development demonstrate remarkable creative power.

But when I have given presentations and lectures on these qualities, the audience at some point grows restless. Parents, for example, recognize the charm of childhood, but this isn't their greatest concern. What they really want to know is how to help their children get into a prestigious college and become highly successful adults. Parents often privately imagine a judgment day is coming for them as parents. When their children are seventeen or eighteen years old and receive their letters from college admissions committees, the parents will be known to the world as successes or failures.

To put one's child on the road to success, today's adults focus on the academic "basics"—math, science, reading, and writing. These are the skills that standardized tests measure each school year and they are critical to the SAT. And these are the skills that our nation's leaders have repeatedly said our students will need for the competitive future. Most of the distinctive childhood strengths—imaginary play, nature exploration, the arts—are peripheral to the basics and are given short shrift. Schools find less and less time for free play and the arts, for example.

To be sure, alert parents will take an interest in such "extra-curricular" activities if their child demonstrates a special talent in one of them. Then the parents give their child special lessons. This is because they hear that elite colleges are not just interested in the "academic grind" but the more "well-rounded package." So parents sign their children up for art classes, music lessons, tennis instruction, and soccer league in the hope of increasing their child's prospects.

But these lessons are often so structured and adult-directed that they dampen children's enthusiasm for the activity. What's more, adults enroll children in so many lessons and leagues that the children become "oversubscribed"; they no longer have time for their own spontaneous activities. They have little time to engage in free play, to draw in their own ways or explore woods and ponds and search for insects. They have little time, that is, for the free activities during which they spontaneously develop the special qualities of the childhood years.

I have found that some parents worry that something is amiss. They find that by the time children are in the second or third grade they have lost much of their enthusiasm for learning. On the topic of free time, one parent told me, "My children are signed up for so many lessons that I sometimes wonder, What's wrong with just playing? But I have to think of the future. With everyone else starting their kids in this competition for the best colleges, I have to do it, too."

How did the future gain such a grip on our minds? To understand this, we must go back in time, to medieval Europe, before the child's future became a prominent concern.

WHEN CHILDREN WERE LITTLE ADULTS

IN THE MIDDLE AGES, families didn't worry much about the child's future, partly because the prospects were limited. Tradition held sway, and people assumed that children would enter the crafts, trades, and occupations of their own social class.

What's more, families spent little time worrying about the child's future because the child entered the adult world at a very young age. According to the great French historian Philippe Ariès (1914–84), children were typically sent off to other villagers to begin apprenticeships when they were only six or seven years old. They learned carpentry, farming, domestic service, weaving, and other crafts and trades on the job. The child lived as a boarder in a master's house and often worked alongside other apprentices who were much older than he or she. No one paid much attention to the child's age, for the child had basically entered adult society. The child wore the same kinds of clothes, played the same games, and participated in the same festivals as the grownups. "Wherever people worked," Ariès said, "and also wherever they amused themselves, even in the taverns of ill repute, children mingled with the adults." The child was a little adult.

Ariès acknowledged that younger children—before the age of six or seven—were treated differently. People recognized their need for protection and care. But on the whole, Ariès suggested, people seemed to think of children as little adults even before they were six or seven years old. This is why medieval paintings and sculptures typically depicted children—even newborns—with adult body proportions and facial characteristics. The children were distinguished only by their size. They were pint-sized adults.

Some historians have challenged Ariès's views. Because medieval written documents are sparse, it is difficult to evaluate all the disagreements, but historians such as Barbara Hanawalt and Shulamith Shahar have gathered enough evidence to indicate that Ariès was sometimes prone to overstatement. It appears that apprenticeships, while common, were not as universal as Ariès claimed. It also appears that six- and seven-year-olds frequently entered the adult workplace more gradually than Ariès implied. For example, the young children sometimes worked fewer hours than the others. Still, I believe that Ariès's critics have done more to qualify his characterization than to refute it.

Moreover, other sources have shown that the same image of children that Ariès highlighted—that of the child as a little adult—has been prevalent throughout the ages. This image is perhaps most evident in preformationistic theories in embryology. For centuries, many scientists believed that a tiny, fully formed human, or homunculus, is implanted in the sperm or egg at conception (see figure 7.1). They believed that the human is "preformed" at the instant of conception and only grows in

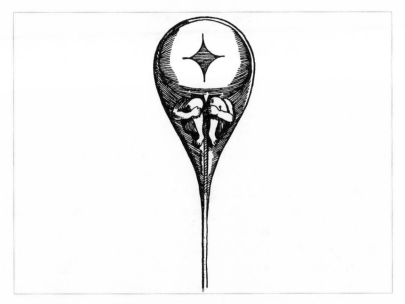

Figure 7.1. A seventeenth-century drawing of a fully formed
human in the sperm. *From Needham 1959, 206.*

size and bulk until birth. Preformationism in embryology dates
back at least to the fifth century B.C. and is found in scientific
thinking throughout the ages. As late as the eighteenth century,
most scientists held preformationist views. They admitted that
they had no direct evidence for a fully formed homunculus, but
they argued that this was only because it is transparent or too
small to see. Preformationism was abandoned only after microscopes showed that the embryo develops gradually.

As we look back on the "little adult" views of earlier times,
it's easy to regard them as quaint and antiquated. But we often
lapse into the same thinking today, as when we expect young
children to be able to sit as still as we can in social settings, or
when we assume that their thinking is the same as ours. For example, while I was recently standing in a supermarket checkout

line, a mother next to me discovered that her toddler had put several items of interest to him in her shopping cart. The mother exclaimed, "What are these things doing in here? You know I can't afford them!"—as if a toddler had an adult's knowledge of budgets.

Some social critics, such as Neil Postman and Marie Winn, have suggested our society as a whole has recently been treating children more like adults. These writers point to several trends, including similarities between children and adults in dress (for example, both wear designer jeans), the way television is exposing children to sex and adult themes, and the way the criminal system has begun treating juvenile offenders like adult criminals.

But many of these trends also meet with resistance, and, in any event, the little-adult conception of childhood hardly holds sway as it did in the past. Modern society simply does not believe that children are ready for adult life. We believe, instead, that children require an extensive period of preparation for the future. Children are not little adults but future adults.

CHILDREN AS FUTURE ADULTS

THE MODERN CONCEPTION of childhood was the outgrowth of sweeping changes in the European economy. During the Middle Ages, most of the occupations—such as farming, carpentry, domestic service, metalwork, and weaving—required skill, but the adults believed that six- and seven-year-olds could at least begin learning them on the job. But after 1500 or so, the occupational world showed clear signs of change. With the invention of the printing press, the growth of commerce and market economies, the rise of cities and nation-states, the occupational world began to take on a "white collar" look. New opportunities arose for merchants, lawyers, bankers, journalists, and government officials—occupations that required reading, writing, and math. A rising middle class saw that it could advance its families' fortunes by providing its children with the academic instruction that these new occupations required. This new demand for education sparked a tremendous growth of schools in the sixteenth and seventeenth centuries.

The upshot was that growing numbers of parents were no longer willing to send their children off to work at the age of six or seven years. Parents wanted their children to go to school first. Parents began keeping their children in school at least until they were twelve years old, and often until they were well into their teens. Parents held their children back from the adult world while they prepared their children for the future.

It was Ariès, once again, who started scholars thinking about this change. Ariès attached particular importance to the growth of schools because schools separated children from adult society. Once parents began sending children to school, "it was recognized that the child was not ready for life, and that he had to be subjected to a special treatment, a sort of quarantine, before he was allowed to join the adults." This separation of children into their own institutions—schools—gave the childhood years their own social identity.

Ariès's insight into the role of schools is important but limited. As Martin Holyes observes, Ariès didn't explain why schools emerged in the first place. In Ariès's view, the rapid growth of schools in the sixteenth and seventeenth centuries was the brainchild of a small group of clergy, lawyers, and moralists. Ariès basically overlooked the more fundamental force—the driving ambition of a rising middle class. Middle-class parents saw that the occupational world was changing and were determined to use schools to prepare their children for it.

In the process, the rising middle class stimulated a revolutionary change in the way Western society viewed time. It initiated the modern view that the most important time dimension is not the past or the present, but the future.

Today we take a strong focus on the future for granted. What parent isn't deeply concerned about his or her child's future success? In our own lives, too, we unquestioningly assume that it is the future that should matter most. Few of us would proudly proclaim that our goal in life is to live day to day or to live in the past. We believe that our primary thoughts and concerns should focus on the future. What is important is our plans, our visions, our dreams.

But as the anthropologist Florence Kluckholn pointed out in her valuable (if generally ignored) 1961 essay on culturual values, a strong focus on the future is hardly universal. Although all cultures must to some extent address all three time dimensions—the past, present, and future—many cultures have placed the greatest emphasis on the past or the present. Indeed, the feudalistic societies of the Middle Ages emphasized the past—tradition. Families didn't think a great deal about improving their lot, for this would violate feudalism's emphasis on the venerable old ways. Feudalism even promoted the idea that the social class divisions were divinely ordained. As an Ulster-woman's poem later expressed it,

> The rich man in his castle,
> The poor man at his gate,
> God made them, high and lowly,
> And ordered their estate.

Thus, when middle-class families thought about schooling as a way of advancing their families' occupational status, their thinking was new and daring. It tore at the core of feudalistic values. Middle-class parents were proposing that it was no longer the past, but the future, that mattered. They were saying this was true with respect to their children, and it eventually became true with respect to Western society in general.

To get a more detailed picture of how the middle class exerted its impact, it will be helpful to look at how it stimulated changes in schools during the early modern period, from about 1500 to 1850.

THE EVOLUTION OF SCHOOLS

DURING THE MIDDLE AGES, schools primarily trained those who went into the clergy, which was only a small fraction of the population. When, in the sixteenth and seventeenth centuries, new schools tried to meet the new demand for education, the schools were largely at a loss as to how to proceed. Most schools treated the children as if they already had adult minds (reflecting the persistence of the "little-adult" image). They assigned their pupils, even seven- and eight-year-olds, classic Latin and Greek texts and expected them to learn the rules of Latin grammar. That the children had no interest in these lessons and didn't understand the material they managed to memorize were facts that bothered few educators.

Children also were frequently dressed like adults and were expected to sit in their seats up to ten or twelve hours a day with few breaks. When the children proved restless, the schoolmasters didn't wonder why this was so. Instead, they saw the need for discipline—for beatings. In fact, whipping quickly became so common in the schools that it became known as the *poena scholastica,* the scholastic punishment.

Here and there, sixteenth- and seventeenth-century observers did display a sensitivity to the child's plight. Shakespeare wrote of the schoolboy "creeping like a snail, unwillingly to school," and Thomas More expressed the child's wish that "these hateful books all/were in a powder burnt to small." There also was a smattering of educators—people such as Vives, Comenius, and Fenalon—who wanted to make education more manageable for children. Among these, Comenius is widely recognized as the most profound, and his experiences and work illustrate the problems that children faced.

John Amos Comenius (1592–1670) was born in Moravia, a part of what later became Czechoslovakia. He had no formal education until he was twelve years old. At that age, both his parents died, and he was sent off to school—first to a village school and then to one that was more advanced. Comenius hated them both. Since, however, he was older than most of the other boys, he was probably in a better position to think more critically about the practices. He later would recall with horror the way the teachers forced the children to struggle with lessons that were far too difficult and, then, seeing that the children couldn't keep up, lost their tempers and beat the children. Comenius likened their behavior to that of a nurse who tries to force an infant to walk before the baby is able to do so, and then beats the baby when she falls.

Even without the beatings, Comenius said, the lessons were so "overburdened with long-winded rules, with commentaries and notes on commentaries," and "knotty questions," that "we, poor wretches, were so confused that we scarcely understood what it was all about." The students were compelled to perform dictations and memorize material until "nausea and, in some cases insanity [was] produced." Comenius himself was an excellent student, but he described himself as "one of the many thousands who have miserably lost the sweetest spring-time of their whole life, and wasted the fresh years of youth on academic trifles."

In response, Comenius devoted his adult life to improving education. His goal, as he announced on the title page of his book, *The Great Didactic* (1657), was to show how all subjects could be learned "Quickly, Pleasantly, and Thoroughly." Comenius argued that students could learn to read and write much more easily if they learned the skills in their mother tongue prior to turning to Latin. He also proposed that all lessons be arranged in gradual steps, progressing from the simple to the difficult, and he developed a series of new textbooks. One of his texts, the *Orbis Pictus* (1658), was the world's first picture-book reader for children. Comenius wanted beginners to be able to see objects while they were learning the objects' names. Comenius, finally, urged schools to open their doors to girls as well as to boys.

But Comenius was far ahead of his time. His work caught the attention of various national dignitaries, but he couldn't get his ideas implemented. He tried to establish a school in Sarospatak, Hungary, but his teachers couldn't follow his scheme, and the school collapsed. Only Comenius's textbooks had an immediate impact. His *Orbis Pictus,* in particular, was extremely popular. Even so, the *Orbis Pictus* stood as an isolated achievement. For over a century after its appearance, there were few efforts to produce similar books, and no one tried to improve on it. It was almost as if the *Orbis Pictus* had been created by an alien intelligence and dropped from the sky.

The primary changes in seventeenth- and eighteeth-century education were not brought about by people who, like Comenius, were concerned about the experiences of children. Rather, the main changes were initiated by those whose eyes were firmly set on the occupational world. Middle-class parents, in particular, focused on the way society was changing and wanted their children to be ready for it. As Ivy Pinchbeck and Margaret Hewitt put it with respect to seventeenth-century England, "The wide-awake, practical parents sent their children to schools which laid claim, rightly or wrongly, to move with the times."

Early instruction in Latin, for example, diminished, but not because schools were impressed by the ideas of Comenius or like-minded educators. Rather, parents and teachers saw that Latin was becoming less important in adult society. As national governments took power away from the church, modern languages became increasingly prominent in official and commercial transactions. Thus, parents wanted their children to learn the languages that would be useful in the changing occupational world, and middle-class families provided markets for new, private-profit schools that put an emphasis on modern languages.

The aristocracy, too, wanted schools that would prepare its children for a changing society. The aristocracy wasn't particularly enthusiastic about the social changes; it stood to lose considerable status and power to the rising middle class. But the aristocracy tried to adapt. Its parents weren't interested in an education that befitted a future monk; they wanted their children to be equipped for the contemporary court and state.

Thus, new schools emerged to meet the aristocracy's needs. These schools still taught Latin, but they stressed the modern languages, and they replaced the ancient studies of the Bible with those of the sciences, giving special attention to practical applications. The schools also stressed history, politics, geography, and jurisprudence—subjects that would aid future leaders in the governance of nations.

Not all seventeenth-century adults focused exclusively on the education of their own children. A number of European religious and political leaders believed that education could benefit the larger social order, especially in the cities, where poverty and lawlessness were widespread. Police actions were doing little good, and it was hoped that a limited amount of education would turn the children of the down-and-outs into pious, serious workers. The result was the growth of a large number of "charity schools," as the British called them, which offered a few years of instruction to poor boys, and sometimes to girls, too. Typically, five- to twelve-year-olds received some religious education as well as instruction in reading, writing, arithmetic, and sometimes a manual trade. Because no one expected the poor children to go far in life, the education was kept modest, and Latin and Greek, which were identified with the upper classes, were omitted. The children were taught in their own languages.

But it soon turned out that these schools, which were designed for the poor, were filled with middle-class children. Visiting a French charity school in 1675, one church official found no children in rags, and when he asked the school's mistress about this, her only reply was that "she didn't know how poor they were." The reason for so many middle-class children, the clergyman Claude Joy suggested, was the schools were free: "When something is free, everyone wants it." This may have been so, but what is striking is the way middle-class families encroached on schools intended for others.

LEGITIMIZING THE FUTURE: THE PROMISE OF TECHNOLOGY

DURING THE EARLY modern era (from about 1500 to 1750), then, it was basically the middle class that propelled the growth of schools and the form they took. It was the rising middle class, the bourgeoisie, who most energetically began using schools to advance its children's future prospects. And in the process, the middle class started Western society thinking that it is the future that really matters.

But those of the bourgeoisie couldn't accomplish this alone. They vigorously pursued a brighter future for themselves and their children, but they did not give a future orientation its moral legitimacy. After all, the bourgeoisie was often considered to be lacking in moral values. Its members were attacked, especially by the aristocracy, as an ignoble collection of families who were only interested in themselves and their own financial interests—as greedy people who had no respect for loyalty, honor, or tradition. Indeed, Elinor Barber says that in eighteenth-century France, the nouveaux riches were themselves often ashamed of their status. Many tried to purchase titles of nobility, while others traced their ancestry to demonstrate that they, too, like the aristocrats, had a lineage—even when their ancestors were criminals.

To gain legitimacy, the bourgeoisie needed an ideology that would give a future orientation its own moral standing. This ideology was supplied by the remarkable intellectuals of the eighteenth-century Enlightenment. Gathering primarily in Paris, this collection of freethinking scholars, economists, publicists, and writers—known by the French name *philosophes*—attacked the traditional authority of the feudal church and state. These institutions, the philosophes argued, filled the world with dogmatism and superstition. And because of this, these institutions not only were stifling free and rational thought; they were impeding progress. If the authority of the feudal regime could be lifted, the philosophes said, reason and science could create a better world for all.

In the realm of economics, for example, François Quesnay (1694–1774) and other philosophes argued that scientific analyses demonstrated the natural benefits of laissez-faire. When individuals are free to pursue their own self-interests, they produce the greatest wealth for the entire society. This, Quesnay emphasized, is a scientific law. In a similar manner, the philosophes believed that they could apply scientific analyses to society and alleviate crime and other social ills.

The principal vehicle of Enlightenment thought was the *Encyclopedia,* which included essays by Quesnay, Voltaire, Montesquieu, and many other great essayists. But the *Encyclopedia*'s top priority was not the publications of theoretical papers. Above all, it championed technology. Under the tireless leadership of its chief editor, Denis Diderot (1713–84), the *Encyclopedia* published twenty-two volumes of text and eleven volumes of illustrations, and almost all the illustrations depicted technological innovations. Superb plates showed the latest canals, workshops, laboratories, tools, and machines. The *Encyclopedia* attempted to document the progress technology already had made and to draw wide attention to technology's tremendous potential.

Diderot, it should be noted, published the first volume of the *Encyclopedia* in 1751, fourteen years before James Watt's new steam engine, which many historians consider the driving force behind the Industrial Revolution. Thus, Diderot saw the promise of technology early on. He visited workshops and learned to operate some of the newest machines himself. He also solicited articles from prominent writers in the field of technology, as well as from people who were actually working in the manual arts and crafts. Sometimes, to be sure, the *Encyclopedia*'s enthusiasm got carried away. As D. C. Coleman observes, some of the illustrations glamorized the new machines, presenting them on a larger scale and locating them in more pristine work settings than was really the case. All the same, the *Encyclopedia*'s compilation of technical information was an extraordinary achievement.

Diderot and many other philosophes displayed uncommon courage. They frequently saw their works banned, and they were even imprisoned because of them. But they persisted because they believed in their ideas and ideals.

At the same time, it is easy to see how their views justified the economic interests of the rising bourgeoisie. If the profit motive of the new capitalists struck people as selfish, the philosophes cast the motive in a new light. It is precisely when individuals are free to pursue their own financial interests that the wealth of the entire society grows. And if anyone were to criticize the bourgeoisie for repudiating the past, the philosophes were rendering this criticism obsolete. It is precisely the past, with its dogmatism and intolerance, that must be overcome. Instead, people should put their faith in progress—especially technological progress. By investing capital in new inventions and products, the bourgeoisie was performing a great service. It was contributing to a brighter future.

During the Enlightenment, there was a major dissenting voice—that of Rousseau. Rousseau contributed some early articles to the *Encyclopedia* (primarily on music), and he shared the other Enlightenment intellectuals' opposition to feudal authority. But Rousseau questioned the new faith in progress. In his view, the forward march of civilizations was making things worse, not better. As work was becoming more specialized, people were becoming more dependent on one another and on external opinions. They were losing their ability to fend and think for themselves. Rousseau argued that instead of placing faith in progress, it would be better if people could somehow recapture aspects of a simpler, rustic life when people were more self-reliant.

As noted in the introduction, Rousseau also questioned the new emphasis on the future in education. When we focus too intently on what children will need for tomorrow's job markets, we overlook the ways they develop as strong, independent individuals. Rousseau urged us to consider nature's ground plan for healthy development. Nature inwardly guides children to develop different capacities at different stages, and we should give them opportunities to develop themselves at their present stage.

When calling attention to nature's developmental plan, Rousseau rejected the two views of childhood we have considered so far. He wanted us to stop thinking about children either as little adults or as future adults. Children are children, with interests and ways of learning befitting their stage of life. "Nature would have them children before they are men," and we should treat them as such.

Rousseau's writings had an impact. They inspired the Romantic movement in the humanities and the child-centered movement in education. But it was the dominant themes of the Enlightenment—the prospect of a better future and the faith in technology to bring it about—that took hold of the modern mind.

A SPECIAL ZEAL

THE UNITED STATES in particular is a future-oriented society. Our nation was created by people searching for a better future—people who, if unhappy with the land they initially colonized, had only to pack up and move westward. Two great inventions of the Industrial Revolution, the steamboat and the railroad, empowered a people on the move; and other technological advances, especially in weapons and explosives, enabled pioneers to conquer new territories. Marvelous new inventions (such as the airplane, telephone, and automobile) convinced us that our hopes for the future were well-founded.

A future orientation permeates our everyday thought. We believe that we must constantly set our sights on what lies ahead. We must approach every task with a plan, a goal, or a vision. We admire trendsetters, those on the cutting edge. We pride ourselves on being a forward-looking people, and we embrace the technological innovations that are going to move us forward. Indeed, we have come to think of the future itself as synonymous with technology and speak of the "high-tech world of tomorrow" and, using the words of computer technology, the "new Information Age."

Images of the future are everywhere. High-tech corporations advertise their products as "the wave of the future" and "links to the world of tomorrow." Even professional publications in fields such as psychology and education try to impress us with titles such as *New Directions in This* and *Emerging Trends in That*. These titles catch our attention, and they stir in most of us a twinge of anxiety, a feeling that we must read this publication or the worst thing that can happen to us will happen: We will be left behind. Through such ads and promotions, we have it drummed into our heads, day after day, that the future is the time dimension that we should be concerned about.

In a society so powerfully and pervasively oriented toward the future, it is difficult to think about education in any other terms. It is difficult to consider education as nurturing children's interests and capacities at their present stage. It has been especially difficult to consider alternatives when our nation's technological supremacy has been threatened. In the past fifty years, this has happened twice.

The first threat occurred in 1957, when the Soviet Union launched *Sputnik,* the first Earth-orbiting satellite. The Russians had taken the lead in the space race. In response, our nation's leaders pressed our schools to start producing the adults who would restore U.S. supremacy. College professors designed the "new math," and "new science" to teach theoretically advanced concepts to young children. But elementary-school children understood little of the new material. In fact, the material was so abstract that parents couldn't offer their children much help, either. So the new curriculum reforms failed. Still, the educational reforms of the early 1960s started pushing academic instruction down into the early years.

The late 1960s and early 1970s, when the nation was deeply involved in the Vietnam War, was a period of radical questioning. In education, some questioned the traditional approaches and undertook new experiments with child-centered education. That is, new schools tried to tailor education to children's spontaneous interests and natural ways of learning. However, these experiments never dominated the educational scene, and by the mid-1970s, a second crisis hit.

Japan and West Germany began to outperform us in automotive and high-tech industries. Once again, our political leaders looked to the schools (rather than to their own policies) as the source of the problem. Our schools, they charged, weren't producing a sufficiently skilled and educated workforce to compete in the global economy. "Back to basics" was the rallying cry, and schools starting focusing intently on the three Rs. State and municipal governments increasingly mandated standardized tests, and remedial instruction for children falling below selected cutoff scores.

Since then, the pressure to raise academic standards and testing requirements has steadily increased. The 1983 federal report *A Nation at Risk* issued a call "to all who care about America and its future" to demand more from our children. A multitude of similar reports followed, and the movement to raise standards has won strong support from both major political parties. During the 1990s the first Bush and the Clinton administrations established ambitious national goals, including the goal that by the year 2000 the United States would be first in the world in math and science. The United States failed to meet this goal, but the standards movement continues to develop momentum. Almost every state government in the nation has developed higher academic standards and more rigorous standardized tests to measure students' progress. Increasingly, states are making high-school graduation and grade promotion contingent on specific test scores. Whenever the standards movement seemed faltering in the slightest, strong advocates, such as Louis V. Gerstner, Jr., the former CEO of IBM, have called the governors together to recommit themselves to preparing students for tomorrow's technologically advanced economy.

Some people have complained that the standards movement consists of too much rhetoric, and not enough concrete demands on schools and children. However, standardized testing dominates instruction and the standards movement's driving goal—to prepare children for a competitive future—is also having a very real impact on children. Children are worrying about the future at younger and younger ages. The *New York Times* recently conducted roundtable discussions with sixth graders in several states and found that many of the children were *already* worried about college admissions. Many of the students were so worried about their academic performances that they were suffering from headaches and loss of sleep. They also complained that the academic demands have become excessive. As one girl said, "It's all being crammed into your brain. It's too much to take." Meanwhile, children are missing out on the experiences—play, artistic activities, the exploration of nature—that are so fulfilling to them as children.

|||||||||||||||||||||||||||||||||||||||||||||||||||||||||||||||||||||||||||||||||

CHAPTER 8

Questioning Technology

Too much computers.

—ALLEN GINSBERG

I F WE wish to help children develop, we must adopt a more critical attitude toward modern technology. We must take a closer look at technology's prize tool, the computer, as well as the values that promote modern technology in general.

COMPUTERS

EDUCATORS ALMOST UNIVERSALLY seek more computers for schools. Indeed, many people consider computers so central that they equate social inequity with disparities in computer access—"the digital divide." There can be no doubt that computers perform amazing feats. They can instantly produce a wealth of information and a variety of graphics. They also are fun. With the touch of a button, we command attractive pictures, text, and statistics, giving us a feeling of magical power.

But computers also create problems—none more basic than

the computer's physical setup. The child at the computer monitor is locked into an artificial, sterile environment. There is
nothing but plastic and metal. There is, as John Davy has said,
"no wind or birdsong . . . no connection with soil, water, sunlight, warmth, no real ecology."

The sterility of the computer environment is particularly
worrisome for young children, prior to the age of seven years or
so, who are in the process of developing their senses. At the
computer monitor, children learn about the world through
symbols—pictures and words—on a screen. The pictures may be
attractive, but children get no sense of how things feel, smell,
taste, weigh, or respond to their movements. A picture of a
pond is no substitute for the sensory stimulation of a real
pond—the breezes and mists off the water, the feel of the mud
and ground at the water's edge. The picture of a bird, or even a
video of one, is no substitute for being near a real bird, watching
its movements, noting how it reacts to sounds, sights, and wind
currents, as well as to one's own presence and movements.

Computer-based knowledge continues to be problematic
after the age of seven or eight, too. Schools increasingly use
computers to present a wide range of facts and concepts, but it is
all on a symbolic level. Computers introduce children to a good
deal of biology, geography, and atmospheric sciences, but what
kind of knowledge is it if the child lacks relevant experience
with water, wind, animals, and other natural elements? Similarly, what does it mean for a child to learn physics—principles
such as velocity, force, and balance—without having had lots
of experience throwing, hammering, seesawing, and climbing.
The child learns words and symbols without having had the
personal, bodily, and sensory experience that makes the symbols
meaningful. The danger is that the child is learning at too cere-
bral a level. The child is becoming a disembodied mind.

When I have told colleagues about the problems with the

computer environment, they have often said, "Yes, but the computer doesn't have to monopolize the child's time. Why can't children learn from the computer and also spend a good deal of time playing outdoors, exploring nature and gaining sensory and physical experience?" In theory this is possible, but in reality today's children are spending more and more time indoors at the computer monitor. When they are not doing homework on the computer, they are surfing the Internet, playing video games, or "talking" to their friends on e-mail. The rest of the time they watch TV. The computer and electronic media stimulate the child to remain in a relatively sterile, indoor environment.

I believe the problem is so serious that parents and educators should limit the time children spend in artificial environments. Many Waldorf schools (child-centered schools founded by Rudolf Steiner) keep computers out of the classroom until the eighth grade. Few other schools would consider anything so restrictive. But we must set some limits on the time spent in artificial, electronic environments in the early years so children will have full opportunities to develop their senses, learn through physical activities, and form bonds with the natural world. One child advocacy group, the Alliance for Childhood, has called for a moratorium on the further introduction of computers into early-childhood and elementary-school education until more is known about their effects.

TECHNOLOGICAL VALUES

BEHIND ADVANCED TECHNOLOGY's tools—behind the computers, electronic microscopes, and cyclotrons—is a set of values, whose existence is often denied. Technology's advocates often claim that technology is value-neutral: it only consists of tools and techniques, which can serve good or bad purposes, depending on whose hands they fall into. But scholars such as Lewis Mumford and Neil Postman have made a strong case that modern technology does advance a set of values. The values aren't the traditional kind, like humility and justice; they are the primacy of the future, speed, efficiency, rational thinking, objective analysis, and the mastery of the environment.

I have found that a consideration of values has immense practical value. For example, in meetings in which the direction of my university is discussed, administrators and faculty leaders often talk about the most efficient way to deliver instruction. Efficiency can be served by larger class sizes, combining campus offerings, distance learning, and by other means. It's often helpful to observe that while efficiency is one value, prized in a technological society, it is only one value. We should also consider other values, such as the value we place on students' ability to think critically and fully. The development of such abilities might require small classes, individual faculty mentoring, and other approaches that aren't necessarily the most efficient.

Let us consider three technological values and their influence on children.

1. The Future

I already have discussed the primacy of the future and how it distorts our view of children. Our eyes are so fixed on children's futures that we overlook the experiences they need at their present stage, such as rich experiences with nature and the arts. What I want to stress here is that our modern preoccupation with the future is a technologically driven value. Technology's advocates want us to believe that our fundamental concern, whether it is with respect to our children or ourselves, ought to be for the future. If, instead, we put greater value on the past or the present, we wouldn't desire all the high-tech innovations that promise to take us well into the new millennium.

The modern value on the future, more than anything else, is responsible for the exalted status of computers in our schools. Educational-policy makers embraced computers long before any research indicated that computers were effective educational tools. Beginning in the 1980s, schools everywhere started purchasing as many computers as possible simply because of the computer's anticipated prominence in tomorrow's workplace. Even today, the research supporting the instructional value of computer technology doesn't begin to justify the esteem in which the computer is held. I would emphasize that although computers may play a major role in the child's future, the future isn't the only important time dimension. The child's present needs and development matter, too. We should consider the full range of experiences the child needs at his or her current stage, and ask, "How well does the computer fulfill and limit these needs?"

2. Rational, Goal-Directed Thinking

Technology also values a specific kind of rational thinking—that which sets clear goals, ignores irrelevant information, and monitors progress each step of the way. This kind of goal-directed, systematic thinking has become very popular in psychology and education. As psychologist David Wood says, "Individuals can only take in so much information about their situation at any moment in time, so they must organize their activities over time (develop a plan). . . . The development of knowledge and skill involves the discovery of what is best paid attention to, borne in mind and acted upon in an appropriate (goal-achieving) sequence."

Such goal-directed thinking is very difficult for children prior to the age of seven or eight years. They are easily distracted from the task at hand. They also have difficulty monitoring their own progress. Accordingly, educational psychologists have produced manuals and kits to teach young children goal-directed, self-monitoring skills, and prestigious scholars believe that these skills will enable children to master reading, math, and science at early ages. Computer advocates also observe that their logical, step-by-step programs can also facilitate such thinking.

But these instructional methods overlook the strength of the young child's approach—the child's open-minded receptivity to the world in all its richness and variety. In the Berkeley nature area, Robin Moore observed that the children like to wander about without any goal in mind, just seeing what is there and taking delight in new experiences. Similarly, the naturalist Cathy Johnson says that she tries to remove "adulthood's blinders" and let herself be open to experience and serendipitous discoveries. "When, instead, I become too single-minded and goal-directed, straight ahead, one foot in front the other, I might as well be a robot or a computer. Humanity fades; the joy is gone."

The rational approach often conceptualizes the goal as a problem—something to be fixed, changed, or explained. It is the approach of the engineer or the technician who needs to figure out how to widen a road, dig a tunnel, or dam a river. But in natural settings, children often simply marvel at things just as they are. In the following poems, consider how the children are happy to observe nature just as it presents itself:

> Whistling, whistling
> Blowing blowing
> Branches swaying
> Blossom blowing
> The wind
> —*Rosemary Stinton (five years old)*

Busy bee! Busy bee!
I hear your voice of humming.
        —*Gillian Hughes (six years old)*

The humanistic psychologist Abraham Maslow and the developmental psychologist Heinz Werner suggest that the most creative adults, including adult scientists, make full use of the childlike receptivity to the world before engaging in more advanced, rational modes of thought. Rational, goal-directed modes of thinking are valuable, but so too is the childlike delight in the world as it unfolds before us. To devalue the childhood experience is to shortchange thinking itself.

3. Speed

A third major technological value is speed. Indeed, speed is so highly valued in the technological worldview that it is one of the major criteria by which technology measures its progress. Jet airplanes are considered superior to propeller-driven aircraft because they travel faster. New computers are better than older models because they crunch numbers faster. New modems are superior to old modems because they connect us with information more quickly.

The premium on speed extends to practically every walk of life. According to the farmer and writer Wendell Berry, the quest for speed is found in public-relations pieces such as the following: "Today we have multi-row planters that slap in a crop in a hurry, putting down seed, fertilizer, insecticide and herbicide in one quick swipe across the field." But Berry believes that the proper cultivation of land requires a slower pace. Berry quotes an old-time English farmer who observes that today's farmers don't even take the time to get a sense of the land before planting. "A good practical man would hold on a few weeks, and get the feel of the land under his feet. He'd walk on it and feel it through his boots and see if it was in good heart, before he planted anything; he'd sow only when he knew what the land was fit for." Unfortunately, Berry says, modern technological farming has driven out the small farmer, whose slower pace made a more sensitive, caring attitude possible.

Most of us probably recognize that the emphasis on speed diminishes our own lives as well, and we sometimes complain about our hurried existences. Nevertheless, we expect and value speed. We want our microwave ovens, fax machines, and instant analysis of the news. When it comes to children's learning, we assume that faster is better. Parents are proud to hear that their children are fast learners—that their kids have been placed in accelerated classes. In fact, to say that a child is "slow" is just a polite way to say that the child is stupid. Even highly respected scholars believe that speed is the essence of good education. In the words of the psychologist Lloyd G. Humphreys, "Effective learning requires starting students at their current level and helping (even pushing) them ahead as rapidly and as far as possible."

A few developmental theorists have maintained that the pace of development has a certain inherent slowness, and that it cannot be rushed. Rousseau and Gesell argued that this is because development is an organic process; children, like plants, grow according to nature's timetable. Gesell and contemporary maturationists believe that the pace of development, which varies from child to child, is controlled by the genes.

Another important developmental theory, that of Jean Piaget, puts less weight on genetic variables. Instead, Piaget sees cognitive development as a spontaneous construction process. Children construct new cognitive structures as they work on problems they find interesting. We can, in the Piagetian view, sometimes accelerate this process by providing children with interesting tasks. But there is a limit. Genuine cognitive development only occurs when children think things out for themselves, and this takes time. "Learning to master the truth for oneself," Piaget said, means "losing a lot of time going through all the round-about ways that are inherent in real activity." Piaget was deeply impressed by how long it took Darwin to construct his theory of evolution, and Piaget and his followers have suggested that cognitive development has a certain natural slowness, with each child working at his or her own optimal pace. Other species may develop more quickly than humans, but humans go farther in the long run.

Piaget's views have produced considerable impatience among psychologists, who have searched for ways of accelerating development. These efforts have produced mixed results, but the computer revolution has offered new hope. Seymore Papert and others have argued that the high-speed digital computer is just the tool for accelerating the development of logical thinking.

But studies on the computer's power to do this have produced mixed results as well. Moreover, informal but thought-provoking research by Craig Brod has raised troubling concerns. On the basis of interviews and observations, Brod suggests that the computer may frequently establish a pace that is too fast for full and deep thought. When children are caught up in the speed and intensity of the computer, they are so busy making decisions and reacting to outputs on the screen that they don't take the time to mull over ideas or reflect on experience.

Brod also reports that youngsters who become deeply involved in computers become impatient with social dialogue. They find discussions too slow. For Piaget, this finding would also be troubling because social discussions can provide children with the experience of having their ideas challenged, motivating them to think more fully and deeply.

When Piaget said that thinking needs time to develop, he was primarily referring to mathematical and scientific thinking. He wasn't considering the activities I have highlighted in this book, such as make-believe play, artistic expression, and the sensory exploration of nature. But the child's development in these areas, too, can only flourish if the child is given unpressured time. Children need stretches of unhurried time to create imaginary dramas, to draw or compose poems, to wander alongside a brook, seeing what they can find. Indeed, children need the opportunity to get in touch with nature's own rhythms, as when a child sits in a daydreamy state by a pond, feeling a oneness with the water.

In the Berkeley schoolyard, the children said that the nature area invited them to sit quietly, listen to the birds, look at the trees, and just think. What the children thought about, we do not know. My guess is that they sometimes thought about their personal problems, and these problems seemed smaller in the context of the beautiful and intricate web of life surrounding them. In any case, just sitting and thinking was calming and helpful, and the thinking required unhurried time.

|||||||||||||||||||||||||||||||||||||||||||||||||||||||||||||||||||||||||||||||||

CHAPTER 9

Responding to the Standards Movement: The Child-Centered Alternative

I'm going to drop out of school.

—ELLIA *(age ten)*

I N MAY 2000 several hundred Massachusetts high-school sophomores boycotted the state's new standardized test. They felt that the great emphasis on testing was taking away from a deeper, more personalized education. This rebellion took courage, and the following springs saw new boycotts in other regions of the country, including Scarsdale, New York; Marin County, California; and New York City. But as striking as the protests have been, they were a long time coming. During the entire decade of the 1990s, the standards and testing movement swept through the nation with scant opposition. Led by the nation's top political and corporate leaders, the standards movement took control of education, and it continues to gain in strength.

To date, forty-nine of the fifty states have developed new curricular goals and standards, and most states have created new standardized tests to hold students accountable to the standards. In addition, states are increasingly establishing penalties for school districts with low test scores, and the states are steadily reducing "social promotion"; they are no longer permitting students with low scores to advance to new grade levels or to graduate from high school. To be sure, a few states have delayed the implementation of their tough new policies. But in January 2002 the federal government weighed in, mandating standardized testing in grades three through eight. So the ultimate success of the boycotts and protests is very much in doubt.

Those who are distressed by the standards movement have found it difficult to formulate persuasive critiques. To a large extent, this is because the standards movement phrases its aims in such convincing terms. How could anyone oppose "higher standards" and "clear goals"? Does anyone question the need for "accountability" and "higher test scores" or the need to end "social promotion"?

Actually, a child-centered philosophy does question these aims. Child-centered education hasn't been very visible in recent years, but it offers an alternative conception of what education should be.

Child-centered education takes many forms, including Montessori schools, the progressive education inspired by John Dewey, open education, Piaget-inspired constructivism, and Rudolf Steiner-inspired Waldorf schools. Despite the variations, child-centered educators share basic positions—positions that differ radically from those of the standards movement.

SHOULD WE SET GOALS AND STANDARDS?

THE STANDARDS MOVEMENT's leaders claim they are bringing a large dose of clearheaded thinking to our muddled educational system. They say education must begin with clear goals. "Education," says Diane Ravitch, a former assistant secretary of education, "means to lead forth, but it is impossible to lead anyone anywhere without knowing where you want to go." Thus, standards advocates have urged educational leaders, with input from local communities, to focus on the desired end products of education—the overall goals. What should children know and be able to do when they graduate? What knowledge and skills will enable them to succeed in the twenty-first-century workplace? Once these goals are defined, it's possible to specify the detailed objectives at each grade.

Standards advocates assume that an emphasis on goals is just common sense, and in a sense it is. It is part of the future orientation so engrained in Western thought. We routinely assume that we should approach life with a plan or a vision—an idea of where we are headed. In addition, clear goals contribute to rational problem solving; once we have defined our goals, we can monitor our progress. Having clear goals just makes sense.

Flying in the face of such conventional wisdom, child-centered educators have argued that our focus should not be on our goals, but on the child as a growing organism. Instead of asking, "What do we want the child to know and be able to do?" we should ask, "What capacities is the child spontaneously motivated to develop at his or her current stage?" Instead of thinking about our own goals, we should consider the child's interests and needs.

In earlier chapters I mentioned how adult goals can impede the child's development. For example, educational-policy makers urge us to raise our academic expectations for young children—to teach the three Rs—even prior to elementary school. However, young children seem to be have a stronger inner need to develop the "nonacademic" side of their personalities, such as their artistic abilities, connections to nature, and fantasy. Early academic pressure can rob children of the chance to develop in these areas. Some people try to show that these nonacademic experiences indirectly help academic learning, too. For example, they say the arts can help children's math or reading. But from a child-centered perspective, this justification isn't necessary. Our task is to help the child develop his or her own emerging capacities, whether they fit our goals or not.

As the psychologists Herbert Ginsburg and Sylvia Opper point out, it is not always for the child-centered educator to know what the individual child needs to develop well. Although children seem to proceed through the same general stages, they develop at different rates and possess unique temperaments, talents, and interests. Thus, a child-centered philosophy calls for an openness on the part of the adult. The educator is not so much a leader as a follower. The educator tries to see what capacities the child herself feels a deep urge to master, and then tries to give the child opportunities to do so.

The child-centered approach is illustrated by the work of Maria Montessori. Montessori, who was the first female physician in Italy, initially experimented with new educational methods for developmentally delayed children and then founded a school for ordinary children in an economically impoverished section of Rome. In developing her methods, Montessori didn't just decide what children need to know and begin teaching them. Instead, she tried to suspend her own ideas and to observe open-mindedly their spontaneous tendencies and interests. When she did this, she saw that children often chose tasks on which they worked with amazing concentration.

Montessori told, for example, of a four-year-old girl who was working on a cylinder task, placing different-sized cylinders in their appropriate holes in a wooden frame. When the girl completed the task, she began again, and she kept repeating it over and over. All the while, she was so engrossed in the task that she was oblivious to her surroundings. After fourteen repetitions, Montessori decided to test her concentration. She asked the rest of the class to sing and march loudly. But the girl simply continued her work. Montessori then lifted the girl's chair, with the girl in it, onto a table. But the child merely gathered up her cylinders in her lap and kept working, hardly aware of the disturbance. Finally, after forty-two repetitions, the child stopped on her own, as if coming out of a dream, and smiled happily.

After this, Montessori observed the same phenomenon on many occasions. When children had access to certain tasks, they worked on them over and over, completely absorbed, as if in a kind of meditation. It seemed that they kept repeating the tasks to solidify a new capacity. And when they finished, they were rested and joyful. They seemed to possess an inner peace that came from the knowledge that they were able to develop something vital within themselves.

Thus, Montessori made it her task to create a school environment that included tasks on which children would concentrate deeply. She observed how children responded to a variety of materials, and observed that children often freely chose the activities that most deeply engrossed them. For example, she noticed that two-year-olds, when free to move about the room, were constantly straightening things up. If a glass of water slipped from a child's hand, the others would run to collect the broken pieces and wipe the floor. The children seemed to have a particularly strong need for order, so she altered the school environment to meet this need. She obtained child-size tables and chairs so the children could arrange them just right; she had the washbasins lowered so the children could wash their own brushes and hands; and she had the cupboards lowered so they could put their materials away where they belonged. Montessori didn't create such an environment because she had some future goal in mind, such as preparing children to be janitors or tidy adults. She created this environment so young children could meet a spontaneous need.

Today the Montessori-school environment is largely set in

the early years. It includes some materials that help children learn to write and develop other academic skills in ways that come naturally to them. Some Montessori teachers also introduce new tasks (apart from the standard curriculum). In any case, the children are always given free choice, for their choices often lead to tasks on which they concentrate intently. In a typical classroom, children of mixed ages—say three- to-six-year-olds or six- to-nine-year-olds—pick out materials and work on them individually or sometimes in small groups.

Sometimes the teacher introduces a task to a child. The teacher spends a good deal of time observing each child and, venturing a guess as to what the child is ready to work on, the teacher introduces it. But the choice is the child's. The Montessori teacher believes that the child has an inner wisdom with respect to what he or she needs to develop. The child, in Montessori's view, is guided by nature, and the teacher must follow the child's lead.

DON'T WE NEED TO END SOCIAL PROMOTION?

STANDARDS ADVOCATES RAIL against social promotion. It's unfair to students, they say, to promote them if they haven't mastered the material in the prior grade. Schools must insist on grade retention—holding students back—when necessary. One might object that holding students back humiliates them and increases dropout rates, but standards advocates consider these concerns secondary. In the long run, they say, it doesn't help the student to have been promoted year after year without having learned what he should have learned far back in the earlier grades.

But the social-promotion issue is an artifact of our schools' traditional, factory-style setup. Children are expected to meet the same standards each year, year after year, as if they were on a conveyor belt. In Montessori classrooms, social promotion is not really an issue. In classrooms of mixed ages, each child chooses from a variety of tasks and proceeds at his or her own pace. There are no uniform end-of-year objectives.

Not all child-centered schools mix the ages, but many encourage children to work individually or in small groups on the tasks they are ready for. Thus, if we were to visit an open-education or a progressive-education classroom, we might see some children working on individual math projects, others reading books of their own choice, and a group of three or four children engaged in building a model canal system. For the child-centered educator, tasks are arranged to meet each child's developing needs—not some uniform, predetermined schedule. Students work at their own pace, and the issue of social promotion only arises in exceptional cases.

WILL EXTERNAL PRESSURES HELP?

AS THE STANDARDS movement presses forward, it constantly raises the issue of students' motivation—or, more accurately, students' lack of motivation. There is broad agreement, within and outside the standards movement, that students in traditional schools don't like their work very much and don't work very hard at it. But the standards movement doesn't call for more intrinsically interesting work—work that students find exciting and meaningful. Instead, the movement calls for more external pressures and incentives. Parents must push children to work harder for the sake of their future; states must threaten children with being held back if they don't perform well on standardized tests; and employers and colleges must let students know they will be rejected if they don't achieve high grades and high test scores in high school. Adults must be able to convince children that their schoolwork has real consequences. Otherwise, says economist and standards advocate James Rosenbaum, adults will be "like lion-tamers without a whip."

Child-centered education rejects an emphasis on external motivators. Child-centered educators believe that children are naturally curious and have an inner urge to work on tasks that enable them to develop themselves. If we provide the right tasks, they will work on them with great energy and enthusiasm.

In the child-centered view, nothing is more important than this spontaneous enthusiasm for learning. It drives intellectual development. When children become engrossed in tasks, they think deeply and fully and their minds expand. It is therefore a great tragedy that conventional schools do so little to stimulate this enthusiasm for learning.

John Dewey and progressive educators have discussed this problem at length. Most schools, they observe, are filled with textbooks, workbooks, and lectures that children find dull and unrelated to their lives. Children memorize a certain amount of material to pass their tests, but they do not think deeply about it and forget most of it when the tests are over.

Progressive educators have found that students work with much greater energy on projects such as building things, conducting experiments, gardening, and producing newsletters. They also learn a good deal of academic material through such projects. For example, they can learn a good deal of math through the design and construction of a model house. And whereas students find the math presented in textbooks and workbooks dull and tedious, they work eagerly on the math involved in building things because the math enables them to fulfill their creative impulses.

THE ISSUE OF INDEPENDENCE

STANDARDS ADVOCATES INSIST that our schools expect too little of children. Schools, they say, must "raise the bar" and demand "more challenging" work. Standards advocates seem to believe that harder is better.

But much of what children are taught already sails over their heads. When children memorize words for a vocabulary test or formulas for a science test, they often don't even care if they understand what they are memorizing; they just want the right answers. So if schools simply make the conventional curriculum more difficult, children will merely memorize more material they don't grasp and find school more unpleasant than they already do. The education journalist Alfie Kohn, after visiting many American schools, has concluded that a grim experience is what many educators actually want children to have.

But as Rousseau pointed out, overly difficult instruction presents another danger: It undermines the child's independence. When, to take a contemporary example, we assign a child a math problem that is too difficult for her, she has no recourse but to turn to a more knowledgeable person or to the back of the book to see if she got the right answer. And because she doesn't fully understand the solution, she must accept on faith whatever the "smarter" person or the book says is true. She learns to depend on external authority rather than to think for herself.

Many child-centered educators have tried to promote independent learning. Montessori not only searched for tasks on which children concentrate deeply, but valued tasks on which children work on their own. She never wanted children to have to turn to adults for assistance or supervision.

A contemporary scholar who is passionate about independent learning is Constance Kamii. Kamii, a follower of Piaget, suggests that teachers should ask questions that arouse children's curiosity and then let the children solve them on their own. If the first-grade children are playing softball, the teacher might ask, "How many points do you need to reach eleven?" If a child brings pudding for the class, the teacher might ask, "Are there just enough cups for all the children?" The teacher should try to ask questions that the children will find inherently interesting and will set their minds in motion, but the teacher always should let the children come up with their own answers. Kamii recommends that teachers even respect children's wrong answers. For it is better for children to make mistakes than to believe that they must turn to an adult to know what is correct.

Kamii has suggested many ways children can develop arithmetic on their own. For example, she has shown how many card, dice, and board games stimulate children's spontaneous thinking. Her general method is called constructivism because children construct their own knowledge, and she suggests that it applies to every aspect of school life. If some children get into an argument during a game, the teacher doesn't impose a solution but might ask, "Can you think of a way that would be fair to everybody?" In this way the teacher prompts the children themselves to work on a question of justice.

The main drawback of Kamii's method is that it allows learning to be slower than most educators like. Kamii tells, for example, about lessons in specific gravity. Elementary-school children are often surprised to see that a pin sinks in water whereas a block of wood (which is larger) floats, and children usually need some time to figure out why this is so. A small group of fifth graders might spend several hours or days experimenting with different objects, seeing which float, as they test out hypotheses. Teachers are therefore tempted to step in and explain the answer (especially if the teacher has other material to cover in preparation for an upcoming standardized test). But to the extent the teacher has a choice, Kamii urges the teacher to wait. It is far better, Kamii says, for the children to keep thinking and wondering than "to be told the answer and to learn incidentally that the answer always comes from the teacher's head."

Kamii has conducted evaluation research on her method of teaching arithmetic in the early elementary grades. She has found that on standardized tests, her children score about the same as children taught by conventional methods. But her children demonstrate a deeper understanding of their work, and they are much more independent minded. When a teacher tried to help one first-grade girl with a hint, the girl said, "Wait, I have to think it in my own head." To Kamii this response is more valuable than any test score.

THE TYRANNY OF TESTING

THE STANDARDS MOVEMENT wouldn't amount to much without standardized tests. Education officials can set lofty goals and develop detailed curriculum standards, but their efforts would be pretty useless if they didn't know whether students are actually meeting the standards. Standardized tests provide this information. As the standards advocates say, tests hold schools and students "accountable."

But in the standards movement, "accountability" means more than just getting information. It means exerting control, trying to make sure schools do what government officials want. Officials use incentives and punishments (such as the threat to replace school principals and superintendents) to pressure schools to raise their scores.

Standards advocates often contend that testing actually gives schools new freedom. If schools are held accountable only for test results, schools will be free to get these results any way they choose. There will be no need for bureaucratic state mandates, such as the number of hours schools must devote to each subject.

In reality, when standardized tests carry high stakes, such as grade promotion or superintendents' jobs, the tests drive the curriculum. And test-driven education has numerous drawbacks.

For one thing, it deprofessionalizes teaching. In the atmosphere of high-stakes testing, teachers no longer make many judgments about tasks and activities students need. Instead, they must give students the textbook and workbook exercises that prepare them for the tests. In surveys, teachers say that as professionals they are "no longer trusted—tests carry the aura of respectability" and "Teachers feel jerked around. The test tells them what to teach."

Some standards advocates counter that there has never been much teacher flexibility anyway. Previously, the standards advocates say, the textbooks and workbooks set the agenda. But teachers consider the loss of freedom to be much greater under high-stakes testing.

This loss of flexibility is especially damaging to child-centered education. Child-centered teachers need the freedom to assess children's interests and provide tasks on which children will work with energy and enthusiasm. But with high-stakes tests on the horizon, teachers must put engrossing activities aside. Students might be engaged in lively and thoughtful discussions during a mock trial. Or they might be absorbed in a research study. But the teacher must say, "I'm sorry, we must stop now to prepare for the upcoming tests." This preparation usually consists of drills and exercises that children find extremely tedious. Test-driven education undermines the child's love of learning.

Standardized testing is particularly inappropriate for children in the early grades. The tests typically use paper-and-pencil, multiple-choice formats that present problems on a purely symbolic level. The tests present children with nothing but words, graphs, and numbers at ages when children think best when dealing with concrete things and ongoing social interactions. For example, whereas an eight-year-old boy may scratch his head over problems using the symbols ½, ⅓, and ⅛, he readily understands fractions when dividing a pie or sorting marbles among friends.

The adults who create standardized tests assume that because they, as adults, can solve problems on a purely abstract or symbolic level, the same is true of children. But it takes time for children to reach this level. By the fourth grade or so, many children have *some* facility with symbolic or abstract thought and can muddle their way through standardized tests, but they still basically find the formats unnatural and puzzling. Needless to say, they also find months of test preparation using these formats less than inspiring. It is not until adolescence that many children begin to find these formats manageable.

But even in adolescence, most students think most energetically and deeply when actively doing things—conducting experiments, producing newsletters, building model towns, role-playing, writing plays. Test preparation typically requires textbook instruction that drains the youngster of cognitive energy.

Now it is true that such interesting, projects-based learning has traditionally been only a small part of the classroom experience—even before the testing movement. But high-stakes testing makes even the possibility of projects-based learning impossible.

What's more, as the standards movement keeps pressing for more advanced instruction, students increasingly struggle with material they only half understand. They must memorize the answers that authorities say are correct rather than making their own discoveries and figuring out problems on their own.

Finally, the test itself often produces feelings of chronic fear and dread. To anyone who believes that there should be joy and excitement in learning, test-driven education is a disaster.

DOES THE STANDARDS MOVEMENT PROMOTE CIVIL RIGHTS?

STANDARDS ADVOCATES, INCLUDING President George W. Bush, contend that high standards and rigorous testing promote civil rights. By holding high expectations for all children and testing them regularly on their performances, we can see if we are failing those whom we have so typically failed—poor children and children of color—and do something about it. President Bush's standardized testing program for grades three through eight is titled the "No Child Left Behind" Act.

In theory the standards advocates have a case. But in practice, standardized testing ends up hurting children of color and financially disadvantaged children. In every instance I know of, these children receive disproportionately lower test scores than their white, middle-class counterparts. As a result, they are made to feel inferior, are barred from exciting gifted and talented programs, and are required to spend long hours on tedious test preparation drills and exercises. In Paterson, New Jersey, a city that consists predominantly of low-income minorities, the state government has tried to raise test scores by eliminating electives such as art and music and teaching only the "basics." Such heavy diets of test-driven education destroy students' enthusiasm for learning. Mounting evidence indicates that high-stakes testing is producing higher dropout rates.

Today's "high standards for all" rhetoric and testing requirements provide government leaders with an inexpensive way of acting as if they want to help children of color. These children disproportionately attend the most overcrowded, underfunded schools, and if government officials really want to help them, their first step is to fund these schools on a par with middle-class suburban schools. As Jonathan Kozol so cogently argues, we need to start achieving social equity in terms of class sizes, books and equipment, teacher salaries, and comfortable physical environments. The standards movement not only fails to address these issues, but makes things worse for disadvantaged children by singling them out for the largest amount of tedious test-driven education.

AUTHENTIC ASSESSMENT

ONE OFTEN HEARS the statement that, "OK, standardized testing might cause some problems, but there has to be some evaluation of our schools. What's the alternative?"

Child-centered educators prefer what educators call "authentic assessment." Authentic assessment includes samples of students' work, demonstrations and performances (such as a design of a scientific study or a musical performance), and portfolios. Portfolios are particularly useful because they enable teachers to chart the individual student's progress, in all its richness and detail, over time. This way, teachers can see how much progress a student is making in various subject areas. Portfolio advocates like to say, "The best indicator of the child's work is the child's work."

Portfolios and other kinds of authentic assessment strike many people as being too subjective. Standardized tests, which provide impersonal, quantitative measures of achievement, seem much more scientific.

Actually, portfolios can be assessed in objective and reliable ways. Independent judges can use checklists and reach agreement on the ratings of students' progress. But the process is time-consuming, and on a large scale it becomes extremely expensive. To make authentic assessment more doable, Alfie Kohn and others suggest that public officials could send evaluation teams to examine *samples* of classes and schools. The evaluation teams could then make suggestions to school districts for ways of improving their schools.

Evaluation teams have been used extensively in Great Britain. Since evaluation teams only sample a small percentage of students' work, they have no basis for making high-stakes decisions about all students. These decisions would have to be returned to the schools and teachers, which would mean returning trust to them as professionals.

CHILD-CENTERED VERSUS CONVENTIONAL EDUCATION

AT PRESENT, AUTHENTIC assessment seems most useful for providing qualitative information for the individual school. But people also want to know about the effectiveness of child-centered education in general, compared to conventional education.

Although child-centered education takes many forms (ranging from Montessori education to the Waldorf's arts-oriented schools), the research results are pretty consistent. One result is rather ironic. Since child-centered educators do not believe in aligning education to tests, we might expect that child-centered children would score lower on them. But generally speaking, child-centered classrooms produce about the same standardized-test scores as conventional schools do.

To child-centered educators, the most important variables are children's feelings and attitudes toward learning. Children's feelings are the principal indicators of natural development. If, for example, a school is generally meeting the child's need to develop her inwardly developing powers, the child will feel positive or even enthusiastic about it. And if the child is enthusiastic about learning, she works at it very hard. Such emotions and attitudes are often difficult to measure, and some of the research methodologies are less than rigorous. But generally speaking, children who attend child-centered schools receive higher ratings on independence, creativity, curiosity, and a liking for school.

This overall pattern of results, with respect to both test scores and attitudes, seems to hold across grade levels, from prekindergarten to high school. It also seems to hold across social classes, although the bulk of the research has examined children in the lower socioeconomic classes.

A CHILD-CENTERED CHECKLIST

THE FOLLOWING IS a list of the emotions and attitudes that child-centered educators consider the expressions of natural development. Parents and teachers might want to refer to this list as they assess the learning and development of particular children.

Interests

Child-centered writers believe that when a child's inner growth and development ready her for a new activity, the first sign will be the child's interest in it. As John Dewey said, "I believe that interests are the signs and symptoms of growing power. I believe they represent dawning capacities."

A child's interest in a task or activity is probably the single strongest indicator that a natural growth process is at work. But as Dewey himself observed, this indicator isn't foolproof. We can sometimes arouse a child's interest in a subject by making it entertaining, but the interest doesn't lead anywhere. The child is

stimulated, but the child doesn't work on any new capacity. We
see many examples of this in today's world. Television, videos,
and movies frequently arouse children's interests, but they leave
children in a passive, inactive state.

Concentration

When tasks enable children to develop their natural capacities,
the children not only show an initial interest in the tasks, but
work on them with sustained enthusiasm and energy. Montessori said children enter states of deep concentration. She observed
that until children find tasks on which to concentrate, they seem
restless and out of sorts. Then they rather mysteriously become
attracted to the tasks (as if moved by an inner guide) and work
on them with a concentration so deep that it looks like a kind of
meditation. The child repeats the task over and over, oblivious
to the world around her, and when she finally stops, she emerges
rested and happy, as if awakening from a pleasant sleep. She
seems to look upon the world as full of fresh new possibilities
and is friendly to everyone. Montessori said the child is happy
and serene because she has been able to fulfill an inner need to
develop herself.

Tranquillity

This quality of serenity or tranquillity deserves a special note,
for the child who strikes us as natural seems at ease with herself
in general—not just after periods of intense concentration. The
child seems relaxed and calm.

Montessori believed that the child is calm and at ease because
she has a basic confidence in her capacities and because she
trusts her environment to keep providing her with opportunities
to develop new capacities.

Independence

A child who is natural and at ease is also independent. The child doesn't anxiously look to others for approval or to know what she should feel or do. Instead, she has an implicit faith in herself as a center of judgment. In Carl Rogers's terms, she trusts her own organism—her own senses, intuitions, feelings, and gut-level impressions. She trusts herself.

Exuberance

Some of the qualities listed so far have a serious tone. Heinrich Pestalozzi, Paul Goodman, and others have emphasized that children's natural behavior is frequently joyful and spirited. In their informal sports and games, children run, leap, dodge, and chase with freedom and exuberance. The poet William Blake was impressed by the spirited nature of children's play. In *Nurse's Song,* the children convince their caretaker to let them play a few more minutes before going home to bed. And then:

> The little ones leaped & shouted & laugh'd
> And all the hills echoed.

Grace

As children develop their naturally emerging capacities—rather than struggling to master those imposed upon them—their behavior often becomes quite graceful. Gracefulness is a quality we associate with many aspects of nature, such as a bird in flight or a deer on the run. The child at play—or dancing, singing, or drawing—often strikes us as graceful, too. Behavior is smooth and flowing. It seems to unfold spontaneously and naturally, almost without effort.

I was once struck by this quality during a picnic at the end of our Little League team's season. During the season we, the adult coaches, did a great deal of teaching—instruction that never seemed to translate into the baseball skill or intelligence we expected. During the picnic I asked the youngsters (ages ten to twelve, mostly boys) if they would like to play kickball while we adults rested. They eagerly formed sides and began playing. It was clearly the children's game—not ours; they took positions and began playing before I could utter a word, and as they tried to outwit one another, they invoked all kinds of rules and conditions that we, the adults, had never heard of. I was struck that these children, whose Little League play was often stiff and hesitating, were suddenly free, exuberant, and intelligent. Above all, they were graceful. They ran, faked, threw, and dodged as if part of one fluid dance.

||||||||||||||||||||||||||||||||||||||||||||||||||||||||||||||||||||||||||

CHAPTER 10

Parents' Questions

THIS BOOK'S central thesis is that we should stop focusing so intently on the child's future and start appreciating the child in her present life. The future is, of course, important, and parents must pay attention to it. But it's a question of degree. Today our focus on the future is all-consuming. We need to balance it with a child-centered approach that values the special strengths of the childhood years.

To help children develop these strengths, we need to give them opportunities to pursue their own deepest interests and engage in activities that matter the most to them. We need to keep an eye out for the activities that they work on with great energy and enthusiasm.

We also need to respect children's independence. Instead of directing, instructing, and correcting children, we are more help-ful when we set the stage for learning. For example, we might give children the time and materials they need for artwork, or we might bring them into contact with the natural world, but then step back and let them make their own discoveries.

A child-centered parent acts something like an experienced gardener. An experienced gardener knows that he doesn't actually grow plants. He tries to create good conditions for growth, such as fertile soil and the right amount of water and sunlight, but beyond this there is a limit to what he can do. The plant grows on its own, under the guidance of inner forces. In a similar way, we as parents can create conditions and opportunities for the child's growth, but we must trust the child to do her own growing. We must allow her to make her own discoveries.

This sounds like a hands-off approach and, as such, it raises common parental concerns.

Will my child fall behind?

Parents worry that if they give their child too much time to pursue her own interests and make her own discoveries, their child will fall behind her peers. "Other young children are getting lots of academic instruction these days," parents worry. "I don't want to put my child at a disadvantage."

Before the age of seven or eight years, much of the early academic instruction is so foreign to the child's natural ways of learning that it doesn't sink in anyway. Children memorize material, but they barely understand it, and they come to dislike learning. The driving force behind intellectual development— the child's enthusiasm for learning—is weakened. So, it's not at all clear that early academic instruction puts the young child at any advantage. If, instead, we give young children time and opportunities for play, the arts, and the exploration of nature, we give them a chance to develop the strengths of their own phase of life.

Children need significant free time after the age of seven or eight as well. I have emphasized the need for time to explore nature, but older children also need time to pursue whatever their special interests might be—to build things, draw cartoons, collect baseball cards, think up jokes and rhymes, play informal sports, make up new games, and just relax and daydream. In child-centered schools, children learn academic concepts through meaningful and exciting projects, and these also take time.

So, with older children, too, the child-centered approach poses the risk that children might progress more slowly in academic subjects than children who are consumed by academic lessons. The research on child-centered schools doesn't indicate any significant risk in schools alone, but if we also give our children lots of free time outside school, it is possible that they might not achieve the highest test scores. But consider the trade-off. An adult-directed child may achieve very high scores, but the child feels intense pressure and only half understands much of what she is learning. She doesn't understand it well enough to judge it for herself. Her education is forced from the outside, and she has little chance to pursue her own deepest interests and exercise her creative powers. She doesn't find learning enjoyable—a fact that not only affects her current life but also bodes ill for the future.

In contrast, the child who can pursue her own deepest interests loves to learn. By making her own discoveries, she learns to trust herself. She values her own intuitions, ideas, and judgments. Through the exploration of nature, she develops powers of patient observation and the inner peace that comes from feeling part of life. She feels happy and fulfilled and reaches out to learn new things.

Parents cannot, of course, simply ignore the demands of school, but it is good to take some time to consider the relative importance of academic achievement versus personal happiness and growth.

If children pursue their own interests, will they learn what they need to function in society?

Many people (psychologists as well as parents) worry that children will never learn many skills and subjects, such as reading, geometry, or history, solely from their intrinsic interest in these topics. Aren't such topics unnatural to children? Don't we have to require them for their own good?

If we don't force things, children will spontaneously become more interested in such topics than we might imagine. Consider reading. Young children know that books contain special secrets and fascinating stories. At some point, they try reading on their own and often make considerable progress. To be sure, we need to monitor their progress. But we should initially exercise patience and give their spontaneous interest a chance to grow. We can indirectly encourage reading by reading aloud stories they like, by having interesting books in the home, and by letting them see how much we ourselves enjoy reading. If, instead, we quickly intervene with our instructions and demands, we're likely to make reading an unpleasant experience. We will sour the child's present experience and limit how much the child will want to read in the future, too.

Children also acquire other skills and concepts more spontaneously than we might think. Children intuitively recognize that geometry is useful when they draw pictures, make outlines for hopscotch, or lay out a football field. Many child-centered educators encourage projects that enable children to learn math and other academic concepts through activities children find natural and meaningful. I recommend that parents consider the value of projects-based learning when they select schools or work to improve those their children currently attend.

How can I resist the school's assignments?

Many parents would like to give their children more free time to pursue their own deepest interests, but school assignments crowd out this time. If teachers assign three hours of homework to a first grader, should the parent openly defy the teacher and tell the child to stop after one hour?

This is probably not the best approach, at least initially. But parents can talk to teachers, principals, and other parents. They can raise their concerns at their school board and PTA meetings. In Piscataway, New Jersey, a suburban school system with seven thousand students, parents were part of a movement that resulted in a school board decision to sharply limit homework on weeknights and practically eliminate it on weekends.

Parents who take up this issue will want to refer to research data on the academic benefits of homework. A good book on this matter, which suggests that the benefits are hardly substantial, is *The End of Homework* by Etta Kralovec and John Buell.

What about my child's request for help with her homework?

If we really value independent thinking, we shouldn't help children with their homework in any major way. We can try to provide good conditions for studying—a quiet space for the child—but assistance or feedback detracts from the child's initiative. We might worry that other parents are helping their children and putting their children at a competitive advantage, but the advantage is ephemeral. The other children know that there is something a bit fraudulent about their achievement. The child who works independently feels an inner integrity.

Often schools, in the name of "parent involvement," ask parents to sign sheets verifying that the child brought home the homework assignment and completed it. I believe this practice is improper. As Haim Ginott pointed out, the child soon resists this kind of surveillance. We should let children exercise their own responsibility. If parents agree with me, they should talk to their child's teacher about the matter.

How can I let my child play outdoors when the streets, play-grounds, and parks are unsafe?

In urban areas, this is a widespread concern. In fact, one reason parents sign their children up for structured, adult-directed activities (such as tennis lessons, ballet lessons, soccer leagues, Little League, and gymnastic lessons) is that the children's activity is supervised. Even if the parent is unhappy with all the adult direction, the activity at least gets the child away from TV.

From a child-centered viewpoint, it would be much better if adults could supervise children's play less obtrusively. One model is what the British call "parkies." These are park attendants or playground directors who keep a watchful eye on the children at play, to make sure the children are safe, and to help out if problems arise. But appreciating the value of children's free and independent play, they don't give a lot of instruction.

In a U.S. playground the adult might hand out balls, bats, and bases and perhaps help get a game started, but then step back and let the children work out the rest on their own. The children choose sides, discuss the particular rules for the game, and, in all likelihood, get into some debates as the game progresses. In Piaget's view, such interactions are vital to children's intellectual and moral development. As children debate and resolve differences, they learn to consider others' viewpoints and develop broader understandings of what is fair and just. Piaget thought children must engage in these discussions and debates among themselves. When adults tell them what to do, they don't develop their minds; they just obey authority.

I strongly recommend that parents lobby their municipal leaders to provide helpful and unobtrusive "parkies" in their neighborhoods. In New York City, one grassroots group is pressing for money for such staff in the annual city budget.

If I make time for play, won't my child just watch TV?

Television has indeed become a powerful attraction. Marie Winn has compared it to a drug from which one needs to withdraw. This isn't easy. Sometimes children hardly venture outdoors, so we need to actively introduce children to the rewards of outdoor activities. For example, to introduce children to nature exploration, we might take them to places that stir their imaginations, such as taking them to the beach, lake, or woods at night. We might take them for hikes that give them a chance to experience a sense of physical accomplishment. Often, if they can spend some time in a relatively wild, remote area, they will experience the profound quiet and inner peace that nature bestows. We can also sign children up for nature studies programs that unobtrusively help children discover the excitement in nature's small details. In such ways, we introduce children to experiences that are much more profound than watching TV.

Child-centered adults follow children's spontaneous interests. Isn't TV a spontaneous interest?

I addressed this issue indirectly in the last chapter but need to say more specifically about it. Spontaneous interests are very important in child-centered theory, but one also has to look at other aspects of the child's experience. As Montessori pointed out, children not only become interested and even engrossed in activities that help them develop their naturally emerging powers; after they complete the activities, they emerge happy and rested. They seem content and at peace because they were able to develop something within themselves. So we look for tranquillity and inner peace as signs that we are providing an environment that enables the child to develop naturally. Television watching produces nothing of the kind. After watching TV children are typically restless and distracted.

Some psychologists have also questioned whether the child's interest in TV is completely spontaneous. Television corporations use sudden shifts in sounds and images that elicit involuntary startle responses. Such techniques artificially capture and recapture the child's attention.

In any event, whenever we consider the value of new technologies for children, we need to consider not only the extent to which they attract children's interest, but the behavior and emotions of the child after using the technology. Ultimately, the child who is benefiting will show some of the characteristics, such as tranquillity, gracefulness, and independence, discussed at the end of the previous chapter.

If I let my child grow slowly, pursuing her own interests, is there any hope for admission to Harvard?

Actually, the most selective colleges are looking for young people who are interesting, which usually means young people who have strong interests. These colleges value applicants who have written a play, choreographed a dance, painted exciting pictures, conducted interesting science experiments, composed songs and poems, shown courage and leadership in athletics, or have taken up a cause for social justice. Child-centered parenting, which nurtures children's own passions and interests, produces this kind of high-school senior. The applicant will not be one who has taken up an extracurricular activity in an unmotivated way, just for the sake of the college application. Instead, the applicant is likely to be a person who has followed her own inner passions from the start.

The best colleges also are interested in young people who think for themselves, and here too the child-centered approach is most appropriate.

Of course, the child-centered approach doesn't aim for Ivy League college admission. It doesn't aim for any future role. Rather, it tries to nurture the child's fullest potentials at each stage. But in the process, it actually establishes the firmest foundation for future growth. It tends to produce creative young people who throw themselves into activities and like to think for themselves—the kinds of people who make a difference in the world.

At the same time, it is entirely possible that such a young person will choose not to spend enormous amounts of time preparing for the SAT or striving for high grades. Thus, the young person might not be a prime candidate for the most selective colleges. Young people will make their own decisions about what kinds of sacrifices and future goals they want to pursue.

I realize it's unsettling to parents to leave the child's future open. But we make a mistake if we overplan for it. Today's parents and educators frequently act like a housebuilder who is so concerned with the final product's appearance that he gives all his attention to the exterior design and neglects to build a strong foundation. As parents, we need to pay closest attention to the qualities that children are naturally motivated to develop at their current phase. As Maria Montessori once said, "We serve the future by protecting the present." Our job is to help the child develop into a strong, happy, independent person each step of the way. Then, as the child moves toward the adult years, we have to turn the future over to the child. Having done our best while the child was in our care, working in alliance with nature's plan for healthy growth, we have to have faith in the child to negotiate life as an adult.

I want children to learn independently, but what should I do when they are emotionally upset and seek my help?

In these cases I recommend the child-centered approach called active listening. It is adapted from Carl Rogers's client-centered therapy, which tries to create conditions in which clients will take the lead in exploring their feelings and come up with their own insights.

During active listening, the parent doesn't offer advice or make moral judgments. Instead, the parent does two things. First, she maintains an attitude of unconditional positive regard, prizing the child as a person. This is usually communicated non-verbally by the way the parent listens and accepts the child's statements. If the parent thinks to herself, "I prize my child as worthwhile for just being who she is," and if the parent listens without judging, this attitude of unconditional positive regard will come through.

Second, the parent reflects or mirror's the child's feelings. The parent tries to restate what the child says, focusing on the feeling edge of the child's statements. If the child says, "That boy's a jerk," the parent might say, "You're feeling angry."

These two behaviors—unconditional positive regard and the reflection of feelings—in themselves help the child. Children (indeed, all people) feel better when they are valued and understood. These two behaviors also create an atmosphere in which the child is free to explore her feelings and think in new ways. Children might not begin thinking in new ways all at once, but sometimes they do.

Here is an example provided by Thomas Gordon. A child comes home upset and tells his mother, "Tommy won't play with me today. He won't ever do what I want to do." The temptation for the mother is to give advice, such as, "Why don't you play with someone else?" or "Why don't you take turns?" Or the parent might be tempted to ask for more information. Gordon says it is better for the parent to stick to active listening, reflecting back the child's feelings, in a dialogue such as this.

CHILD: Tommy won't play with me today. He won't ever do what I want to.

MOTHER: You're kinda angry with Tommy.

CHILD: I sure am. I never want to play with him again.

MOTHER: You're so angry you feel like never seeing him again.

CHILD: That's right. But if I don't have him for a friend, I won't have anyone else to play with.

MOTHER: You would hate to be left with no one.

CHILD: Yeah. I guess I have to get along with him some way. But it's so hard for me to stop getting mad at him.

MOTHER: You want to get along better but it's hard for you to keep from getting mad at Tommy.

CHILD: I never used to—but that's when he was always willing to do what I wanted to do. He won't let me boss him anymore. . . .

MOTHER: Tommy's not so easy to influence now.

CHILD: He sure isn't. He's not such a baby now. He's more fun though. . . .

The mother's contribution to this dialogue may seem less than profound, but she maintains an accepting attitude and reflects his feelings in a way that makes him feel understood. She resists the temptation to solve her child's problem for him; instead, she gives him the freedom to move toward his own insights and solutions. Parents who are interested in such methods might start with two classic books, Thomas Gordon's *Parent Effectiveness Training* and Haim Ginott's *Between Parent and Child.*

What about the goal that is popular today—promoting a life-long love of learning?

This goal is appealing because it creates a bridge between the child's future and the child's present life. We cannot produce an adult who loves to learn without nurturing this attitude in the child's current life. If we pursued this goal, life would be happier for children.

But there is a pitfall. Once our thoughts turn to the future, it's easy to focus on the kind of learning we, as adults, value. For example, we might start thinking about their academic achievement in reading, math, or science and then, secondarily, how we can instill positive feelings about these topics. I suggest instead that we initially suspend our ideas about what children need to know and give them opportunities to pursue the activities they themselves find rewarding. If we can put more trust in their inner impulses to grow and learn in their own ways, we will see that the future often takes care of itself.

Since people talk about the future of the planet, isn't the future more important than suggested?

My primary concern in this book has been with our excessive focus on the child's future success as an individual. From my talks with parents, I am convinced that many are living with a constant nightmare that, as one told me, "My child will wind up a fruit delivery man." I have tried to argue that we need to soften this concern. My hope is that we might ease up on the competitive academic pressures we are placing on children and, by appreciating their special qualities as children, give them a chance to develop more fully.

But there is another, broader concern with the future: the well-being of our planet's ecosystems. I consider this to be a critical matter. Ironically, if we would give children greater opportunities to develop one of their special strengths—their affinity to nature—we would be in much better shape. If, instead, we just continue on our current course, living in increasingly artificial, technological environments, it is doubtful that many of us will feel close enough to nature to act decisively to protect it. As the poet Gary Lawless worries,

> When the animals come to us,
> asking for our help,
> will we know what they are saying?

The evidence indicates that we are most capable of developing a sensitivity to nature as children. Children impersonate animals and dream about animals. They communicate with animals, as well as plants and other aspects of nature, in their poems. Children want to learn about nature and develop their kinship to it. We need to put children in contact with nature so they can do so.

What about questions not addressed in this chapter?

As a parent, you will have many other specific questions about your child's development—more questions than I can address here. It will help to keep the general child-centered philosophy in mind. That is, consider more than your child's external accomplishments, such as admission to a prestigious preschool or to your public school's gifted and talented program. More fundamental are your child's feelings about learning—feelings such as curiosity, enthusiasm, concentration, independence, and overall peacefulness. These emotions are important in their own right, and they also indicate that the child is actualizing his or her naturally emerging powers. As parents we often have doubts, but if we are helping children develop in accordance with nature's ground plan for healthy development, we can trust that we are doing things right.

APPENDIXES

|||||||||||||||||||||||||||||||||||||||||||||||||||||||||||||||||||||||||||||||||||||

Portraits

of

Natural

Children

Appendix A

||||||||||||||||||||||||||||||||||||||||||||||||||||||||||||||||||||||||||||||||||||||||||

A Child of Nature:
Huckleberry Finn

*I won't be rich, and I won't live in them cussed smothery houses. I like
the woods, and the river . . . and I'll stick to 'em too.*

— HUCK FINN

MARK TWAIN'S *The Adventures of Huckleberry Finn* is perhaps
the best-known novel in American literature. Its merits and
faults have been widely discussed. But it deserves another look
for what it can teach us about the child's feeling for nature.

Huck lives on the fringes of society. A motherless boy, whose
father is incapable of guiding him, he fends for himself. As
Twain introduces him in *The Adventures of Tom Sawyer:*

> Huckleberry came and went, at his own free will. He slept
> on doorsteps in fine weather and in empty hogsheads [barrels]
> in wet; he did not have to go to school or church, or call any
> being master or obey anybody; he could go fishing or swim-
> ming when and where he chose. . . . He was always the first
> boy that went barefoot in the spring and the last to resume
> leather in the fall; he never had to wash, nor put on clean
> clothes; he could swear wonderfully. In a word, everything
> that goes to make life precious, that boy had. So thought
> every harassed, hampered, respectable boy in St. Petersburg.

Huck is between twelve and fourteen years old. Some scholars believe that Twain made Huck this age so Huck would be old enough to move about freely in the adult world, while his relatively uneducated status would permit him to see the world with the innocence and openness of a somewhat younger child.

Huck, to be sure, isn't completely isolated from society. He plays with the other boys and has assimilated the language and folklore of his rural subculture. He has even internalized the conventional conscience of the pro-slavery South. In *The Adventures of Huckleberry Finn* he is tormented by guilt because he is helping Jim escape slavery and he almost turns Jim in. But in the end, Huck follows his heart, rather than society's teachings, and he helps Jim. Huck is an eager, free, and open boy who is entirely without pretense. As he narrates his story, we feel we are listening to a real child who tells us just what he sees and thinks—not what anyone might expect of him. He is a natural child.

Huckleberry Finn opens with Huck in the process of being "sivilized" by the Widow Douglas. One night, when life in the widow's house is becoming more than he can stand, he gives us this beautiful and haunting picture of the night.

> I felt so lonesome I most wished I was dead. The stars were shining, and the leaves rustled in the woods ever so mournful; and I heard an owl, away off, who-whooing about somebody that was dead, and a whippowill and a dog crying about somebody that was going to die; and the wind was trying to whisper something to me, and I couldn't make out what it was, and so it made the cold shivers run over me. Then away out in the woods I heard that kind of a sound that a ghost makes when it wants to tell about something that's on its mind and can't make itself understood. . . .

Huck's description is superstitious, and, more notably, it is animistic. When, for example, Huck says that leaves rustled "ever so mournful" and the wind "was trying to whisper something to me," he attributes emotions and intentions to the leaves and wind. Most of us, living in a modern, scientific society, view animism as irrational and childish. Indeed, the esteemed developmental psychologist Jean Piaget considered animism to be one of the common defects of children's thinking. Animism, he said, reflects children's inability to distinguish their own subjective states from the rest of the world.

But the matter isn't so simple. Some psychologists, especially those in the Gestalt tradition, have pointed out that animistic sensibilities are valued by artists. Poets and painters don't try to separate themselves from the rest of the world. Instead, they try to feel an underlying unity between themselves and the world so they can sense the expressive qualities of things. They want to feel the joy of a songbird's melody, the sadness of the weeping willow, and the mournful sound of the wind rustling in the trees.

From a poetic standpoint, then, Huck's assumption that he is in personal communication with nature is valuable. When Huck says that "the wind was trying to whisper something to me, and I couldn't make out what it was," we might consider his attitude irrational and childish, but it's an attitude that many adult poets have longed to recapture. In a 1942 poem, Hermann Hesse said,

> Sometimes, when a bird cries out,
> Or the wind sweeps through a tree,
> Or a dog howls in a far-off farm,
>
> My world turns and goes back to the place
> Where, a thousand forgotten years ago,
> The bird and the blowing wind
> Were like me, and were my brothers. . . .

Huck's sensitivity to nature emerges throughout the novel. After his alcoholic and abusive father returns, Huck flees in a canoe to Jackson Island, slipping onto shore just before dawn. He tells us that he took a nap before breakfast and what he saw when he woke up:

> The sun was up so high when I waked that I judged it was after eight o'clock. I laid there in the grass and the cool shade thinking about things, and feeling rested and ruther comfortable and satisfied. I could see the sun out at one or two holes, but mostly it was big trees all about, and gloomy in there amongst them. There was freckled places on the ground where the light shifted down through the leaves, and the freckled places swapped about a little, showing there was a little breeze up there. A couple of squirrels set on a limb and jabbered at me very friendly.

In passages such as this, we get the sense of how comfortable Huck feels in natural settings, and how carefully he reads the signs of nature. He judges the hour by the height of the sun, and he infers the presence of a slight breeze above him by the sunlight's movement on the ground. Underlying Huck's observations is his affection for nature, which is evident when he reports that two squirrels sat on a limb and "jabbered at me very friendly." This was probably a misreading of the squirrels' noises, but it indicates how readily Huck assumes a friendly relationship with nature.

Huck's feeling for nature deepens once he meets Jim on the island and the two fix up an old raft and begin floating down the Mississippi River, headed for Cairo, Illinois. They travel by night (hiding during the daylight), and by the second night they find themselves getting in tune with the river's rhythm. "It was kind of solemn, drifting down the big, still river, laying on our backs looking up at the stars, and we didn't ever feel like talking loud, and it warn't often we laughed—only a little kind of low chuckle." As the novel progresses, Huck repeatedly talks about how the river's stillness affects their mood, producing a quiet in them, too. Even when ashore, Huck says Jim and he spent hours "lazying around, listening to the stillness."

I noted this effect of nature's stillness in the previous chapter. People often feel it when they spend time in woods or natural settings alone. Several years ago I inspected a small tract of woods in the suburb of Teaneck, New Jersey, trying to decide whether it would be valuable for children to explore and whether I could organize a campaign to preserve it. The woods were littered and surrounded by traffic. But as I was about to leave, I lingered a moment, perceived a complete stillness at the top of the trees, and was surprised to feel the stillness also in my chest. To some poets and writers, such effects have a spiritual dimension. Nature's peace becomes ours.

In any event, with his love for the river deepening, Huck is moved to give us a detailed description of sunrise on the water. He says that Jim and he typically tied up the raft before dawn, took a swim to cool off, and then sat on the sandy bottom in knee-deep water to watch the daylight come.

Not a sound anywheres—perfectly still—just like the whole world was asleep, only sometimes the bullfrogs a-cluttering, maybe. The first thing to see, looking away over the water, was a kind of dull line—that was the woods on t'other side; you couldn't make nothing else out; then a pale place in the sky; then more paleness spreading around, then the river softened up away off, and warn't black any more, but gray . . . and by and by you could see a streak on the water which you know by the look of the streak that there's a snag there . . . and you see the mist curl up off the water and the east redden up . . . then the nice breeze springs up, and comes fanning you from over there, so cool and fresh and sweet to smell on account of the woods and the flowers; but sometimes not that way, because they've left dead fish lying around, gars and such, and they do get pretty rank; and next you've got the full day, and everything smiling in the sun, and the songbirds just going it!

Here again, Huck's description includes a bit of animism, which comes at the very end. When the full morning breaks out, "[Y]ou've got the full day, and everything smiling in the sun." The metaphor is so apt that it almost goes unnoticed. When Huck adds, "[A]nd the songbirds just going it!" we share Huck's delight in the energy and radiance of the morning.

We are indebted to the literary historian Leo Marx for calling attention to the fresh, immediate, and poetic quality of Huck's descriptions. "All his senses are alive," Marx says, and "a highlight is thrown upon the minute particulars."

Marx speculates that Huck's account is fresh and vivid because Huck is part of the scene and tells us exactly what he sees. He doesn't idealize or embellish. He even describes the smelly fish. Marx also speculates that the portrait of the dawn feels authentic because it is written in the vernacular. It is told by a boy who "'belongs' to the landscape in the sense that his language is native to it."

I would add that Huck also belongs to the landscape in the sense that he feels an emotional identity with it and is, at just the right moments, given to animism. That is, he animistically sees nature as sharing the same energy and expressive forces that we feel. Just as we often feel fresh and vibrant at daybreak, when we are first warmed by the sun's life-sustaining rays, so do birds, plants, and other life-forms. They, too, are energized and radiant. And there is no better way of describing what happens than to say that everything is "smiling in the sun."

Of course nature isn't always pleasant and serene. But Huck even takes delight in violent storms.

One night a great storm arises while the two con men, the king and the duke, are aboard the raft. They quickly maneuver to get the beds inside the raft's wigwam (which Jim and Huck had built). Huck and Jim are left to keep watch. But Huck says,

> I wouldn't 'a' turned in anyway if I'd had a bed, because a body don't see such a storm as that every day in the week, not by a long sight. My souls, how the wind did scream along! And every second or two there'd come a glare that lit up the white-caps for half a mile around, and you'd see the islands looking dusty through the rain, and the trees thrashing around in the wind; then comes a *h-whack*—bum! bum! bumble-umble-umbum-bum-bum-bum—and the thunder would go rumbling and grumbling away, and quit—and then *rip* comes another flash. . . .

Huck's enthusiasm leaps off the page. His account does not, in this case, rely primarily upon animistic metaphors (although the wind does "scream along"). Instead, he uses another means of identifying with nature, onomatopoeia; he reproduces the storm's sounds (such as *"h-whack"*). Huck goes on to tell us that the waves actually washed up on him, but he didn't mind. He was completely immersed in the experience. In contrast, the king and the duke, whose only interests are self-interests, insulated themselves from the storm and missed the whole scene.

During the storm Huck mentions that he didn't have to worry about unseen snags in the river because the lightning kept lighting up the sky and exposing them. But the biggest danger isn't the snags. It's one of the great inventions of the Industrial Revolution—the steamboat.

As Leo Marx points out, Mark Twain was very ambivalent

about industrial technology. Twain had himself been a steamboat pilot, even taking his pen name from the steamboat term for two fathoms. But the steamboat keeps intruding on the stillness of the river.

Sometimes Huck uses animistic metaphors to describe the steamboat, but the metaphors are often those of a body that is sick or out of sorts. Huck and Jim see "a steamboat *coughing* along upstream" and see them "*belch* a whole bunch of sparks" from their chimneys [italics mine].

About a third into the novel, a steamboat comes up too fast on the raft.

> She was a big one, and she was coming in a hurry, too, looking like a black cloud with rows of glowworms around it; but all of a sudden she bulged out, big and scary, with a long row of wide-open furnace doors shining like red-hot teeth, and her monstrous bows and guards hanging right over us. There was a yell at us, and a jingling of bells to stop the engine, a pow-wow of cussing, and whistling of steam—and as Jim went overboard on one side and I on the other she come smashing straight through the raft.

Huck has difficulty describing the big, scary steamboat. He attempts to draw upon metaphors from nature, saying it came "looking like a black cloud with rows of glowworms around it" and had "furnace doors shining like red-hot teeth," but the images are unreal. Huck seems to recognize that his nature images aren't just right. He says the steamboat was looking "*like* a black cloud" and shining "*like* red-hot teeth" [italics mine]. In his portraits of nature, Huck simply tells us what he sees and doesn't use the term *like*. But the steamboat is artificial, and Huck must struggle to describe it. He is no longer in his element.

After he wrote that the steamboat crashed into the raft, Twain stopped working on the novel for three years. The basic difficulty, Leo Marx suggests, is that Twain sensed that the pursuit of a joyful and spontaneous life on the river couldn't coexist with the coming industrial technology. Twain sensed that the change was going to destroy the pastoral life.

Twain did continue the book, of course, and he added many loving descriptions of the river environment. But if he did have a premonition about technological development, it was right. As our technology has advanced, we have transformed nature in ways that few nineteenth-century thinkers would have imagined possible. We have dammed rivers, cut down forests, bulldozed mountains, and crisscrossed the land with paved roads. We have built almost entirely artificial environments of concrete, steel, and plastic. Wherever we live, we increasingly get our information from the electronic media. We have almost completely cut ourselves off from the natural world.

We might imagine that people still have considerable contact with wild areas when they travel outside their urban or suburban neighborhoods. But this is hardly the case. By 1968, Edward Abbey had described how even our wilderness state parks were becoming the products of industrial tourism, "complete with police, administrators, paved highways, automobile nature trails, official scenic viewpoints, designated campgrounds, Laundromats, cafeterias, Coke machines, flush toilets, and admission fees." And as the research of Gary Nabhan and Sara St. Antoine in the Sonoran Desert suggests, other remote areas are succumbing to modern trends. In the Sonoran Desert region, the children no longer spend much time learning about nature by exploring their surroundings. Instead, they learn about wildlife indoors—watching television, films, and videos.

Our modern society seems determined to insulate itself from nature. Like the king and the duke in *Huckleberry Finn,* we seek comfort in artificial environments. We close ourselves off in temperature-controlled homes, office buildings, and automobiles, and we look upon nature's storms, winds, and snows as disruptions to our daily routines.

As I indicated in chapter 3, our estrangement from nature is probably making it difficult for our children to grow well. Nature stimulates children's creativity and their senses and powers of observation, and we must wonder what happens to children who are isolated from the natural world.

Nature also seems to give children a sense of calm and belonging in the world, a theme that *Huckleberry Finn* illustrates well. Huck gives us a sense of how a child might feel an emotional continuity with nature. He listens to the moods and messages of the wind; he senses the friendliness of squirrels; he feels the joy of the birds and the plants at daybreak on the river. The river's stillness, moreover, creates stillness in him. Even storms are welcome and exciting events for Huck, and he immerses himself in them. Children who have no such feelings for nature—who feel completely apart from nature—must be very empty and alone inside.

Today, of course, adults cannot be expected to let children grow up like Huck Finn. We cannot let children skip school in order to spend time by a river or in the fields, hills, or vacant lots.

Still, Huck is such a wonderfully drawn character that he can provide us with a useful image as we consider many current issues. Thinking that we do want a little bit of Huck Finn in children, we might fight harder against real-estate developments that will destroy the natural areas in our region. We might think twice about the wisdom of longer school years and school days if the result will be less time for summer camps and leisurely nature experiences. We might take a firmer stand against so much TV watching and take kids to parks instead. We might ask school boards to scale back their enormous investments in the latest technology and put some funds into nature studies and outdoor experiences.

Appendix B

||||||||||||||||||||||||||||||||||||||||||||||||||||||||||||||||||||||||||||||||||||

Children Facing School:
Sally Brown and Peppermint Patty

Learning is not worth a penny if courage
and joy are lost along the way.

— PESTALOZZI

TODAY'S POLITICAL, corporate, and educational leaders keep
calling for higher academic standards and student achievement.
Our schools, they say, must demand more from children if they are
going to be ready for the competitive global economy. And almost
everyone agrees. The call for tougher standards receives wide support in public opinion polls, and local school boards and parent
groups are deeply concerned about their students' test scores.

In this climate, too little is said about children's feelings about
school. Historically, children seem to have never liked school
very much. It has always taken its toll on the natural curiosity
and enthusiasm for learning with which children begin life. But
today, as the standards movement rolls on, the pressures on children are becoming quite oppressive.

Because a concern for children's feelings toward school is so
rarely heard these days, I am grateful when anyone does raise it.
And I find it particularly meaningful that one of our most popular humorists, Charles Schulz, devoted many of his *Peanuts*
comic strips to children's natural reactions to school.

In a sense, it might seem that Schulz didn't depict natural children. For part of the comic strip's humor comes from the way young children raise philosophical questions that are beyond their years. The children, who range in age from infancy to about eight years, question each other on "the purpose of life" and what they think "is the biggest problem we have in the world today." Sally Brown, after dropping an ice-cream cone that took her a long time to select, compares life to a "Shakespearean tragedy."

Nevertheless, the *Peanuts* characters illustrate many of the distinctive features of childhood. For one thing, the cartoons are filled with animism; the children attribute emotions and consciousness to almost everything in their surroundings. They talk to trees, falling leaves, balloons, beachballs, and the school building, and most of these objects react as if they understand what the children are saying. Snoopy, a dog, thinks and acts like a human being. Schulz's children, like children in general, don't make the same distinctions adults do; they don't separate the human from the nonhuman, the animate from the inanimate. For children, everything is full of life and feeling.

Peanuts's best-known insight into childhood is Linus's need for his security blanket. In psychoanalytic theory, the blanket is known as a "transitional object"—Donald Winnicott's term for the blankets, teddy bears, and other objects toward which many infants develop a special attachment. Winnicott called such objects "transitional" because they help the child make the transition from being merged with the mother to becoming independent from her. Winnicott began writing about transitional objects in the early 1950s, gradually convincing mental-health workers that these objects can be a part of normal child-development. Schulz introduced Linus and his blanket at the same time, making a much larger audience more tolerant of children's need for transitional objects.

Schulz said that he took deep pride in the Linus cartoons, which struck an early blow for "kids' rights." His cartoons about children's difficulties in school are just as important.

SALLY BROWN

THE CHILD WHOM we most fully see starting school is Charlie Brown's sister, Sally. When Sally learns that she must go to kindergarten, she is shocked and tries to get out of it. In one cartoon she hands Charlie Brown a pencil and a sheet of paper and asks him to write, "To Whom It May Concern: Please excuse Sally Brown from kindergarten . . . She is needed at home." But he tells her he cannot write that, and she becomes a nervous wreck.

Actually, Sally finds the first day of kindergarten enjoyable ("and we sang songs, and we painted pictures . . . and listened to stories. . . ."), and she likes school so long as she can approach tasks in terms of the natural tendencies of the young child. In particular, she enjoys the tasks that she can construe as drawing. When practicing the letter *i* (writing *iiiii*), she tells her brother that she is actually drawing ocean waves with a tiny sea gull flying over each wave. As she works on her written assignments, she perceives the simplest marks and lines as living things. In one cartoon she tells her brother, "These are dittos chasing dottos," and in another she tries to show him "some sixes that like to pretend they're noses."

In these cartoons Sally illustrates the imaginative, artistic perception of lines and numerals that impressed some of the great developmental psychologists, including Heinz Werner. These cartoons demonstrate Schulz's insight into the young child's spontaneously artistic bent. But Sally soon discovers that she cannot turn every school assignment into an artistic production.

In one cartoon she energetically draws flowers and pretty shapes around a sentence, explaining to Charlie Brown that she is supposed to "decorate a sentence." When he tells her that her assignment was to *diagram* a sentence, she sighs.

Moreover, school subjects become abstract and beyond her understanding. Math, in particular, gives her fits, and she resorts to guessing. When Charlie Brown, helping her with her times tables, asks her, "What is two times seven?" Sally ventures, "One million?" When he asks, "How much is three times zero?" she guesses, "Four thousand? Six? Eleventy twelve? Fifty-quillion? Overly eight? Twiddley-two?"

So the strains of school get to her. At the end of her first summer vacation, Charlie Brown informs her that school starts Monday. Sally says, "Not for me. I went last year." At the end of another summer, when she learns that school begins in three weeks, she shouts, "Panic in the Streets!"

A major part of Sally's difficulty is that school, as John Dewey emphasized, is scholastic in the worst sense. It requires the child to learn material that has no relationship to the child's active life. Sally clearly has no interest in when Charles Dickens was born or in the height of Mount Whitney. She stands in front of the class to read her report on John Deere, who "in 1837 invented the self-polishing steel plow," but confesses to the teacher, "No, Ma'am, I've never seen a plow. I've never even seen a farmer."

In Sally's experience, school consists only of information that one must memorize or face the consequences. One morning she is awakened by her brother and exclaims, "I can't go to school! I'm not ready!! I don't know where Italy is! I can't spell 'cavalry'! Who was the father of Richard the Fiftieth? Is my boiled egg ready? . . . I need answers!" Charlie Brown tries to reassure her that she doesn't have to know the answers because "That's why you go to school . . . School is for learning." But Sally says, "HA!" And when Sally has to write a report on

PEANUTS reprinted by permission of United Feature Syndicate, Inc.

"What I learned in school this year," she doesn't refer to book learning but to real life. "This year I learned to keep my eye on my lunch so it doesn't get ripped off."

Despite all her frustrations, Sally keeps displaying exuberance, humor, and imagination. In numerous comic strips she lightens the school routine by making up a joke, at which she laughs uproariously. After each, the teacher says something that causes Sally to reply soberly, "Yes, Ma'am," and get back to business. But we aren't surprised when she tries another joke in another comic strip.

For example, in one class Sally raises her hand and says, "Ma'am, I have a suggestion for a class project. Why don't we all get together and raise a ruckus? They're easy to raise . . . All you have to do is shout, and they grow! HA HA HA HA HA! Yes, Ma'am . . ."

Sally Brown illustrates the conflict between the creative impulses of childhood and the demands of school. In this battle Sally is holding her own. She keeps cracking jokes and coming up with new ideas. And this is what is so appealing about her. We don't appreciate Sally because of her success in school— because of any gold stars, good marks, or high achievement test scores. We appreciate her because she illustrates the unvanquished spirit of childhood struggling against an oppressive system.

We might wonder, though, how long Sally will be able to keep up this fight. Will she be as full of life and wit after another year or two of school? Schulz wasn't likely to tell us the answer;

he seemed set on keeping Sally at about the same age. But his comic strip also features a slightly older child who is struggling with school—Peppermint Patty.

PEPPERMINT PATTY

PEPPERMINT PATTY, who in one cartoon says she is seven years old, is a tomboy who loves sports and games, excels at baseball, and likes to use the colorful language of the blue-collar worker. If, when she joined Peanuts in the late 1960s, the characters were a bit too sophisticated and precious, she brought them back to earth by picking up the phone one day and introducing herself to Charlie Brown with the words "Hi, Chuck!"

Peppermint Patty isn't a simple character. She retains a considerable amount of childhood naïveté. She's the only *Peanuts* character, for example, to believe that Snoopy is actually a kid, albeit a funny-looking one. She also is open with emotions and doesn't hesitate, for instance, to express her thrill at the beauty of a lake. But she's also a forceful presence in the world of children—especially on the playground and the sandlot and in summer camp. If a boy is so foolish as to tease her or one of her friends, she issues threats such as "Tell him to shut up [or] I'll shorten his life span." And if pushed too hard, she can knock a boy off his feet with a single blow.

Patty is a throwback to an earlier era, before television and video games, when children seemed more active in their free time. In this respect, she differs from Sally Brown, who has fallen under the spell of TV. In one cartoon series, Patty stays a few days at Charlie Brown's house, and after the first dinner, Patty is surprised that he and Sally spend their evenings watching TV. "You mean you don't talk? How about playing some checkers or something? Or making fudge? Or catching fire-

PEANUTS reprinted by permission of United Feature Syndicate, Inc.

flies? . . . How about paints, Chuck? Maybe we could do some watercolors?" But Charlie and Sally Brown simply sit down in front of the TV set, and Patty just sighs.

But Patty cannot muster the same energy inside the classroom. She finds school so difficult and boring that she often just sleeps at her desk, and she received nothing but D minuses. When the teacher calls on her, she often guesses wildly or tries to fake the answer, saying, for example, that the answer is "so obvious" she wouldn't want to take advantage of the teacher by giving it. In other episodes, she tries holding a piece of crystal over her test paper to make the answers come out right, tries putting ribbons in her hair to win the teacher's favor, and signs her name "Betty" "to protect the innocent."

None of these tactics works, of course, and she keeps receiving D minuses.

On a rare occasion, the school departs from its usual routine and provides an experience that arouses Patty's enthusiasm. One day the school takes her class to a young people's classical-music concert, and Patty is surprised to find herself deeply moved by the music. But afterward the class is assigned a five-hundred-word essay on the concert, and she concludes that she should have expected as much. After all, she tells Charlie Brown, "I guess that's what education is for, huh, Chuck? To keep us from enjoying ourselves."

Peppermint Patty, then, illustrates the extent to which many children can only be spontaneous and happy outside the classroom.

Children themselves often seem to recognize that many of the qualities they value—qualities such as athletic skill, humor, compassion, bravery, and leadership—mainly flourish outside the formal academic setting. This is why the peers they most admire aren't those who receive the highest grades. In *Peanuts,* Marcie, though herself a straight-A student, calls Peppermint Patty "Sir."

Nevertheless, the adult society puts a tremendous value on academic achievement, and Peppermint Patty's poor performance in school begins to undermine her self-worth. As she tells her friend Marcie, "I'm getting dumber every day, and it's all just too embarrassing."

In two remarkable series of cartoons, Schulz forsakes much of his characteristic light humor and lets us know just how painful Patty's feelings are.

The first series begins when Patty is sent to the principal's office. She doesn't know why, but she senses she's in for another humiliation. As she opens the door, she says, "I think they purposely put the door knob up high to make you feel inferior." The reason for the visit, she learns, is that she has violated the school dress code by wearing sandals. But the sandals are precious to her because Patty, who doesn't have a mother, was given them by her father with the words, "You certainly may have them because you are a rare gem." Feeling a deepening sense of inferiority in school, Patty can ill afford to let go of the sandals. Ordinarily she would be expected to fight the dress code, but this time she just breaks down and cries.

In a second series Patty tells Marcie, "I can't take it anymore," and drops out of school. She plans to spend her days with Snoopy, atop his doghouse (which she believes is Charlie Brown's guest cottage). Sensing something dangerous about Patty's move, Marcie herself stays out of school, trying to persuade her friend to return. Finally, Marcie pulls Patty down from the dog house, dismantling the structure in the process and yelling, "It's not a guest cottage, Sir, it's a dog house! And Snoopy is not a funny-looking kid with a big nose!! He's a beagle! **When are you going to face up to reality?!**"

Peppermint Patty is undoubtedly fortunate to have a friend who cares deeply about her and who prevents her from dropping out of school. But there is no reason why Patty had to be driven to this point. There is no reason why a child must spend several hours a day struggling with tasks she finds overly difficult and meaningless and to come to feel inferior as a person because she performs poorly on them. Yet this is the situation countless children face.

Schools, to be sure, must teach certain material. They must provide students with the knowledge and skills they will need as adults. But schools also should respect the child's spontaneous interests and natural ways of learning. They should respect the child's enthusiasm for physical activities, creative projects, the arts, and play, and they should give children opportunities to learn through these activities. It has been the goal of child-centered schools to tailor education to children's natural tendencies, and we should encourage more schools to do so.

Notes

PREFACE

PAGE

xi Parents' observation that their children were eager to learn prior to school: see Kamii and DeVries 1980, 14.

xii Examples of contemporary testing critics who seek broad goals for the future: Miner 1999–2000; Shorofsky 2000. Among the rare writers today who emphasize the child's present life: Egan 1997; Kozol 2000, 138–42.

xii Child-centered writers who questioned preparation for the future: Rousseau 1762/1974; Dewey 1916/1966, 54–56; Montessori 1949/1967; Ames 1971; Elkind 1981, 199.

INTRODUCTION: OUR OBSESSION WITH THE CHILD'S FUTURE

1 The two-mothers anecdote is in Berger 1986, 49.

1 *A Nation at Risk*: National Commission on Excellence in Education, 1983.

2 The standards movement has not made life pleasant for children: Kohn 1999, 86–92; Bastian 2000.

2 "At risk": Swadener and Lubek (1995) attack the concept of *at risk* for perpetuating negative stereotypes but their substitute concept, *at promise,* also implies the value of childhood is to be found in future achievements.

2 "As the U.S. population ages": Sherman 1994, 91.

3 Competition for New York City preschools: R. Gardner 1999.

3 Elkind 1989, 34.

3 Early brain stimulation and SAT scores: Bruer 1999, 17.

4 Pediatricians say kids are stressed out: Wallace 2000.

4 Strain of fourth-grade tests drives off teachers: Goodnough 2001.

4 Rousseau 1762/1974.

4 Young children's artistic bent: H. Gardner 1973, 1980.

5 The child between three and eight: Many distinctive qualities are described in the five- to seven-year shift: Sameroff and Haith 1996; White 1965.

6 In a nationwide household survey, parents reported nearly 20 percent of children between three and seventeen years suffered from at least one developmental, learning, or emotional disorder: Zill and Shoenborn 1990. Other surveys have reported comparable findings: Shaffer et al. 1996.

6 Between 1985 and 1997, *Who's Who Among American High School Students* annually asked high-achieving students if they had considered suicide. Over a quarter typically said they had. Among the nation's students in general, the figure seems to be about 19 percent: Centers for Disease Control and Prevention 2000.

6 Attention deficit disorder: Baren 1994; Wenar and Kerig 2000.

6 Rawlings 1938. My quotes are from the motion picture based on book.

8 Elkind 1981.

Chapter 1. Following Nature's Plan: Child-Centered Parenting in the Early Years

11 *Teach Your Child How to Think,* de Bono 1994. *Teach Your Child Decision-Making,* Clabby and Clabby 1994. *Teach Your Child the Language of Social Success,* Duke, Norwicki, and Martin 1996.

11 Spock 1945/1968; Erikson 1959, 63, 99.

11 Gesell and Ilg 1943.

12 On maturation: Gesell 1945.

13 On differences in temperament: Gesell and Ilg 1943, 44–45. Researchers have not pursued Gesell's idea that temperament is linked to growth rate. However, his temperament typology overlaps with more recent studies of temperament, including the highly influential studies of Thomas and Chess 1977.

13 On Piaget's theory: Crain 2000, chap. 6.

14 Bell and Ainsworth 1972. Other studies on responding to child's signals: Ainsworth et al. 1978, chap. 8; Mahler, Pine, and Bergman 1975; Crain 2000, 57.

15 Emerson 1876/1966, 216.

15 Ginott 1965.

16 Nabhan and Trimble 1994.

17 Ames on grandparents: Ames and Chase 1974.

18 Baumrind 1971a, 1971b. For a critique of Baumrind's findings, see Lewis 1981.

19 On early academic instruction: Hirsh-Pasek 1991; Marcon 1994, 27; Weikart and Schweinhart 1991.

20 On scaffolding: Vygotsky 1934/1986; Berk and Winsler 1995.

21 The birth-to-three movement: Bruer 1999; Eliot 1999, 29–32.

23 "Full court developmental press": Bruer 1999, 17; *Start Smart:* Schiller 1999.

24 Eliot 1999: stimulate but don't overstimulate, p. 448; rotate toys, p. 448; sustain interest and encourage attention, p. 453; demanding but not pressuring, p. 455.

25 The toddler's "love affair with the world," a "precious period": Mahler, Pine, and Bergman 1975, 70; "a pinnacle of perfection": Kaplan 1978, 182.

28 Our unobtrusive presence: Kierkegaard 1844/1946.

28 Montessori 1936/1966.

28 Base from which to explore: Ainsworth et al. 1978.

29 Parents' "quiet availability": Mahler, Pine, and Bergman 1975.

29 "Watching all the time, acting only when the baby demands it": Tinbergen and Tinbergen 1972.

30 Stern 1985.

CHAPTER 2. THE CHILD AS A DRAMATIST

31 Brontë, 1845/1988.

32 Piaget 1946/1962.

32 Ames and Leonard 1946.

33 Newson and Newson 1968, 176.

33 Estimates of number of children who create imaginary companions up to age seven: Taylor 1999, 32.

34 Sizeable minority of imaginary companions are animals: Taylor 1999, 13; Gleason, Sebanc, and Hartup 2000.

34 Children impersonate animals: Taylor 1999, 17; Ames and Leonard 1946, 154.

35 Personality characteristics of children with imaginary companions: Taylor 1999, chap. 3; Singer and Singer 1990, 102; Gleason, Sebanc, and Hartup 2000.

35 "Not a symptom of emotional problems": Taylor 1999, 157.

35 "He has Candy, a dog": Newson and Newson 1968, 176.

35 Imaginary companions do things children dislike: Taylor 1999, 19.

36 Imaginary pony didn't show up at the horse show: Taylor 1999, 153.

36 Antonia Mills study in India: Taylor 1999, 159.

36 Reincarnation speculation: Newson and Newson 1968, 181.

37 Taylor doubts children believe companions are real: Taylor 1999, 153.

37 Taylor says children's "mastery of fantasy" is impressive: Taylor 1999, 116.

38 "The high season of imaginative play" (ages 2½ to 6 years): Singer and Singer 1990, 64. Other evidence: Fein 1981; Newson and Newson 1976 (cited in Taylor 1999, 129); Questioning Santa: Kamii and DeVries 1980, 14.

39 Five- to seven-year shift: Sameroff and Haith 1996; Brain growth: Eliot 1999, 414.

39 Paracosms: Taylor 1999, 136–41; Singer and Singer 1990, 111–16.

39 Information on imaginary activities after early childhood is sparse. Taylor (1999, 131) indicates most imaginary companions disappear after early childhood. For accounts of other imaginary events after early childhood, see Taylor, chaps. 7 and 8; Singer and Singer 1990, chaps. 10 and 11.

40 Do adults initiate fantasy play in children? For positive evidence see Berk and Winsler 1995, 62–70.

40 "Oh, you want to go in your house": Haight and Miller 1993, 30. "Pat your baby, tell your baby": Miller and Garvey 1984, 116.

41 Children initiate first episodes of fantasy play: Haight and Miller 1993; Miller and Garvey 1984.

41 Adults can facilitate fantasy play: Haight and Miller 1993; Smilansky and Shefatya 1990. But intrusiveness can dampen it: Fiese 1990; Levenstein and O'Hara 1993.

41 Parents promote fantasy play by positive attitude: Singer and Singer 1990, 61; Levenstein and O'Hara 1993.

41 Props: Curry and Arnaud 1984.

42 Rich fantasy in natural hideouts: Kirby 1989. Greater imaginative play in green settings in poor neighborhoods: Taylor, Wiley, Kuo, and Sullivan 1998.

42 "Oh, I'm a mere customer": Newson and Newson 1968, 168.

42 Adult interventions break spell: Taylor 1999, 126–27.

42 "Child retains role of director": Taylor 1999, 127.

CHAPTER 3. THE CHILD AS A NATURALIST

43 Thoreau 1862/1982, 321.

43 Wordsworth 1807/1985.

43 Shelley 1820/1994.

43 Blake 1794/1988.

43 "Primal sympathy": Wordsworth 1807/1985, 77.

44 "Waters on a starry night": Wordsworth 1807/1985, 72.

45 Roger Hart described the replacement of wild areas with homogenized lawns and blacktop in rural New England in the early 1970s: Hart 1979, 283–84, 321, 487–88; Hart 1986.

45 Nabhan and St. Antoine 1993; Nabhan and Trimble 1994.

46 Montessori 1948/1967; Cobb 1959; Pearce 1977.

47 Biophilia hypothesis: Wilson 1993; Kellert 1993.

47 Orr quote: Orr 1993, 427–28.

47 Hart poll: Koennen 1992. Harris poll: Harris 1993. See also Nabhan and Trimble 1994, 40.

48 Environmental concerns in children's ideal governments: Crain and Crain 1976; Suh 2002.

49 Animals in children's stories: Abrams 1977, 65. Animal dreams: Foulkes 1999; Van de Castle 1983.

50 "Symbolic defect" and "cognitive immaturity": Foulkes 1982, 82, 115. Gary Snyder's view: Turner 1995, 44.

51 A few teens dream of animals: Foulkes 1982, 186.

51 Shelter building in New England: Hart 1979. In England and West Indies: Sobel 1993.

51 Questionnaires have produced mixed results on young children's particularly strong concern for nature: Chawla 1988; Kahn 1999. A simpler questionnaire may show young children's especially strong concern: Harvey 1989.

52 Nature stimulates powers of observation. Hart 1979, 318, 321; Moore 1986a; 1989.

53 Blacktop was "boring," but now we "go on little trips and look at things": Moore 1986b, 57.

53 One child likes to look at plants: Moore 1989.

53 "I love to look at the frogs" and "It's like a cool breath of air": Moore 1987.

53 "You would never say, 'Let's go outside and learn about a cement yard'": Moore 1989, 205.

54 Building shelters: Hart 1979; Kirby 1989; Moore 1986a; Sobel 1993.

55 Children's poems: Rogers 1979.

56 Nature instills peace: Hart 1979, 167, 171, 205, 334.

56 "It feels good there. Really quiet": Moore 1989, 201.

56 "It makes me feel at home," "Being alone doesn't bother me now," "It's just a good-natured place," "It seems like one big family there": Moore 1989, 201–3.

57 The still pond "makes me feel speechless": Moore 1987, 17.

57 Chawla 1990.

57 Thurman 1979.

57 "There was something about the night": Thurman 1979, 7.

58 "I had a sense that all things": Thurman 1979, 226.

58 A "certain overriding immunity": Thurman 1979, 8.

58 Attention disorders: Wenar and Kerig 2000; Baren 1994.

59 Green settings alleviate attention disorders among poor children: Wells 2000. Among middle-class children: Taylor, Kuo, and Sullivan 2001.

59 Children's quotes on fighting on blacktop: Moore 1989, 196–97, 206–7.

60 "I thought the earth/remembered me": Oliver 1979.

60 "Wherever the Lakota went, he was with Mother Earth": Standing Bear 1933/1979, 192.

61 Loneliness in modern society: Durkheim 1930/1951; Fromm 1941.

61 Alienation in the family: Bronfenbrenner 1986.

61 Psychoanalysts on early roots of alienation: Mahler, Pine, and Bergman 1975; Winnicott 1965. Kohut's thoughts are summarized in Greenberg and Mitchell 1983.

62 Schachtel 1959.

63 "Be not too much his parent. Trespass not on his solitude": Emerson 1876/1966, 217.

64 "Rough ground": Moore 1986a, 242–44.

65 "Rip up some asphalt": Moore 1986a, 243.

65 The Learning Through Landscapes organization in the United Kingdom: Adam 1990. On U. S. parks: Stine 1997.

65 "Loose parts": Hart 1979, 349.

65 The toys and equipment "our technological society throws before them": Hart 1979, 284.

67 Nature-study books for children: Russell 1990; Evans and Williams 1993.

67 Sitting still when there is apparently nothing to see: Standing Bear 1933/1979, 69–70.

67 Play leaders: Roger Hart, personal communication.

CHAPTER 4. THE CHILD AS AN ARTIST

69 "Once I drew like Raphael": Picasso quoted in H. Gardner 1980, 8.

69 The flowering of the young child's art in many realms: H. Gardner 1980, 94–99; 1982, 341.

69 Gestalt psychology on art: Arnheim 1954/1971; Kellogg 1969.

70 On circles: Arnheim 1954/1971, 166–67.

71 For a detailed description of how a child works to stop expanding his circles, see H. Gardner 1980, 35.

72 Sunbursts and mandalas. Kellogg 1969, 109; Kellogg 1979, 17.

74 Tadpoles: Golomb 1974; Golomb 1992, 77–90.

76 The tadpole controversy: Freeman (1977) sees a deficit in planning;

the Gestalt theorist Schaefer-Simmern (1973) sees the tadpole as an aesthetically pleasing form.

76 Simplicity is a goal of art: Arnheim 1992, 209.

76 Tadpole drawers know human anatomy, and quote from child, "Has cheeks, chin . . .": Golomb 1973, 239–40.

77 While drawing, the child is often oblivious to others: Golomb 1974, 104, 187.

77 Impersonal forces govern drawing: H. Gardner 1980, 33.

77 "Never seen hands coming from the head": Golomb 1973, 222.

77 "The Golden Period": H. Gardner 1980, 99.

79 The Klee reproduction is from the Paul Klee Foundation, Berne. Figure 4.9 is from H. Gardner 1980, 5.

79 Picasso quote: H. Gardner 1980, 8. Mattise quote: Elderfield 1984, 57. Thomas Mann quote: H. Gardner 1973, 20–21. Kandinsky quote: Goldwater 1966, 128.

79 H. Gardner (1973, 20–21) lists an impressive number of people from various disciplines who call attention to the parallels between ordinary children and creative adults. Goldwater (1966) discusses how children's art influenced Klee, Miró, Kandisky, Dubuffet, and other twentieth-century masters.

80 Klee's comments: Gardner 1980, 8.

80 Thomas and Silk 1990.

80 Comments by Delacroix and Baudelaire: Goldwater 1966, 213–14. Research on child art with Chinese judges: Pariser and van den Berg 1997; Kindler 2000; Davis 1997.

80 Drawings become "increasingly faithful to their target, increasingly neat . . .": H. Gardner 1980, 148.

81 Art is more "flavorful" in young childhood: H. Gardner 1990, 21–22; Davis 1997.

82 Five- to seven-year shift: White 1965; Sameroff and Haith 1996.

83 On Piaget's theory: Crain 2000, 145.

85 "Father talks 'boom'": Werner 1948, 262.

85 Ideas of H. Gardner and his colleagues on promoting artistic development: Gardner 1982a, 213; Gardner 1990; Gardner and Winner 1982; Davis and Gardner 1992.

86 Drawing falls off with age: Davis and Gardner 1992, 119; Gardner 1990, 19; Winner 1982, 119.

86 Arts included in national standards: U.S. Department of Education 1994. See also the Consortium of National Arts Education Associations 1994.

87 "[In] kindergarten, the child is 'taught' what is acceptable . . .": Sarason 1990, 127.

87 Sophisticated books on art education still assume we can improve the young child's work: Smith and the Drawing Study Group 1998; Wilson and Wilson 1982.

CHAPTER 5. THE CHILD AS A POET

91 "If I find a moon . . .": Conkling 1920.

91 Chukovsky's comments and illustrative poems: Chukovsky 1925/1971, 64–65.

92 Johnson 1928, 108, 256.

93 Research has supported Johnson: Schwartz 1977; 1981; Weir 1962; Sutton-Smith 1981, 13–14.

93 Stern 1985, 146–61.

93 "Bells are ringing . . .": Rogers 1979, 19.

94 "Open, open the gates . . .": Chukovsky 1925/1971, 80.

94 "When I read poetry to kindergartners . . .": Heard 1989, 1.

94 Children's metaphors are especially inventive: Gardner et al. 1975;
Billow 1981.

94 Nature's inspiration: The two books containing poems by New York
City schoolchildren are by Heard (1989) and Koch (1970). Heard
contains twenty-two poems by children in the five- to eight-year-old
range (kindergarten to third grade), and I estimate 56 percent speak
about the natural world to a significant extent. Koch's book contains
some poems that he may have influenced to some extent. Excluding
these, I looked at seventy-four poems in the five- to eight-year age
range, and I would classify 74 percent as dealing significantly with
nature. (The poems are on pp. 66–75, 87–91, 107–12, 148–54, 156–59,
199–202, and 299–301.)

95 The poems " 'Whump!' goes the wind," "Fruit trees whisper," "The
thunder is tremendous," "There is going to be the sound of voices,"
"It was such a lovely day," "Bu'fly, Bu'fly," and "Sparkle up, little
tired flower" are from Rogers 1979.

97 Piaget's view on animism: Crain 2000, 127–28; Piaget 1926/1963.

98 Physiognomic perception: Werner 1956; Crain 2000, chap. 5.

99 Figure 5.1: Such illustrations are found in Werner and Kaplan 1963,
and Kohler 1947, 132–46.

100 Perception fulfills "its spiritual mission": Arnheim 1954/1971, 434.

100 Modern society distances us from nature: See, for example,
Wordsworth 1985, "The world is too much with us."

100 Goethe: see Roszak 1973, 302–17.

100 "Teach us to listen": Deming 1991, 76.

101 "A horse is a wild animal": Gardner 1980, 116.

102 "I am setting in between three/green trees": Brendan's poem in
Moore 1989, 204.

102 "A poem has got to be born": Gillian Hughes's poem in Rogers 1979.

103 Baby talk, "Hello, Heelloo": Stern 1977, 3.

103 Poem by Lucinda Broadbent: Rogers 1979.

104 Children sometimes like difficult poems: Heard 1989, 1, 4–5,

104 "Children have a natural talent": Koch 1970, 29.

105 Heard's technique: Heard 1989, 41.

CHAPTER 6. THE CHILD AS A LINGUIST

107 "The child has succeeded . . .": Chomsky 1959, 57.

107 Chomsky's first groundbreaking book was *Syntactic structures* (1957).

108 Children learn nine words a day: Clarke 1983, 811.

108 Adam's tag questions: Brown and Herrnstein 1975, 471,

109 Chomsky's discovery of the auxiliary verb rule: Chomsky 1957.

110 Immigrant child's ability: Chomsky 1959.

111 Chomsky on biological programmed, species-specific ability and universal grammar: Chomsky 1975, 1–44.

111 Over the years, Chomsky has changed his ideas on how much work the child engages in when mastering language. In Chomsky 1959, the child actively raises and tests hypotheses; in Chomsky 1986, the child learns language on the basis of minimal experience.

112 Newborns dance to speech: Condon and Sander 1974.

112 Early vocalizations similar throughout the world: Sachs 1976.

112 On single words: Sachs 1976.

112 Early intonations differ for questions versus statements: Halliday, cited in Bickerton 1981.

113 Table 6.1 is adapted from Brown and Herrnstein 1975, 478, and Slobin 1979, 86–87.

113 Pivot grammar was proposed by Braine 1963, then critiqued (see Brown 1973, 90–111).

114 Pauses indicate the child knows that humans work with phrases: Brown and Bellugi 1964; word endings: Crain 2000, 349.

114 "She holded them loosely": Cazden 1972, 92

115 Children's negatives: Klima amd Bellugi 1966.

115 "[T]he language of childen has its own systematicity": Klima and Bellugi 1966, 191.

116 "Where I can put them?": Bellugi-Klima 1968.

116 Slobin 1981.

117 Pidgins and Creoles: Bickerton 1981; 1999.

118 Children's sign language: Pinker 1994, 36–37.

119 Fowler's teaching methods are summarized in Eliot 1999, 385–86.

119 Example of motherese from Adam's speech: Brown and Bellugi 1964, 135.

120 Evaluation of motherese: Crain 2000, 354.

120 Increasing children's vocabulary: Hart and Risley 1995.

121 Increasing vocabulary can alleviate "damaging consequences of poverty": Feldman 1998, 266–67.

CHAPTER 7. HOW DID THE FUTURE GAIN
ITS GRIP ON THE MODERN MIND?

123 "I hear from afar . . .": Rousseau 1762/1974, 43.

125 Ariès 1960/1962.

126 "Wherever people worked": Ariès 1960/1962, 368.

126 Hanawalt 1986.

126 Shahar 1990.

126 Preformationism in embryology: see Needham 1959; Balinsky 1981.

128 The contemporary tendency to see children as little adults: Postman 1982; Winn 1981.

128 The economic and occupational changes in sixteenth- and seventeenth-century Europe: Roberts 1976; Stone 1965.

129 The growth of schools: Pinchbeck and Hewitt 1969, 36–37, 281; Ariès 1960/1962, 412–13; Bowen 1987, 129–30.

129 "It was recognized that the child was not ready for life": Ariès 1960/ 1962, 412.

129 Hoyles 1979.

130 Kluckhohn 1961.

130 "The rich man in his castle": Roberts 1976, 537.

131 Schools at a loss as to how to proceed: Pinchbeck and Hewitt 1969, 37–38, 279–83, 298; Boyd 1963, 304–5.

131 *Poena scholastica:* Ariès 1960/1962, 259, 263.

131 Shakespeare 1599/1994, 651.

131 "These hateful books all": Thomas More cited in Tucker 1974, 251–52.

132 Comenius's life: Sadler 1969, 5; Keatinge 1967, 3.

132 Comenius on schools of his day: Comenius 1657/1967, 139, 122, 136, 79–80.

133 "Quickly, Pleasantly, and Thoroughly": Comenius 1657/1967, cover page.

133 On Comenius's *Orbis Pictus* and other efforts: Bowen 1981, 103–4; Keatinge 1967, 76–79; Boyd 1968, 245; Tucker 1974.

133 "Wide-awake, practical parents": Pinchbeck and Hewitt 1969, 285.

134 Decline of Latin: Pinchbeck and Hewitt 1969, 285.

134 Aristocracy's schools: Boyd 1968, 261–63.

134 Charity schools: Ariès 1960/1962, 306.

136 Nouveaux riches: Barber 1955, 59–60.

136 The *philosophes:* Brinton, Christopher, and Wolf 1976, chap. 17.

136 The *Encyclopedia:* Brinton, Christopher, and Wolf 1976, chap. 17; Coleman 1969; Shakleton 1969.

138 Rousseau's doubts about progress: Rousseau 1755/1964.

139 "Nature would have them children before they are men": Rousseau 1762/1974, 54.

140 *New Directions in This:* see Keniston 1971.

141 *A Nation at Risk:* National Commission on Excellence in Education 1983.

141 National goals: Ravitch 1995.

141 Forty-nine states have new standards and most states have tests to measure progress toward the standards: *Education Week* 2001.

141 Louis V. Gerstner, Jr., called governors/business leaders conferences in Palisades, N.Y., in 1996 and 1999.

142 Sixth graders are already worried about college admissions: Wilgoren and Steinberg 2000.

CHAPTER 8. QUESTIONING TECHNOLOGY

143 Ginsberg 1996.

144 Davy 1984.

145 Computer moratorium: Alliance for Childhood 2000.

145 The claim that technology is value-neutral: see Reinecke 1991.

146 Mumford 1970; Postman 1992.

147 On schools' desire for computers in absence of supporting data: Roszak 1986, 63; Mayer, Dyck, and Vilberg 1986; Armstrong and Casement 2000.

147 Wood 1991, 105.

147 On young children's distractibility: Gardner 1982b, 437–38.

147 How-to books on goal-directed thinking: de Bono 1994; Wilson and Jan 1993.

148 Prestigious scholars advocate goal-directed, self-monitored thinking: Sternberg and Spear-Swerling 1996; Palicsar and Brown 1989.

148 On Berkeley schoolyard: Moore 1986b.

148 Johnson 1990, 21–22.

148 Poems by Rosemary Stinton and Gillian Hughes: Rogers 1979, 54, 73.

149 Maslow 1969; Werner 1956.

149 Berry 1981, 106.

150 Humphreys 1990, 939.

151 "Learning to master truth for oneself": Piaget 1973, 107; Piaget on Darwin: Piaget 1970.

151 Papert 1980.

151 Studies on computer's effects on thinking: Mayer, Dyck, and Vilberg 1986; Armstrong and Casement 2000.

151 Brod 1984.

152 On Berkeley schoolyard: Moore 1986b.

CHAPTER 9. RESPONDING TO THE STANDARDS
MOVEMENT: THE CHILD-CENTERED ALTERNATIVE

153 Massachusetts testing boycott: King 2000.

153 Scarsdale, New York, boycott: Zernike 2001.

153 Marin County, California, boycott: St. John 2001.

153 New York City boycott: Hartocollis 2002.

153 State testing: Education Week 2001.

154 Ravitch 1995, 25.

156 Ginsburg and Opper 1988, 239.

156 Montessori 1936b/1966, 239. For a discussion of her theory and
     methods, see Crain 2000, chap. 4.

160 "Like lion-tamers without a whip": J. Rosenbaum quoted in Rav-
     itch 1995, 119.

160 Dewey 1897/1959.

161 Kohn 1999, 108–9.

161 Overly difficult instruction undermines independence: Rousseau
     1762/1974, 83, 131, 169, 199.

161 Kamii 1985, 1989, 1994.

163 It's better for children to keep wondering than "to be told the
     answer": Kamii 1973, 225.

163 "Wait, I have to think it in my own head": Kamii 1985, 235.

164 Less bureaucratic state mandates: Tucker and Codding 1998, 231.

164 Restrictions on teachers: Kohn 1999, 86–88.

164 "Teachers feel jerked around": Corbett and Wilson 1991, 84. *Quality
     Counts, 2001* (*Education Week* 2001, January 11, 5) reported that 66

percent of teachers in a national survey said "state tests were forcing them to concentrate too much on what's tested to the detriment of other important topics."

164 Textbooks create national curriculum: Gerstner 1995, 187.

164 Standardized testing is inappropriate in the early grades: National Association for the Education of Young Children 1986.

165 My statement that by the fourth grade many children have *some* facility with abstract thought: I am basically following Piaget. I believe Piaget, despite criticisms, outlined the major shifts in cognitive development. See Crain 2000, chap. 5.

166 High-stakes testing and dropout rates: Kornhaber and Orfield 2001, 13.

167 Kozol 1991.

167 Portfolios and authentic assessment: see Sacks 1999, chap. 11.

168 Evaluating samples of schools: Kohn 1999, chap. 10.

168 Evaluating child-centered education: On open education, Horwitz 1979; Walberg 1984; Giaconia and Hedges 1982; Rothenberg 1989. On Montessori education, Crain 2000, 83. On progressive education, Aiken 1942.

169 "I believe that interests are the signs and symptoms of growing power": Dewey 1897/1959.

169 But interests alone don't always lead anywhere: Dewey 1902/1959, 100, 110.

170 Concentration: Montessori 1949/1967, 202–3, 219–20, 272–73.

170 Tranquillity: Montessori 1949/1967, 218–20, 264, 272–73.

171 Independence: Rogers 1961, 169.

171 Exuberance: Pestalozzi 1780/1912, 20; Pestalozzi cited in Downs 1975; Goodman 1960, 6, 42; Blake 1789/1992, 8–9.

171 Grace: Pestalozzi 1780/1912, 20; Goodman 1960, 6, 42.

CHAPTER 10. PARENTS' QUESTIONS

177 Kralovec and Buell 2000.

178 Ginott 1965.

178 Piaget's views of children's informal discussions: Crain 2000, 126, 137.

179 Winn 1977.

179 Montessori 1949.

181 "We serve the future by protecting the present": Montessori 1949, 149.

182 Mother-child dialogue in Gordon 1975, 67–68.

184 Ginott 1965.

184 For thoughtful advocacy of lifelong learning, see Calkins 1997.

185 Lawless 1991.

APPENDIX A. A CHILD OF NATURE: HUCKLEBERRY FINN

189 "I won't be rich": Twain 1876/1988, 434.

189 "Huckleberry came and went, at his own free will": Twain 1876/ 1988, 313–14.

190 Huck's age: Twain 1884/1960, 133; Donyo 1991, 40.

190 Shelly Fisher Fishkin (1993) has argued that Twain modeled Huck partly after a loquacious ten-year-old African-American boy Twain called Sociable Jimmy.

190 Like listening to a real boy: See Doyno (1991, 40–43) for an account of how Twain paid attention to the voices of real children.

190 Twain said he patterned Huck after a boyhood friend named Tom Blankenship, an "unschooled, unsufficiently fed, good-hearted boy

who was really the only independent and happy person in his town" (Clemens 1959, 68).

190 "I felt so lonesome . . .": Twain 1884/1960, 27–28.

191 On animism: Crain 2000, 127–28, 94–98; Werner 1956.

191 "Sometimes, when a bird cries out": Hesse 1942/1980, 86.

192 "The sun was so high . . .": Twain 1884/1960, 65–66.

192 "It was kinda solemn, drifting down the big, still river . . .": Twain 1884/1960, 97.

193 "Lazying around . . .": Twain 1884/1960, 156.

193 "Not a sound anywheres . . .": Twain 1884/1960, 155–56.

194 "All his senses are alive": Marx 1964, 333.

194 Huck "belongs" to the landscape: Marx 1964, 333.

195 "I wouldn't 'a' turned in anyway . . .": Twain 1884/1960, 167.

196 Steamboat "coughing" and "belching": Twain 1884/1960, 156.

196 "She was a big one": Twain 1884/1960, 129–30.

197 Abbey 1968, 193.

197 Nabhan and St. Antoine 1993.

APPENDIX B. CHILDREN FACING SCHOOL: SALLY BROWN AND PEPPERMINT PATTY

199 "Learning is not worth a penny . . .": Pestalozzi 1951, 33.

199 Public support for higher standards: Throughout the 1990s, polls showed overwhelming support from adults. National Education Summit Briefing Book 1999.

199 Lack of attention to children's feelings and interests: See Kane 1995.

200 "The purpose of life": Schulz 1962.

200 "The biggest problem" and "Shakespearean tragedy": Schulz 1991a.

201 Winnicott 1951.

201 "Kids' rights": Mendelson in association with Schulz 1979.

201 Sally wants out of kindergarten: Schulz 1992a.

201 "And we sang songs . . .": Schulz 1992a.

201 Draws a sea gull flying over each wave: Schulz 1982.

201 "Dittos chasing dottos": Schulz 1991b.

201 "Sixes that like to pretend they're noses": Schulz 1979.

201 Werner 1948.

202 "Decorate a sentence": Schulz 1983.

202 "One million?": Schulz 1991c.

202 "Twiddely-two?": Schulz 1991c.

202 "I went last year": Schulz 1970a.

202 "Panic in the Streets": Schulz 1983.

202 "The height of Mount Whitney": Schulz 1984.

202 "I've never even seen a farmer": Schulz 1990a.

202 "I can't go to school! I'm not ready!!": Schulz 1990b.

203 "Keep my eye on my lunch so it doesn't get ripped off": Schulz 1993a.

203 "Ma'am, I have a suggestion for a class project": Schulz 1993a.

204 Peppermint Patty is seven years old: Schulz 1983.

204 "Hi, Chuck!": Schulz 1970b

204 Beauty of a lake: Schulz 1991a.

204 "I'll shorten his life span"; knocks boy off his feet: Schulz 1991b.

204 Play some checkers?: Scholz 1990c.

205 Answer "so obvious": Schulz 1991d.

205 Puts crystal over test paper: Schulz 1991a.

205 Puts ribbons in her hair: Schulz 1993b.

205 "To protect the innocent": Schulz 1992b.

205 Education's purpose is "to keep us from enjoying ourselves": Schulz 1993b.

206 Marcie calls Peppermint Patty "Sir": Schulz 1980.

206 "It's all just too embarrassing": Schulz 1990c.

206 Door knob up high to make you feel inferior: Schulz 1990d.

206 Peppermint Patty has no mother: Schulz 1990c.

206 "You are a rare gem": Schulz 1990d.

206 Ordinarily fights the dress code: Schulz 1983.

206 This time cries: Schulz 1990d.

206 Drops out of school: Schulz 1990c.

207 "When are you going to face up to reality?!": Schulz 1990c.

References

Abbey, E. 1968. *Desert solitaire.* New York: Ballantine.

Abrams, D. M. 1977. *Conflict resolution in children's storytelling.* Doctoral diss., Teachers College, Columbia University, New York.

Adam, E. 1990. *Final report.* Learning Through Landscapes, 3d Floor, Southside Offices, The Law Courts, Winchester, Hampshire S023 9DL, England.

Aiken, W. M. 1942. *The story of the Eight-Year Study.* New York: McGraw-Hill.

Ainsworth, M. D. S., S. M. Bell, and E. F. Stayton. 1974. Infant-mother attachment and social development: Socialization as a product of reciprocal responsiveness to signals. In *The integration of the child into the social world.* Edited by M. P. M. Richards. New York: Cambridge University Press.

Ainsworth, M. D. S., M. C. Blehar, E. Waters, and S. Wall. 1978. *Patterns of attachment.* Hillsdale, N.J.: Lawrence Erlbaum Associates.

Alliance for Childhood, 2000. *Computers and childhood: A call for action.* P. O. Box 444, College Park, MD 20741. www.allianceforchildhood.net.

Ames, L. B. 1971. Don't push your preschooler. *Family Circle Magazine, 79*: 60.

Ames, L. B., and J. A. Chase. 1974. *Don't push your preschooler.* New York: Harper & Row.

Ames, L. B., and J. Leonard. 1946. Imaginary companions and related phenomena. *Journal of Genetic Psychology, 69:* 147–67.

Ariès, P. 1960/1962. *Centuries of childhood: A social history of family life.* Translated by R. Baldick. New York: Vintage Books.

Armstrong, A., and C. Casement. 2000. *The child and the machine.* Beltsville, Md.: Robins Lane.

Arnheim, R. 1954/1971. *Art and visual perception.* Berkeley: University of California Press.

———. 1992. *To the rescue of art: Twenty-six essays.* Berkeley: University of California Press.

Balinsky, B. I. 1981. *An introduction to embryology.* 5th ed. Philadelphia: Saunders.

Barber, E. G. 1955. *The bourgeoisie in eighteenth century France.* Princeton, N.J.: Princeton University Press.

Baren, M. 1994. ADHD: Do we finally have it right? *Contemporary Pediatrics, 11:* 97–124.

Bastian, S. 2000. Scores, scores, scores: How the drive to measure student achievement and assess school effectiveness is changing education. Presentation to forum, 13 June. Open Society Institute, New York City.

Baumrind, D. 1971a. Current patterns of parental authority. *Developmental Psychology Monograph, 4,* No. 1, part 2.

———. 1971b. Harmonious parents and their preschool children. *Developmental Psychology, 4:* 99–102.

Bell, S. M., and M. D. S. Ainsworth. 1972. Infant crying and maternal responsiveness. *Child Development, 43:* 1171–90.

Bellugi-Klima, U. 1968. Linguistic mechanisms underlying child speech. In *Proceedings of the conference on language and language behavior.* Edited by E. M. Zale. Englewood Cliffs, N.J.: Prentice-Hall.

Berk, L. E., and A. Winsler. 1995. *Scaffolding children's learning: Vygotsky and early childhood education.* Washington, D.C.: National Association for the Education of Young Children.

Berger, P. L. 1986. *The capitalist revolution.* New York: Basic Books.

Berry, W. 1981. *The gift of good land.* San Francisco: North Point Press.

Bickerton, D. 1981. *The roots of language.* Ann Arbor, Mich.: Karoma.

———. 1999. Creole languages, the language biogram hypothesis, and language acquisition. In *Handbook of child language acquisition.* Edited by W. C. Ritchie and T. K. Bathia. San Diego: Academic Press.

Billow, R. M. 1981. Observing spontaneous metaphors in children. *Journal of Experimental Child Psychology, 31:* 430–45.

Blake, W. 1794/1988. Songs of Experience. In *William Blake: Selected Poetry.* Edited by W. H. Stevenson. London: Penguin.

———. 1789/1992. Nurse's song. In *Songs of innocence and songs of experience,* 8–9. New York: Dover.

Bowen, J. 1981. *A history of Western education.* Vol. 3, *The Modern West.* New York: St. Martin's Press.

Boyd, W. 1963. *The educational theory of Jean-Jacques Rousseau.* New York: Russell and Russell.

———. 1968. *A history of Western education.* 9th ed. London: Adam and Charles Black.

Braine, M. D. S. 1963. The ontogeny of English phrase structure: The first phase. *Language, 39:* 1–14.

Brinton, C., J. B. Christopher, and R. L. Wolff. 1976. Chap. 17 in *A history of civilization, 300 to 1815.* 5th ed. Englewood Cliffs, N.J.: Prentice-Hall.

Brod, C. 1984. *Technostress: The human cost of the computer revolution.* Reading, Mass.: Addison-Wesley.

Bronfenbrenner, U. 1986, February. Alienation and the four worlds of childhood. *Phi Delta Kappan, 67:* 430–36.

Brontë, E. J. 1845/1988. Julian M. and A. G. Rochelle. In *The Brontë Sisters: Selected Poems*. Edited by S. Davies. Manchester, England: Fyfield Books.

Brown, R. 1973. *A first language*. Cambridge: Harvard University Press.

Brown, R., and U. Bellugi. 1964. Three processes in the child's acquisition of syntax. *Harvard Educational Review, 34:* 133–51.

Brown, R., and R. J. Herrnstein. 1975. *Psychology*. Boston: Little, Brown.

Bruer, J. T. 1999. *The myth of the first three years*. New York: Free Press.

Calkins, L. with L. Bellino. 1997. *Raising lifelong learners*. Cambridge, Mass.: Perseus Books.

Cazden, C. 1972. *Child language and education*. New York: Holt, Rinehart and Winston.

Centers for Disease Control and Prevention (CDC) 2000, 9 June. Youth risk behavior surveillance—United States, 1999. *Morbidity and Mortality Weekly Report, 49* (No. SS-5). Atlanta: U.S. Department of Health and Human Services.

Chawla, L. 1988. Children's concerns for the natural environment. *Children's Environments Quarterly, 5:* 13–20.

———. 1990. Ecstatic places. *Children's Environments Quarterly, 7:* 18–23.

Chomsky, N. 1957. *Syntactic structures*. The Hague: Moulton.

———. 1959. Review of B. F. Skinner's *Verbal Behavior. Language, 35:* 26–58.

———. 1975. *Reflections on language*. New York: Pantheon.

———. 1986. *Knowledge of language*. New York: Praeger.

Chukovsky, K. 1925/1971. *From two to five*. Translated and edited by M. Morton. Berkeley: University of California Press.

Clabby, J. F., and J. J. Elias. 1987. *Teach your child decision-making*. Garden City, N.Y.: Doubleday.

Clarke, E. V. 1983. Meanings and concepts. In *Handbook of child psychology.* Vol. 3. Edited by J. H. Flavell and E. M. Markman. New York: Wiley.

Clemens, S. 1959. *The autobiography of Mark Twain.* New York: Harper.

Cobb, E. 1959. The ecology of imagination in childhood. *Daedalus, 88:* 537–48.

Coleman, D. C. 1969. The economics of an age of change. In *The eighteenth century: Europe in the age of Enlightenment.* Edited by A. Cobban. New York: McGraw-Hill.

Comenius, J. A. 1657/1967. *The great didactic.* Translated by W. M. Keatinge. New York: Russell and Russell.

Condon, W. S., and L. W. Sander. 1974. Neonate movement is synchronized with adult speech: Interactional participation and language acquisition. *Science, 183:* 99–101.

Conkling, H. 1920. *Poems by a little girl.* New York: Frederick A. Stokes.

Consortium of National Arts Education Associations. 1994. *National standards for arts education.* Reston, Va.: Music Educators National Conference.

Corbett, H. D., and B. L. Wilson. 1991. *Testing, reform, and rebellion.* Norwood, N.J.: Alex Publishing Corporation.

Crain, W. 2000. *Theories of development: Concepts and applications.* 4th ed. Upper Saddle River, N.J.: Prentice-Hall.

Crain, W. C., and E. F. Crain. 1976. Age trends in political thinking: Dissent, voting, and the distribution of wealth. *Journal of Psychology, 92:* 179–90.

Curry, N. E., and S. H. Arnaud. 1984. Play in developmental preschool settings. Chap. 15. *Child's play: Developmental and applied.* Edited by T. D. Yawkey and A. D. Pelligrini. Hillsdale, N.J.: Lawrence Erlbaum.

Davis, J. H. 1997. The what and the whether of the U: Cultural implications of understanding development of graphic symbolization. *Human Development, 40:* 145–54.

Davis, J., and H. Gardner. 1992. The cognitive revolution: Consequences for the understanding and education of the child as an artist. In pt. 2 of *The arts, education, and aesthetic knowing*. Edited by B. Reimer and R. A. Smith. Chicago: University of Chicago Press.

Davy, J. 1984. Mindstorms in the limelight. In *The computer in education: A critical perspective*. Edited by D. Sloan. New York: Teachers College Press.

de Bono, E. 1994. *Teach your child how to think*. New York: Penguin.

Deming, B. 1991. Spirit of love. In *Earth prayers*. Edited by E. Roberts and E. Amidon. San Francisco: HarperSan Francisco.

Dewey, J. 1897/1959. My pedagogic creed. In *Dewey on education: Selections*. Edited by M. S. Dworkin. New York: Teachers College Press.

———. 1902/1959. The child and the curriculum. In *Dewey on education: Selections*. Edited by M. S. Dworkin. New York: Teachers College Press.

———. 1916/1966. *Democracy and education*. New York: Free Press.

Downs, R. B. 1975. *Heinrich Pestalozzi: Father of modern pedagogy*. Boston: Twayne Publishers.

Doyno, V. A. 1991. *Writing Huck Finn: Mark Twain's creative process*. Philadelphia: University of Pennsylvania Press.

Duke, M. P., S. Norwicki, and E. A. Martin. 1996. *Teach your child the language of social success*. New York: Peachtree.

Dunn, J., and N. Dale. 1984. I a daddy: 2-year-olds' collaboration in joint pretend with sibling and with mother. In *Symbolic play*. Edited by I. Bretherton. Orlando, Fla.: Academic Press.

Durkheim, E. 1930/1951. *Suicide*. Translated by J. A. Spaulding and G. Simpson. New York: Free Press.

Education Week. 2001, January 11. Executive Summary. *Quality Counts 2001*.

Egan, K. 1997. The arts as the basis of education. *Childhood Education, 73*: 341–45.

Elderfield, J. 1984. *The drawings of Henri Matisse.* London: Thames and Hudson.

Eliot, L. 1999. *What's going on in there? How the brain and mind develop in the first five years of life.* New York: Bantam.

Elkind, D. 1981. *The hurried child.* Reading, Mass.: Addison-Wesley.

———. 1989. *Miseducation: Preschoolers at risk.* New York: Knopf.

Emerson, R. W. 1876/1966. Education. In *Emerson on Education: Selections,* 216–17. Edited by H. M. Jones. New York: Teachers College Press.

Erikson, E. H. 1959. *Identity and the life cycle.* Psychological Issues, 1. New York: International Universities Press.

Ervin, S. M. 1964. Imitation and structural change in children's language. In *New directions in the study of language.* Edited by E. H. Lenneberg. Cambridge: MIT Press.

Evans, D., and C. Williams. 1993. *Living things.* London: Darling Kindersley Education.

Fein, G. 1981. Pretend play in childhood: An integrative review. *Child Development, 52:* 1095–1118.

Feldman, R. S. 1998. *Child development.* Upper Saddle River, N.J.: Prentice-Hall.

Fiese, B. H. 1990. Playful relationships: A contextual analysis of mother-toddler interaction and symbolic play. *Child Development, 61:* 1648–56.

Fishkin, S. F. 1993. *Was Huck black?* New York: Oxford University Press.

Freeman, N. 1977. How young children try to plan drawings. In *The child's representation of the world.* Edited by G. Butterworth. New York: Plenum.

Fromm, E. 1941. *Escape from freedom.* New York: Holt.

Foulkes, D. 1982. *Children's dreams: Longitudinal studies.* New York: Wiley.

———. 1999. *Children's dreaming and the development of consciousness.* Cambridge: Harvard University Press.

Gardner, H. 1973. *The arts and human development.* New York: Wiley.

———. 1980. *Artful scribbles.* New York: Basic Books.

———. 1982a. *Art, mind, and brain.* New York: Basic Books.

———. 1982b. *Psychology: An introduction.* 2d ed. Boston: Little, Brown.

———. 1990. *Art education and human development.* Los Angeles: J. Paul Getty Trust.

Gardner, H., M. Kincher, E. Winner, and D. Perkins 1975. Children's metaphoric productions and preferences. *Journal of Child Language,* 2: 125–41.

Gardner, H., and E. Winner. 1982. *First intimations of artistry.* In *U-shaped behavioral growth.* Edited by S. Strauss. New York: Academic Press.

Gardner, R., Jr. 1999, November 15. Failing at four. *New York* magazine, 32: 28–31, 112.

Gerstner, L. V., Jr. 1995. *Reinventing education.* New York: Dutton.

Gesell, A. 1945. *The embryology of behavior.* New York: Harper & Row.

Gesell, A., and F. L. Ilg. 1943. *Infant and child in the culture of today.* In A. Gesell & F. I. Ilg, *Child development.* New York: Harper & Row, 1949.

Giaconia, R. M., and L. V. Hedges. 1982. Identifying features of effective open education. *Review of Educational Research, 54:* 579–602.

Ginott, H. G. 1965. *Between parent and child.* New York: Avon.

Ginsberg, A. 1996. Ruhr-Gebiet. In *Selected Poems, 1947–1995.* New York: HarperCollins.

Ginsburg, H., and S. Opper. 1988. *Piaget's theory of intellectual development.* 3rd ed. Englewood Cliffs, N.J.: Prentice-Hall.

Gleason, T. R., A. M. Sebanc, and W. W Hartup. 2000. Imaginary companions of preschool children. *Developmental Psychology, 36:* 419–28.

Goldwater, R. 1966. *Primitivism and modern art.* New York: Vintage Books.

Golomb, C. 1973. Children's representations of the human figure: The effects of models, media, and instruction. *Genetic Psychology Monographs, 87:* 197–251.

———. 1974. *Young children's sculpture and drawing.* Cambridge: Harvard University Press.

———. 1992. *The child's creation of the pictorial world.* Berkeley: University of California Press.

Goodman, P. 1960. *Growing up absurd.* New York: Vintage.

Goodnough, A. 2001, 14 June. Strain of fourth-grade tests drives off veteran teachers. *The New York Times,* front page.

Gordon, T. 1975. *Parent effectiveness training.* New York: New American Library.

Greenacre, P. 1957. The childhood of the artist. *The Psychoanalytic Study of the Child, 12:* 27–72.

Greenberg, J. R., and S. A. Mitchell. 1983. *Object relations in psychoanalytic theory.* Cambridge: Harvard University Press.

Haight, W. L., and P. J. Miller. 1993. *Pretending at home.* Albany: State Univesity of New York Press.

Hanawalt, B. A. 1986. *The ties that bound: Peasant families in medieval England.* New York: Oxford University Press.

Harris, L. 1993, Spring. *Children and the environment: A survey of 10,375 children in grades 4 through 12.* Philadelphia: Pew Charitable Trusts.

Hart, B., and T. R. Risley. 1995. *Meaningful differences in the everyday experience of young American children.* Baltimore: Brooks.

Hart, R. A. 1979. *Children's experience of place.* New York: Irvington.

———. 1986. The changing city of childhood. The 1986 Catherine Molony Memorial Lecture, The City College Workshop Center, New York.

Hartocollis, A. 2002, 6 March. Boycotts and a bill protest mandating state tests. *New York Times,* B9.

Harvey, M. R. 1989. Children's experiences with vegetation. *Children's Environments Quarterly, 6:* 36–43.

Heafford, M. 1967. *Pestalozzi: His thought and relevance today.* London: Methuen and Co.

Heard, G. 1989. *For the good of the earth and sun.* Portsmouth, N.H.: Heinemann.

Hesse, H. 1942/1980. Sometimes, when a bird cries out. In *News from the universe: Poems of twofold consciousness.* Edited and translated by R. Bly. San Francisco: Sierra Club Books.

Hirsch, E. D., Jr. 1988. *Cultural literacy.* New York: Vintage Books.

Hirsh-Pasek, K. 1991. Pressure or challenge? How academic environments affect children. In *Academic instruction in early childhood: Challenge or pressure?* Edited by L. Rescorla, M. C. Hyson, and K. Hirsh-Pasek. New Directions for Child Development, No. 53. San Francisco: Jossey-Bass.

Horwitz, R. A. 1979, Winter. Psychological effects of the "open classroom." *Review of Educational Research, 49:* 71–86.

Hoyles, M. H. 1979. History and Politics. In *Changing childhood.* Edited by M. H. Hoyles. London: Writers and Readers Cooperative.

Humphreys, L. G. 1990. A depressing picture of blacks' future status. *Contemporary Psychology, 35:* 938–40.

Johnson, C. 1990. *On becoming lost: A naturalist's search for meaning.* Salt Lake City: Cobbs-Smith Publishers.

Johnson, H. 1928. *Children in the nursery school.* New York: Day.

Kahn, P. H. 1999. *The human relationship to nature.* Cambridge: MIT Press.

Kamii, C. 1973. Piaget's interactionism and the process of teaching young children. In *Piaget in the classroom.* Edited by M. Schwebel and J. Raph. New York: Basic Books.

————. 1985. *Young children reinvent arithmetic.* New York: Teachers College Press.

————. 1989. *Young children continue to reinvent arithmetic: 2nd grade.* New York: Teachers College Press.

————. 1994. *Young children continue to reinvent arithmetic: 3rd grade.* New York: Teachers College Press.

Kamii, C., and R. DeVries. 1980. *Group games in early education.* Washington, D.C.: National Association for the Education of Young Children.

Kane, J. 1995. Educational reform and the dangers of triumphant rhetoric. In *Educational reform for a democratic society.* Edited by R. Miller. Brandon, Vt.: Resource Center for Redesigning Education.

Kaplan, L. J. 1978. *Oneness and separateness.* New York: Touchstone.

Keatinge, M. W. 1967. Introduction—Biographical. In *The great didactic of John Amos Comenius.* Edited by M. W. Keatinge. New York: Russell and Russell.

Kellert, S. R. 1993. The biological basis for human values of nature. In *The biophilia hypothesis.* Edited by S. R. Kellert and E. O. Wilson. Washington, D.C.: Island Press.

Kellogg, R. 1969. *Analyzing children's art.* Palo Alto, Calif.: Mayfield.

————. 1970. Understanding children's art. In *Readings in psychology today.* Edited by P. Cramer. Del Mar, Calif.: CRM Books.

————. 1979. *Children's drawings/children's minds.* New York: Avon.

Keniston, K. 1971. *Youth and dissent.* New York: Harvest Book.

Kierkegaard, S. 1844/1946. *The concept of dread.* Translated by W. Lowrie. Princeton, N.J.: Princeton University Press.

Kindler, A. M. 2000. From U-curve to dragons. *Visual Arts Research, 26:* 15–28.

King, J. D. 2000. MCAS test draws fire. In *Failing our kids.* Edited by K. Swope and B. Miner. Milwaukee: Rethinking Schools.

Kirby, M. 1989. Nature's refuge in children's environments. *Children's Environments Quarterly, 6:* 7–12.

Klima, E., and U. Bellugi. 1966. Syntactic regularities in the speech of children. In *Psycholinguistics papers.* Edited by J. Lyons and R. J. Wales. Edinburgh: Edinburgh University Press.

Kluckhohn, F. 1961. Dominant and variant value orientations. In *Personality in nature, society, and culture.* 2d ed. Edited by C. Kluckhohn and H. A. Murray. New York: Knopf.

Koch, K. 1970. *Wishes, lies, and dreams.* New York: Perennial Library.

Koennen, C. 1992, 18 February. How kids are writing the green agenda for parents. *Los Angeles Times,* E1.

Kohler, W. 1947. *Gestalt psychology.* New York: Mentor.

Kohn, A. 1999. *The schools our children deserve.* Boston: Houghton Mifflin.

Kornhaber, M. L., and G. Orfield. 2001. High stakes testing policies: Examining their assumptions and consequences. In *Raising standards or raising barriers?* Edited by G. Orfield and M. L. Kornhaber. New York: The Century Foundation.

Kozol, J. 1991. *Savage inequalities.* New York: Crown Publishers.

———. 2000. *Ordinary resurrections.* New York: Crown Publishers.

Kralovec, E., and J. Buell. 2000. *The end of homework.* Boston: Beacon Press.

Lawless, G. 1991. When the animals come to us. In *Earth prayers.* Edited by E. Roberts and E. Amidon. San Francisco: HarperCollins.

Levenstein, P., and J. O'Hara. 1993. The necessary lightness of mother-child play. In *Parent-child play.* Edited by K. MacDonald. Albany, N.Y.: State University of New York Press.

Lewis, C. C. 1981. The effects of parental firm control: A reinterpretation of findings. *Psychological Bulletin, 90:* 547–63.

Lipton, L., and P. Yarrow. 1963. "Puff the Magic Dragon." Honabe Melodies and Silver Dawn Music. New York: Cherry Lane Publishers.

Mahler, M. S., F. Pine, and A. Bergman. 1975. *The psychological birth of the human infant.* London: Hutchison & Co.

Marcon, R. A. 1994, November. Doing the right thing for children: Linking research and policy reform in the District of Columbia public schools. *Young Children, 50:* 8–20.

Marx, L. 1964. *The machine in the garden.* London: Oxford University Press.

Maslow, A. H. 1969. *The psychology of science: A reconnaissance.* Chicago: Gateway, Henry Regnery.

Mayer, R. E., J. L. Dyck, and W. Vilberg. 1986. Learning to program and learning to think: What's the connection? *Communications of the ACM, 29* (7): 605–10.

Mendelson, L., in association with C. M. Schulz. 1979. *Happy Birthday, Charlie Brown.* New York: Random House.

Miller, P., and C. Garvey. 1984. Mother-baby role play: Its origins in social support. In *Symbolic play.* Edited by I. Bretherton. Orlando, Fla.: Academic Press.

Miner, B. 1999–2000, Winter. National summit: What wasn't said. *Rethinking Schools.*

Montessori, M. 1909/1964. *The Montesssori Method.* Translated by A. E. George. New York: Schocken.

———. 1936/1966. *The secret of childhood.* Translated by M. J. Costelloe. New York: Ballantine Books.

———. 1948/1967. *The discovery of the child.* Translated by M. J. Costelloe. New York: Ballantine Books.

———. 1949/1967. *The absorbent mind.* Translated by C. A. Claremont. New York: Delta Book.

Moore, R. C. 1986a. *Childhood's domain.* London: Croom Helm.

———. 1986b. The power of nature orientations of girls and boys toward biotic and abiotic play settings on a reconstructed schoolyard. *Children's Environments Quarterly, 3:* 52–69.

———. 1987. "Like diamonds melting": Children's play and learning in aquatic settings. *Children's Environments Quarterly, 4:* 11–18.

———. 1989. Before and after asphalt: Diversity as an ecological measure of quality in children's outdoor environments. In *The ecological context of children's play.* Edited by M. N. Bloch and A. D. Pelligrini. Norwood, N.J.: Ablex.

Mumford, L. 1970. *The myth of the machine.* Vol. 2. San Diego: Harvest/HJB.

Nabhan, G. P., and S. St. Antoine. 1993. The loss of floral and faunal story: The extinction of experience. In *The biophilia hypothesis.* Edited by S. R. Kellert and E. O. Wilson. Washington, D.C.: Island Press.

Nabhan, G. P., and S. Trimble. 1994. *The geography of childhood.* Boston: Beacon Press.

National Association for the Education of Young Children. 1986a. *Good teaching practices for 4- and 5-year-olds.* Brochure no. 522. Washington, D.C.: National Association for the Education of Young Children (202-232-8777).

———. 1986b, September. Position statement on developmentally appropriate practice in early childhood programs serving children birth through age 8. *Young Children.*

National Commission on Excellence in Education. 1983. *A nation at risk: The imperative for educational reform.* Washington, D.C.: U.S. Government Printing Office.

National education summit briefing book. 1999. Achieve, Inc.; 400 North Capitol Street, NW; Suite 351; Washington, DC 20001.

Needham, J. 1959. *A history of embryology.* 2d ed. Cambridge: Cambridge University Press.

Nevers, P., V. Gebhard, and E. Billmann-Mahecha. 1997. Patterns of reasoning exhibited by children and adolescents in response to moral dilemmas involving plants, animals, and ecosystems. *Journal of Moral Education, 26:* 169–86.

Newson, J., and E. Newson. 1968. *Four years old in an urban community.* Chicago: Aldine.

————. 1976. *Seven years old in an urban community.* London: George Allen and Unwin.

Oliver, M. 1979. Sleeping in the forest. *Twelve moons.* Boston: Little, Brown.

Orr, D. W. 1993. Love it or lose it: The coming biophilia. In *The biophilia hypothesis.* Edited by S. R. Kellert and E. O. Wilson. Washington, D.C.: Island Press.

Palicsar, A. S., and L. Brown. 1989. Instruction for self-regulated reading. In *Toward the thinking curriculum: Current cognitive research.* Edited by L. B. Resnick and L. E. Klopfer. Alexandria, Va.: Association for Supervision and Curriculum Development.

Papert, S. 1980. *Mind-storms: Children, computers, and powerful ideas.* New York: Basic Books.

Pariser, D., and A. van den Berg. 1997. The mind of the beholder: Some provisional doubts about the U-curved aesthetic development thesis. *Studies in Art Education, 38:* 158–78.

Pearce, J. C. 1977. *Magical child.* New York: Dutton.

Pestalozzi, H. 1780/1912. Evening hours of a hermit. In *Pestalozzi's educational writings.* Edited by J. A. Green. London: Longmans, Green.

————. 1951. *The education of man: Aphorisms.* Translated by H. Norden and R. Norden. New York: Philosophical Library.

Piaget, J. 1926/1963. *The child's conception of the world.* Translated by J. Tomlinson and A. Tomlinson. Savage, Md.: Littlefield, Adams and Co.

————. 1946/1962. *Play, dreams, and imitation in childhood.* New York: Norton.

————. 1970. Piaget's theory. In *Carmichael's manual of child psychology.* 3d ed. Edited by P. H. Mussen. New York: Wiley.

————. 1973. *To understand is to invent.* New York: Grossman.

Pinchbeck, I., and M. Hewitt. 1969. *Children in English society.* Vol. 1. London: Routledge and Kegan Paul.

Pinker, S. 1994. *The language instinct.* New York: William Morrow.

Postman, N. 1982. *The disappearance of childhood.* New York: Laurel.

————. 1992. *Technopoly: The surrender of culture to technology.* New York: Knopf.

Ravitch, D. 1995. *National standards in American education.* Washington, D.C.: Brookings Institution Press.

————. 2000. *Left back: A century of failed school reforms.* New York: Simon and Schuster.

Rawlings, M. K. 1938. *The yearling.* New York: Collier Macmillan.

Reinecke, I. 1991. Electronic illusions: A skeptic's view of our high tech future. In *Questioning technology.* Edited by J. Zerzan and A. Carnes. Philadelphia: New Society.

Roberts, J. M. 1976. *The pelican history of the world.* New York: Penguin Books.

Rogers, T. 1979. *Those first affections: An anthology of poems composed by children between the ages of two and eight.* London: Routledge and Kegan Paul.

Roszak, T. 1973. *Where the wasteland ends.* Garden City, N.Y.: Anchor Books.

————. 1986. *The cult of information.* New York: Pantheon.

Rothenberg, J. 1989. The open classroom reconsidered. *The Elementary School Journal, 90:* 69–86.

Rousseau, J.-J. 1755/1964. Discourse on the origin and foundations of inequality. In *Jean-Jacques Rousseau: The first and second discourses.* Edited by R. D. Masters. Translated by R. D. Masters and J. R. Masters. New York: St. Martin's Press.

————. 1762/1974. *Emile.* Translated by B. Foxley. London: Dent.

————. 1781/1953. *The Confessions.* Translated by L. M. Cohen. Middlesex, England: Penguin.

Russell, H. R. 1990. *Ten minute field trips.* 2d ed. Washington, D.C.: National Science Teachers Association.

Sachs, J. S. 1976. Development of speech. In *Handbook of perception.* Vol. 7. Edited by E. C. Carterete and M. P. Friedman. New York: Academic Press.

Sacks, P. 1999. *Standardized minds.* Cambridge, Mass.: Perseus.

Sadler, J. 1969. *Comenius.* London: Macmillan.

St. John, K. 2001, May 4. Marin students boycott state test. *San Francisco Chronicle.*

Sameroff, A. J., and M. M. Haith. 1996. *The five to seven year shift.* Chicago: University of Chicago Press.

Sarason, S. B. 1990. *The challenge of art to psychology.* New Haven, Conn.: Yale University Press.

Schachtel, E. G. 1959. *Metamorphosis.* New York: Basic Books.

Schaefer-Simmern, H. 1973. The mental foundation of art education in childhood. In *Child art: The beginnings of self-affirmation.* Edited by H. Lewis. Berkeley, Calif.: Diablo Press.

Schiller, P. 1999. *Start smart: Building brain power in the early years.* Beltsville, Md.: Gryphon House.

Schulz, C. M. 1962. *All this and Snoopy, too.* Greenwich, Conn.: Fawcett Publications.

———. 1970a. *Charlie Brown and Snoopy.* New York: Fawcett Crest.

———. 1970b. *Peanuts classics.* New York: Holt, Rinehart and Winston.

———. 1980. *Dr. Beagle and Mr. Hyde.* New York: Holt.

———. 1982. *This is the best time of the day, Charlie Brown.* New York: Ballantine Books, Fawcett Crest.

———. 1983. *You can't win them all, Charlie Brown.* New York: Ballantine Books.

———. 1984. *Take charge, Snoopy.* New York: Fawcett Crest.

———. 1990a. *You're weird, sir.* New York: Henry Holt and Company, Owl Books.

———. 1990b. *Speak softly, and carry a beagle.* New York: Henry Holt and Company, Owl Books.

———. 1990c. *How long, Great Pumpkin, how long?* New York: Henry Holt and Company, Owl Books.

———. 1990d. *It's great to be a superstar.* New York: Henry Holt and Company, Owl Books.

———. 1991a. *Hats off to you, Charlie Brown.* New York: Fawcett Crest.

———. 1991b. *Summers fly, winters walk.* New York: Henry Holt and Company, Owl Books.

———. 1991c. *A smile makes a lousy umbrella.* New York: Henry Holt and Company, Owl Books.

———. 1991d. *Could you be more pacific?* New York: Topper Books.

———. 1992a. *A kiss on the nose turns anger aside.* New York: Henry Holt and Company, Owl Books.

———. 1992b. *It's hard work being bitter.* New York: Henry Holt and Company, Owl Books.

———. 1993a. *Don't hassle me with your sighs, Chuck.* New York: Henry Holt and Company, Owl Books.

———. 1993b. *The way of a fussbudget is not easy.* New York: Henry Holt and Company, Owl Books.

Schwartz, J. I. 1977. Metalinguistic awareness: A study of verbal play in young children. American Education Research Association. ERIC/ EECE ED 149-852.

———. 1981. Children's experiments with language. *Young Children, 36:* 16–26.

Shackleton, R. 1969. Free inquiry and the world of ideas. In *The eighteenth century: Europe in the age of Enlightenment*. Edited by A. Cobban. New York: McGraw-Hill.

Shaffer, D., P. Fisher, M. K. Dulcan, M. Davies, J. Piacentini, M. E. Schwab-Stone, B. B. Lahey, K. Bourden, P. S. Jensen, H. R. Bird, G. Canino, and D. A. Regier. 1996, July. The NIMH Diagnostic Interview Schedule for Children, Version w.3 (DSIC-2.3): Description, acceptability, prevalence rates, and performance in the MECA study. *Journal of the Academy of Child and Adolescent Psychiatry, 35.*

Shahar, S. 1990. *Childhood in the middle ages.* London: Routledge.

Shakespeare, W. 1599/1994. *As you like it.* In *The comedies of William Shakespeare.* New York: Modern Library.

Shelley, P. B. 1920/1994. Ode to the West Wind. *Percy Bysshe Shelley: Selected Poems.* New York: Gramercy Books.

Sherman, A. 1994. *Wasting America's future: The Children's Defense Fund report on the costs of child poverty.* Boston: Beacon Press.

Shorofsky, R. 2000, 2 February. Letter to the editor. *New York Times.*

Singer, D. G., and J. Singer. 1990. *The house of make-believe: Children's play and developing imagination.* Cambridge: Harvard University Press.

Slobin, D. I. 1979. *Psycholinguistics.* 2d ed. Glenview, Ill.: Scott, Foresman.

———. 1985. Cross-linguistic evidence for the language-making capacity. In *The cross-linguistic study of language acquisition.* Vol. 2, *Theoretical issues.* Edited by D. I. Slobin. Hillsdale, N.J.: Lawrence Erlbaum.

Smilansky, S., and L. Shefatya. 1990. *Facilitating play.* Silver Spring, Md.: Psychosocial and Educational Publications.

Smith, N., and the Drawing Study Group. 1998. *Observation drawing with children.* New York: Teachers College Press.

Sobel, D. 1993. *Children's special places.* Tucson, Ariz.: Zephyr Press.

Spock, B. 1945/1968. *Baby and child care.* New York: Pocket Books.

Standing Bear, L. 1933/1979. *Land of the Spotted Eagle.* Lincoln: University of Nebraska Press.

Stern, D. N. 1977. *The first relationship.* Cambridge: Harvard University Press.

———. 1985. *The interpersonal world of the infant.* New York: Basic Books.

Sternberg, R. J., and L. Spear-Swerling. 1996. *Teaching for thinking.* Washington, D.C.: American Psychological Association.

Stine, S. 1997. *Landscapes for Learning.* New York: Wiley.

Stone, L. 1965. *The crisis of the aristocracy.* Oxford: Oxford University Press.

Suh, S. H. 2002. Political thinking of children in Chile. Unpublished manuscript. The City College of New York.

Sutton-Smith, B. 1981. *The folkstories of children.* Philadelphia: University of Pennsylvania Press.

Swadener, B. B., and S. Lubek, eds. 1995. *Children and families "at promise."* New York: State University of New York Press.

Taylor, A. F., F. E. Kuo, and W. C. Sullivan. 2001. Coping with ADD. *Environment & Behavior, 33:* 54–77.

Taylor, A. F., A. Wiley, F. E. Kuo, and W. C. Sullivan. 1998. Growing up in the inner city: Green spaces as places to grow. *Environment & Behavior, 30:* 3–28.

Taylor, M. 1999. *Imaginary companions and the children who create them.* New York: Oxford University Press.

Thomas, A., and S. Chess. 1977. *Temperament and development.* New York: Bruner/Mazel.

Thomas, G. V., and A. M. J. Silk. 1990. *An introduction to the psychology of children's drawings.* New York: New York University Press.

Thoreau, H. D. 1862/1982. Walking. In *Great short works of Henry David Thoreau.* Edited by W. Glick. New York: Harper & Row.

Thurman, H. 1979. *With head and heart*. New York: Harcourt Brace Jovanovich.

Tinbergen, E. A., and N. Tinbergen. 1972. Early childhood autism: An ethological approach. *Advances in Ethology: Supplement to the Journal of Comparative Ethology, 10:* 37.

Tucker, M. J. 1974. The child as a beginning and end. In *The history of childhood*. Edited by L. de Mause. New York: Psychohistory Press.

Tucker, M. S., and J. B. Codding. 1998. *Standards for our schools*. San Francisco: Jossey-Bass.

Turner, J. 1995. Gary Snyder and the practice of the wild. In *Deep ecology for the 21st century*. Edited by G. Sessions. Boston: Shambhala.

Twain, M. 1876/1988. *The adventures of Tom Sawyer*. In *The Family Mark Twain*. New York: Dorset Press.

————. 1884/1960. *The adventures of Huckleberry Finn*. New York: Dell.

U.S. Department of Education. 1994. *Goals 2000: Educate America Act*. Washington, D.C.

Van de Castle, R. I. 1983. Animal figures in fantasy and dreams. Chap. 15 in *New perspectives on our lives with companion animals*. Edited by A. H. Katcher and A. M. Beck. Philadelphia: University of Pennsylvania Press.

Vygotsky, L. S. 1934/1986. *Language and thought*. Translated by A. Kozulin. Cambridge: MIT Press.

Wallace, S. 2000, October 17. Relaxation techniques go a long way in helping stressed out kids. *AAP* [American Academy of Pediatrics] *News*.

Weikart, D. P., and L. J. Schweinhart. 1991. Disadvantaged children and curriculum effects. In *Academic instruction in early childhood*. Edited by L. Rescorla, M. C. Hyson, and K. Hirsh-Pasek. New Directions for Child Development, No. 53. San Francisco: Jossey-Bass.

Weir, R. 1962. *Language in the crib*. The Hague: Mouton.

Wells, N. 2000. At home with nature: Effects of "greenness" on children's cognitive functioning. *Environment & Behavior, 32:* 775–96.

Wenar, C., and P. Kerig. 2000. *Developmental psychopathology.* 4th ed. Boston: McGraw-Hill.

Werner, H. 1948. *Comparative psychology of mental development.* 2d ed. New York: Science Editions.

———. 1956. On physiognomic perception. In *The new landscape.* Edited by G. Kepes. Chicago: Theobald.

Werner, H., and B. Kaplan. 1963. *Symbol formation.* New York: Wiley.

White, S. H. 1965. Evidence for a hierarchical arrangement of learning processes. In *Advances in child development and behavior.* Edited by L. P. Lipsitt and C. Spiker. New York: Academic Press.

Whittier, J. G. 1855/1993. The barefoot boy. In *One hundred and one famous poems.* Edited by R. J. Cook. New York: Barnes and Noble.

Who's Who Among American High School Students. Lake Forest, Ill.: Education Communications, Inc. (708-295-6650).

Wilgoren, J., and J. Steinberg. 2000, 3 July. Even for sixth graders, college looms. *New York Times,* sec. 1, A1.

Wilson, E. O. 1993. Biophilia and the conservation ethic. In *The biophilia hypothesis.* Edited by S. R. Kellert and E. O. Wilson. Washington, D.C.: Island Press.

Wilson, J., and L. W. Jan. 1993. *Thinking for themselves.* Armidale, Australia: Eleanor Curtain.

Wilson, M., and B. Wilson. 1982. *Teaching children to draw.* Englewood Cliffs, N.J.: Prentice-Hall.

Winn, M. 1977. *The plug-in drug.* New York: Viking.

———. 1981. *Children without childhood.* Middlesex, England: Penguin.

Winner, E. 1982. *Invented worlds.* Cambridge, Mass.: Harvard University Press.

Winnicott, D. W. 1951/1958. Transitional objects and transitional phenomena. In *Through pediatrics to psycho-analysis*. London: Hogarth Press.

————. 1965. *The maturational process and the facilitating environment*. New York: International Universities Press.

Wood, D. 1991. Aspects of teaching and learning. In *Learning to think*. Edited by P. Light, S. Sheldon, and M. Woodhead. London: Routledge.

Wordsworth, W. 1807/1985. Ode: Intimations of immortality from recollections of early childhood. In *Wordsworth: Poems selected by W. E. Williams*. London: Penguin.

Zernike, K. 2001, April 13. Top-scoring suburb set to boycott test. *New York Times*.

Zill, N., and C. A. Shoenborn. 1990, November 16. Developmental, learning, and emotional problems. *Advance Data*, 190. Washington, D.C.: U.S. Department of Health and Human Services.

Acknowledgments

Many colleagues contributed to this book. Discussions with Roger Hart, Robin Moore, and Louise Chawla increased my knowledge of the ways children benefit from rich contact with the natural world. I also am grateful to Howard Gardner, Jeffrey Kane, Douglas Sloan, Lillian Weber, Peter Sacks, Hubert Dyasi, Joy Turner, and Margaret Loeffler for their personal encouragement and insights into childhood.

Many of the ideas in this book took shape during the nine years in which I served on the Teaneck, New Jersey, Board of Education. During this time, a number of us in the community held intense discussions on how we, as adults, can best help children grow and learn. I am particularly grateful for the contributions by my friends Beverly and Alan Lefkowitz, Lloyd Houston, and by my wife, Ellen.

I also am indebted to the staff at Times Books, and I would like to express special thanks to Erika Goldman. Her editorial advice and commitment to the major theme of this book—an appreciation of childhood—have been invaluable.

I wish to thank those who gave permission to include material from my earlier works:

Montessori Life for portions of "The Child's Tie to Nature" (Summer 1993), "How Nature Helps Children Develop" (Spring 1997), and "Children Facing School: Sally Brown and Peppermint Patty" (Spring 1999).

Mothering magazine for excerpts from "Our Unobtrusive Presence" (Winter 1987).

Encounter: Education for Meaning and Social Justice for parts of "The Importance of Nature to Children" (Summer 2000).

Pearson Education for excerpts from *Theories of Development: Concepts and Applications,* 4th edition (Upper Saddle River, N.J., 2000).

In addition, Gary Lawless granted permission to quote from his poem, "When the Animals Come to Us," *First Sight of Land* (Blackberry Books, 1990). Howard Gardner gave permission to reproduce the child's drawing on page 5 and Kay's poem on page 116 of *Artful Scribbles* (1980). The University of California Press granted permission to reproduce portions of figures 125 and 128 in Rudolf Arnheim, *Art and Visual Perception* (1954/1971) and poems in Kornei Chukovsky, *From Two to Five* (1925/1971). Routledge gave permission to include poems from Timothy Rogers, *Those First Affections: An Anthology of Poems Composed Between the Ages of Two and Eight* (1979). The McGraw-Hill Companies, Inc., granted permission to reproduce drawings of faces on page 94 of Rhoda Kellogg, *Analyzing Children's Art* (1969). And Jane Meyerding gave permission to quote from Barbara Deming's poem, "Spirit of Love," in Jane Meyerding, editor, *We Are All Part of One Another: A Barbara Deming Reader* (New Society Publishers 1984).

Index

Abbey, Edward, 197
academics:
  the "basics," 124, 141, 166
  early, 15, 19
  emphasis on, xiii, 2, 15, 124
  learning of, through pursuit of
    spontaneous interests, 176
  meaningless materials, learning,
    202, 207
  "new math" and "new science,"
    140
  nonacademic activities enriching,
    155–56
accountability in standards
  movement, 163–64
active listening, 182–84
adult-directed approaches, 17–24
adult world, age that children enter:
  in the Middle Ages, 125–28
  modern conception of, 128–31
Adventures of Huckleberry Finn
  (Twain), 189–98
after-school activities, 6, 124–25,
  178, 180–81

Ainsworth, Mary, 13, 14, 28
Alliance for Childhood, 145
Ames, Louise Bates, 8, 17, 32
animals:
  drawing, 74, 75
  dreaming of, 5, 49–51, 185
  as imaginary companions, 34
  impersonating, 185
  in poetry, 96
animism, 84, 191, 194, 195
  in *Peanuts* cartoons, 200
  in poetry, 97–102
anxiety:
  parental, 4, 10–11, 23
  test-driven education and, 2,
    142, 165–66
  in young children, 11
apprenticing of children, 125,
  126
Ariès, Philippe, 125, 126, 129
aristocracy, 136
  educational goals of the, 134
Arnheim, Rudolf, 69–72, 75, 76, 99,
  100

arts, the, 174, 191
  artistic abilities, 4, 155
  lobbying in the schools for, 89–90
  nature as inspiration for, 47,
    54–55
  promoting artistic development,
    85–90
  Sally Brown (*Peanuts* character)
    and, 201–2
  society's treatment of, 85, 124
  see also specific artistic forms, e.g.,
    drawing
attachment theorists, 13–14
attention deficit/hyperactive
    disorder, 58–59
attention disorders, 58–59
authentic assessment, 167–68
"authoritative parent," 17–18

babies, *see* infants and toddlers
baby talk, 103
Barber, Elinor, 136
Baudelaire, Charles Pierre, 80
Baumrind, Diana, 17–18
Bell, Sylvia, 14
Bellugi, Ursula, 115
Berk, Laura E., 20
Berkeley, California, transforming
    blacktop schoolyard into nature
    area in, 53–54, 56, 58, 59–60,
    101–2, 148, 152
  replicating the project, 64–65
Berry, Wendell, 149–50
Between Parent and Child (Ginot), 15,
    184
Bible studies, 134
Bickerton, Derek, 117
biological maturation, 12
biophilia hypothesis, 46–47
birth-to-three movement, 21–24
Blake, William, 43, 96, 171
brain development:
  ability to master language and,
    110–11
  birth-to-three movement, 21–24

critical periods, 22–23
  environmental development and, 3
Braine, Martin, 113
"Brilliant Beginnings" instruction
    kits, 23
Broadbent, Thomas, 96
Brod, Craig, 151
Brontë, Anne, 39–40
Brontë, Charlotte, 39–40
Brontë, Emily Jane, 31, 39–40
Brown, Roger, 108, 119
Bruer, John T., 22, 23
Buell, John, 177
Bush, George H. W., administration
    of, 141
Bush, George W., 19, 166

calmness, 170, 179–80, 186
  nature's calming effect, 56–58, 60
"charity schools," 134–35
Charlie Brown (*Peanuts* character),
    202, 204, 205
Chawla, Louise, 57
child-centered approach, 7–8, 11–17,
    27, 141, 153–72, 154, 173–74,
    207
  authentic assessment, 167–68
  checklist, 169–72
  comparison of conventional
    education and, 168–69
  computers in the schools and, 145
  deeper understanding fostered by,
    163
  enthusiasm for learning and, *see*
    learning, enthusiasm for
  feelings of children about learning
    and, 160, 168–69
  focus on interests and needs of the
    child, 155, 156
  independence fostered by, 161–63,
    171, 175
  interest in a task or activity, 169–70
  permissiveness and, 14
  projects-based learning, 160, 165,
    176

questions and answers about, *see* questions and answers for parents about child-centered education

rejection of emphasis on external motivators, 160

Romantic movement and, 139

social promotion issue and, 158–59

childhood's importance in its own right, xiii, 6–7, 17

Children's Defense Fund, 2–3

Chinese art experts, values of, 80

Chomsky, Noam, 107–12, 116, 118, 120

Chukovsky, Kornei, 91–92, 94

circle, first drawings based on the, 70–72

civil rights argument for standards movement, 166–67

Clinton, Hillary Rodham, 21

Clinton administration, 141

Cobb, Edith, 46, 47

Coleman, D. C., 137

college admissions:
  extracurricular activities and, 124
  parents' concern with, 3, 124, 180–82
  standardized testing and, 159

color, children of, 166–67

Comenius, John Amos, 132–33

computers, 45, 143–45, 147, 151
  problems of learning with, 143–45

concentration, child-centered education and, 156–57, 158, 170, 186

concrete operations, stage of, 38, 83–84

Conkling, Hilda, 91, 95, 96, 100

conservation-of-liquids task, 83–84

constructivism, 154, 162

corporate leaders, *see* politicians and corporate leaders

Correll, Richard, 95

Crain, Sally, drawings of, 77–78, 81, 82

Crain, William, 74, 81, 99

creativity, 65
  demands of school and, 203
  nature as stimulant of, 54–55, 198

creole languages, 117–18

criminal system, juvenile offenders and, 128

curiosity, 13, 19, 26, 160, 162, 186, 199

D'Addona, John, 95, 100

dance, 4, 69

Davy, John, 144

Delacroix, Eugène, 80

Deming, Barbara, 100–101

democratic family, 18

depression, 6

developmental stages, xiii, 4–5, 7–8, 150
  attachment theorists, 13–14
  concrete operations, stage of, 38
  inborn schedule of, 11, 12, 13
  individual pace in progressing through, 156
  maturational theorists, 12–13
  Piaget's theory of, 38, 83–84, 150–51
  taking cues from your infant, 11–12

Dewey, John, xii, 7, 154, 160, 169, 202

Diderot, Denis, 137

disadvantaged children, *see* poverty, children living in

"Don't Push Your Preschooler," 8

dramatic play, 4, 39, 69, 123, 124, 152, 155
  adult's role in, 40–42
  animals in, 49
  imaginary companions, *see* imaginary companions

drawing, 4, 69–90, 123
  age of precision (eight to twelve years), 80–85
  ages five to eight, 4

drawing (*cont.*)
   gestalt theory and, 69–70
   the golden period (five to eight
      years), 77–80
   nature as stimulant for, 55
   parental intervention and
      comments, 16, 86–87, 88–89
   the primordial circle (two to three
      years), 70–72
   promoting artistic development,
      85–90
   schools' emphasis on technical
      skills and accuracy, 82
   sunbursts and mandalas (at three
      years), 72–73
   tadpoles (at three to five years),
      74–77
dreams:
   of animals, 5, 49–51
   distinguishing reality from, 38, 84
dress, similarities between children
    and adults in, 125, 128
dropouts, 2, 166, 206–7
Dungeons and Dragons, 40
Durkheim, Emile, 60–61

economics, Enlightenment period
    and, 136, 137–38
ecosystems, concern for future of,
    185
educational system, *see* schools
egocentrism, 97
electronic toys, 6
Eliot, Lise, 24, 119
Elkind, David, xii, 3, 7, 8
e-mail, 145
Emerson, Ralph Waldo, 15, 63
Encyclopedia, 136–37
End of Homework, The (Kralovec and
    Buell), 177
England, education in seventeenth-
    century, 133
Enlightenment, 136–37
environmental concerns of children,
    47–49

Erikson, Erik H., 8, 11, 82
evaluation teams, 168
exploration:
   by toddlers, 25–26
   unobtrusive presence of parents
      and, 28–29
extended family, 10
external authority, dependence for
    answers on, 161–62
external pressures of standards
    movement, 159
extracurricular activities, 6, 124–25,
    178, 180–81
exuberance, 171

family life, 61
federal government and standardized
    testing, 2, 154
Fenalon (educator), 132
feudalism, 130
fighting, 59–60
firstborn children, imaginary
    companions and, 34
"five-to-seven-year shift," 5, 39, 82
   rational thinking and, 39, 82, 84
flash cards, 23
formal operations stage, 84
Foulkes, David, 49, 50, 51
Fowler, William, 119
free choice in child-centered
    education, 158
Freeman, Norman, 76
free time, 125, 174–75, 177
Fromm, Erich, 61
From Two to Five (Chukovsky), 91
future, goal of preparing children for
    the, xii, 1, 2–3, 15, 123–42, 155,
    173
   historical circumstances that led
      to, 125–42
   pervasiveness of, in the United
      States, 139–42
   problem with preoccupation
      with, xiii
   question and answer about, 184–85

as technologically driven value, 146–47

Gardner, Howard, 4, 69, 71, 77, 79, 80, 81, 85, 86, 90
  daughter of, 101
Garvey, Catherine, 41
geometric-technical perception, 98
geometry, 176
Germany, 142
Gerstner, Louis V., Jr., 141
Gesell, Arnold, 11, 12, 13, 150
Gestalt theory, 191
  drawing and, 69–70, 76
ghosts, belief in, 40
Ginott, Haim, 15, 178, 184
Ginsberg, Allen, 143
Ginsburg, Herbert, 156
Gleason, Tracy, 34
Goethe, Johann Wolfgang von, 100
"golden period of artistic development" (five to eight years), 77–80
Golomb, Claire, 77
Goodman, Paul, 171
Gordon, Thomas, 182–84
gracefulness, 171–72, 180
grade promotion:
  in Montessori schools, 158–59
  testing and, 2, 141, 153–54, 158
grammar, *see* language
grandparents, 10, 17
Great Britain, evaluation teams in, 168
Great Didactic, The (Comenius), 132–33
Greenacre, Phyllis, 25

Haight, Wendy, 41
Hanawalt, Barbara, 126
Hancock, Wendy, 55
Harris poll, Louis, 48
Hart, Betty, 120
Hart, Roger, 52, 54, 58, 61, 65, 67
Hart Research Associates, Peter D., 47–48

Hartup, Willard, 34
Head Start, 19
Heard, Georgia, 94, 104, 105
Hesse, Herman, 191
Hewitt, Margaret, 133
hideouts, 41–42, 51, 54, 65, 67
high-school dropouts, 2
high-school graduation, contingency on test scores of, 141
Hirsh-Pasek, Kathy, 19
Holyes, Martin, 129
homework, 5, 88
  child's request for help with, 177–78
  opposition to excessive, 177
homunculus, 126–27
Huckleberry Finn, 189–98
Hughes, Gillian, 102, 149
Humphreys, Lloyd G., 150

imaginary companions, 4, 31–40
  of adults, 40
  adult's role, 40–42
  age of child and, 38
  cultural beliefs about, 36–37
  fate of, 38–40
  as guardian angels, 37
  reality of, 35–38
immigrants, language abilities of children of, 122
independence, 61, 173, 180, 181, 186
  active listening to foster, 182–84
  allowing children to decide their own future, 181–82
  assistance with homework and, 177–78
  "authoritative parent" and, 18
  child-centered education, fostered by, 161–63, 171, 175
  heeding babies' signals and, 14
independent learning, 67
Industrial Revolution, 137, 139
infants and toddlers:
  attraction to nature, 43–44

infants and toddlers (*cont.*)
    child-centered parenting of,
        11–17
    language development, 112–15
    mother-infant dialogues, 93
    as natural explorers, 24–27
    poetry of, 93
    rhythmic jabbering of, 92–93
    spoiling, 14
inferiority, feelings of, 121, 206, 207
inner-city children:
    imaginative play by, 42
    see also inner-city children
instructional materials for
        preschoolers, 3, 23
interest in a task or activity, 169–70,
        179, 180
    see also spontaneous interests
Internet, surfing the, 145
invisible companions, *see* imaginary
        companions
IQ tests, 3, 120
isolation, 61
Ivy League colleges, 180–82
    nursery school admissions and, 3

Japan, 142
job preparation:
    apprenticeships, 125, 126
    children living in poverty and, 2–3
    education aimed at, 1, 133–35,
        141–42
    "white collar" occupations, shift
        toward, 128–29
Johnson, Cathy, 148
Johnson, Harriet M., 92–93
Joy, Claude, 135
Jung, Carl, 73
juvenile offenders, criminal system's
        treatment of, 128

Kaluli of New Guinea, 120
Kamii, Constance, 7, 161–63
Kandinsky, Wassily, 4, 79
Kaplan, Louise, 25

Kellogg, Rhoda, 69–70, 72, 73, 75, 76
Kent, Frances, 93
Kierkegaard, Søren, 28
kindergarten:
    academics emphasized in, xi, 5
    drawing in, 87
Kirby, Mary Ann, 41–42
Klee, Paul, 4, 78, 79, 80, 86
Klima, Edward, 115
Kluckhorn, Florence, 130
Koch, Kenneth, 104
Kohn, Alfie, 161, 168
Kohut, Heinz, 61
Kozol, Jonathan, 167
Kralovec, Etta, 177
Kuo, Frances, 59

labeling, parents' overreliance on,
        62–63
laissez-faire, 136
Lakota Indians, 60, 67
language:
    biological programming and
        ability to pick up, 110–11
    Chomsky's research on, 107–12,
        116, 118, 120
    creoles, 117–18
    genetically determined period,
        special powers of children for,
        118–19
    growth of child's grammar,
        research on, 112–17
    infants and, 112
    motherese, 119–20
    negatives, use of, 115
    one-word utterances, 112
    overregulation of rules, 114–15
    pidgins, 117–18
    "pivot grammar," 113
    putting three or more words
        together, 114–15
    rules of, children's ability to
        master, 107–12, 121–22, 123
    second, children's ability to pick
        up a, 118, 122

self-directed speech, 39
sign language, 118
tag questions, 108–10, 116
teaching of, 119–22
transformations, between three
and six years of age, 116–17
two-word utterances, 113
vocabulary growth, 108, 120–22
word endings, children's
formation of rules for, 114
Language Instinct, The (Pinker), 118
Latin, teaching of, 134
Latin American cultures, imaginary
companions in, 37
Lawless, Gary, 185
learning, enthusiasm for, 169, 184,
185, 186, 199
child-centered approach and, 160,
174, 175
test-driven education's
undermining of, 164, 174
Learning Through Landscapes, 65
Leonard, Janet, 32
Linus (*Peanuts* character), 200, 201
"little adults," concept of children
as, 125–28, 139
schools and, 131–32
local community, defending nature
in the, 63–64
loneliness, 60–61, 198
lullabies, 103

magic, questioning of, 38–39
Mahler, Margaret, 25, 29, 61
mandalas, drawing, 73
Mann, Thomas, 79
Marin County, California, boycott
of standardized testing in, 153
Marx, Leo, 194–95, 197
Maslow, Abraham, 149
maternal presence of nature, 60, 61
math, 176, 202
constructivist approach to, 162
see also academics
Matisse, Henri, 79

maturational theorists, 12–13
memorization, 160, 161, 165, 174,
202
mental health, contact with nature
and, 58–60
Middle Ages, the:
concept of children as "little
adults" in, 125–28
emphasis on the past in, 130
schools in, 131
middle class:
"charity schools," attending, 135
emergence of, 129
emphasis on the future and job
preparation, 129–30, 133,
135–38
evolution of schools and, 130–31,
135
Miller, Peggy, 41
mirroring the child's feelings, 182
Montesquieu, Baron de la Brede et
de, 136–37
Montessori, Maria, xii, 7, 28, 46, 47,
156–58, 161, 170, 179, 181
Montessori schools, 154, 157–58, 168
Moore, Robin, 52–53, 56, 58,
59–60, 61, 64–65, 65, 148
moral behavior, setting limits on, 15
More, Thomas, 131–32
motherese, 119–20
mother/infant dialogues, 93, 103
movies, 170
Mumford, Lewis, 146
Myth of the First Three Years, The
(Bruer), 22
myths, questioning of, 38–39

Nabhan, Gary, 16, 45, 197
Nation at Risk, A, 1, 141
Native Americans, 60, 66–67
natural interests, *see* spontaneous
interests
nature, 5, 43–68, 124, 139, 152, 155
benefits for children of contact
with, 52–61, 193, 198

nature (*cont.*)
  biophilia hypothesis, 46–47
  children's special sensitivity to, 5–7,
      43, 47–51, 123, 148–49, 185
  child's perspective of, 16
  conclusion, 68–69
  decreased exposure of children to,
      45–46, 59, 101
  defending, in your local
      community, 63–64
  Huckleberry Finn as child of,
      189–98
  as inspiration for poetry, 47,
      54–55, 67, 94–96, 101, 185
  insulation from, 197–98
  limited research on decreased
      exposure of children to, 46
  loneliness and estrangement from,
      60–61, 198
  maternal presence of, 60, 61
  mental health and contact with,
      58–60
  nature studies, encouraging,
      66–67, 179, 198
  opportunities to play in, 41–42,
      62, 103, 174–75, 179, 185, 198
  peaceful feelings instilled by,
      56–58, 61, 193
  recommendation for enriching
      children's contact with, 62–68
Needham, J., 127
negatives, child's use off, 115
Nesham, Roberta, 96
Newson, John and Elizabeth, studies
    of, 32–33, 36–37, 38, 42
New York City, New York:
  boycott of standardized testing in,
      153
  park attendants in, 179
New York Times, 4, 141
No Child Left Behind Act, 166
nursery schools:
  competition for "the right," 3
  Montessori and Piagetian, 27
Nurse's Song, 171

observation, powers of, 175, 198
  nature as stimulant of, 52–54, 59
occupations, *see* job preparation
Oliver, Mary, 60
oneness with the world, feelings of,
    56–58
only children, imaginary
    companions and, 34
onomatopoeia, 195
open education, 154
Opper, Sylvia, 156
Orbis Pictus (Comenius), 133
order, children's need for, 157
Orr, David, 47

Papert, Seymore, 151
paracosms (imaginary worlds), 39–40
paranormal, belief in the, 40
Parent Effectiveness Training (Gordon),
    184
parents and parenting:
  adult-oriented approaches, 17–24
  anxiety of, 4, 10–11, 23
  artistic development, promoting
      children's, 85–90
  child-centered approach, *see*
      child-centered approach
  excessive pushing by, 8
  helping with homework, 177–78
  imaginative play and, 40–42
  intervention and correction, 8, 16,
      26–27, 85, 86–87, 121–22, 173
  labeling, overreliance on, 62–63
  language, teaching of, 119–22
  media pressures on, 10–11
  nature, enriching children's
      contact with, 62–68, 103, 179
  poetry, facilitating children's, 102–6
  providing opportunities, 8, 41–42,
      62, 87–88, 102–6, 173, 174–75,
      185
  questions and answers, *see*
      questions and answers for
      parents about child-centered
      education

safety issues, 63, 178
scaffolding and, *see* scaffolding
spontaneous interests of children and, 9, 15–16
unobtrusive presence of, 27–30, 63, 104–6, 178
park attendants ("parkies"), 178–79
past, cultures with emphasis on the, 130
Paterson, New Jersey, 166
patience, 30, 52, 62
peacefulness, sense of, 186
child-centered education and, 157, 170, 175, 179–80
nature's instilling a, 56–58, 61, 193
Peanuts characters, attitude toward school of, 199–207
Pearce, Joseph Chilton, 46
Peppermint Patty (*Peanuts* character), 204–7
permissiveness, 14–15
Pestalozzi, Heinrich, 171, 199
philosophes of the Enlightment, 136–38
physiognomic perception, 98
Piaget, Jean, 7, 8, 32, 85, 150–52, 154, 178, 191
animism, view of, 97
developmental stages according to, 38, 83–84, 150–51
intellectual development and child's curiosity, 13
Picasso, Pablo, 4, 69, 79, 86
pidgin languages, 117–18
Pinchbeck, Ivy, 133
Pinker, Steven, 118
Piscataway, New Jersey, 177
"pivot grammar," 113
playground directors, 178–79
poetry, 4, 69, 91–106, 152, 191
animistic, 97–102
avoiding evaluation of, 105–6
"baby talk," 93, 103
exhilaration expressed in, 92
facilitating children's, 102–6

infant rhythmic jabbering and, 92
listening to children's, 105
musical elements in, 93
nature as inspiration for, 47, 54–55, 67, 94–96, 101–2, 148–49, 185
reciting, 104
of toddlers, 93
visual imagery and feelings in, 93–94
politicians and corporate leaders:
early academics and, 19
educational "reforms" and, xiii, 1, 141, 199
education to benefit the larger social order and, 134
portfolios, 167–68
positive regard, unconditional, 182
Postman, Neil, 128, 146
poverty, children living in:
"charity schools," 134–35
funding of schools attended by, 166–67
future problems of, focus on, 2
imaginative play by, 42
vocabulary growth of, 121
preformationistic theories in embryology, 126–27
preoperational thought, stage of, 83–84
preschools, academics in, 19
present:
cultures with emphasis on the, 130
education focusing on the, *see* child-centered approach
see also future, goal of preparing children for the
pretend play, *see* dramatic play; imaginary companions
primordial circle, drawing of, 70–72
progress, Enlightenment's faith in, 139
progressive education, 154, 160
projects-based learning, 160, 165, 176

promotion to the next grade, *see* grade promotion
PTA meetings, 177

Quesnay, François, 136
questions and answers for parents
    about child-centered education, 174–86
    about an orientation to the future, 184–85
    about child falling behind, 174–75
    about college admissions, 180–82
    about emotionally upset child seeking parent's help, 182–84
    about free time leading to more TV watching, 179
    about homework, 177–78
    about learning what is needed to function in society, 176
    about promoting a love of learning, 184
    about TV watching, 179–80

railroads, 139
rational problem-solving skills, 5, 155
rational thinking:
    "five-to-seven-year shift," 39, 82, 84
    technology and, 147–49
Ravitch, Diane, 154–55
Rawlings, Marjorie Kinnan, 6
reading, 176
    see also academics
real-estate development, 63, 64, 198
reflecting child's feelings in active listening, 182–84
Reiner, Rob, 21
restlessness, 6
Risley, Todd, 120
Rogers, Carl, 171, 182
Rogers, Timothy, 94
Romantic movement, 139
Romantic poets, 5, 43, 100
Rosenbaum, James, 160

Rousseau, Jean-Jacques, xii, xiii, 4, 7, 123, 138–39, 150, 161
rules, social games with, 39, 178

safety:
    in natural settings, unobtrusive protection of child's, 63
    outdoor play and, 178
St. Antoine, Sara, 45, 197
Sally Brown (*Peanuts* character), 200, 201–4
Sarason, Seymour, 87
SATs (scholastic aptitude tests), 124
scaffolding, 19–21, 40
Scaffolding Children's Learning (Berk and Winsler), 20–21
Scarsdale, New York, boycott of standardized testing in, 153
Schachtel, Ernest, 62
Schaefer-Simmern, Henry, 76
school day, lengthening the, xiii, 6, 198
schools, 9
    advancement of the middle class and, 130–31
    the arts, teaching of the, 86, 87, 89–90, 124, 166
    authentic assessment of, 167–68
    boredom with typical curriculum of, xi, 160
    "charity," 134–35
    child-centered, 154, 157–58, 168
    cold war and, 140
    computers in the, 163–65, 198
    dropouts, 2, 166, 206–7
    evolution of, 131–35
    "little adult" image of children and, 131–32
    minority children, attended by, 166–67
    Peanuts characters and children's feelings about, 199–207
    separation of children from adult society, 129

in sixteenth and seventeenth
century, growth in demand for,
129, 131
Vietnam era, effect of, 140–41
whippings in, 131
see also academics; standards
movement; teachers;
test-driven education
Schultz, Charles, and *Peanuts*
cartoons, 199–207
science, *see* academics; technology
Sebanc, Anne, 34
second language, children's ability to
pick up a, 118, 122
self-worth, school performance and,
206, 207
Shahar, Shulamith, 126
Shakespeare, William, 131
Shelley, Percy Bysshe, 5, 43
shelters, building, 51, 54, 65, 67
sign language, 118
Silk, Angele, 80
Singer, Dorothy, 38, 39, 40
Singer, Jeremy, 38, 39, 40
singing, 4, 69
lullabies, 103
Sleeping in the Forest, 60
Slobin, Dan, 116–17
Snoopy (*Peanuts* character), 200, 207
Snyder, Gary, 50
Sobel, David, 51, 54
sociability:
games with rules, 39
imaginary companions and, 35
social class divisions:
feudalistic beliefs about, 130
schooling as way overcoming,
130–31
social promotion, *see* grade
promotion
Soviet Union, 140
speed as technological value,
149–52
Spock, Dr. Benjamin, 11
spoiling an infant, 14

spontaneous interests, 15–16, 21,
179–80, 204–205, 207
learning of academics and, 176
opportunities to develop, xiii, 9,
15, 173, 175
Sputnik, 140
standards movement, xi, xii, 1–2, 8,
141–42, 153–67
accountability, 163–64
arguments of proponents of,
154–55, 161
civil rights argument for,
166–67
external pressures and incentives
of, 159–60, 163–64, 199
popular support for, 199
see also test-driven education
Standing Bear, Luther, 60, 67
*Start Smart: Building Brain Power in the
Early Years*, 23–24
state parks, 197
steamboat, 139, 195, 196
Steiner, Rudolf, 145, 154
Stern, Daniel, 30, 93, 103
Stinton, Rosemary, 148
storytelling, 69
studying, conditions for, 177
suicidal ideation, 6
Sullivan, William, 59
sunbursts, drawing, 72–73
Sung Ha Suh, 48–49
suns, drawing, 74
symbols:
early use of, 32
test-driven education, symbolic
thought required by, 162
synesthesia, sense of, 85

tadpoles, drawings of (three to five
years), 74–77
controversy over, 76–77
tag questions, 108–10, 116
Taylor, Andrea, 42, 59
Taylor, Marjorie, 33–34, 35, 37, 39,
40, 42

teachers:
  deprofessionalizing of, standards
    movement and, 164
  independent learning, fostering,
    161–63
  role in child-centered education,
    158
Teaneck Board of Education, xi,
    xiii
technology, xiii, 143–52
  computers in the schools, 143–45,
    198
  Diderot's *Encyclopedia* and, 137
  emphasis on the future in
    education and, 135–38
  Twain's feelings about, 195–97
  values associated with, 145–52
teenage pregnancy, 2
television watching, 6, 35, 45, 66,
    170, 179–80, 198, 204–5
temperament, inborn, 13, 156
test-driven education, xi, xii,
    141–42, 153–67, 199
  anxiety triggered by, 2, 142,
    165–66
  boycotting, 153, 154
  deprofessionalizing of teaching by,
    164
  in early grades, inappropriateness
    in, 164–65
  federal government and, 2, 154
  grade promotion and, 2, 141,
    153–54, 158
  performance on standardized
    tests of children learning in
    child-centered environment,
    163, 168, 175
  state penalties for low-test scores,
    153
  symbolic or abstract thought
    required for, 165
  see also standards movement
textbooks, 160
Thomas, Glyn, 80
Thoreau, Henry David, 43

Those First Affections (Rogers), 94
Thurman, Howard, 57–58, 61
toddlers, *see* infants and toddlers
transformational grammar, 116
transformations, language,
    116–17
transitional objects, 200
trees, drawing, 74
trust, responding to babies' signals
    and development of, 14
Twain, Mark, 189–98

unconditional positive regard,
    182
unemployment, 2
unity of life, 73
University of Wyoming, 49
unobtrusive presence of parents,
    27–30, 63, 104–6, 178
urban areas, safety of outdoor play
    in, 178

Van de Castle, Robert, 50
video games, 6, 45, 59, 66, 145
videos, 170
Vives, Juan Luis, 132
vocabulary, 108, 120–22
Voltaire, 136
Vygotsky, Lev, 19–20
  theory of internalization of
    language, 39

Waldorf schools, 145, 154, 168
Wasting America's Future (Children's
    Defense Fund), 2–3
Watt, James, 137
Wells, Nancy, 59
Werner, Heinz, 98, 149, 201
What's Going On in There?
    (Eliot), 24
White, Sheldon, 82
Whittier, James Greenleaf, 5
Wilson, E. O., 46, 47
Winn, Marie, 128, 179
Winner, Ellen, 85

Winnicott, D. W., 61, 200
Winsler, Adam, 20
Wood, David, 147
word endings, children's formation
    of rules for, 114–15
Wordsworth, William, 5, 43,
    44, 100
workbooks, 160

workplace, preparation for, *see* job
    preparation

Yearling, The (film), 6–7
Yearling, The (Rawlings), 6

"zone of proximal development,"
    teaching children in the, 19–20

About the Author

WILLIAM CRAIN, PH.D., is a developmental psychologist, author, and social activist. A professor of psychology at the City College of New York, he is the author of a major textbook in the field, *Theories of Development: Concepts and Applications* (Prentice-Hall, 4th edition, 2000). He is the editor of the journal, *Encounter: Education for Meaning and Social Justice*. William Crain lives in New York City.